AF594501

IN THE PRESENT MOMENT

IN

PRESENT

BUDDHISM, CONTEMPORARY ART, AND SOCIAL PRACTICE

HAEMA SIVANESAN

THE MOMENT

Figure.1
Vancouver / Toronto / Berkeley

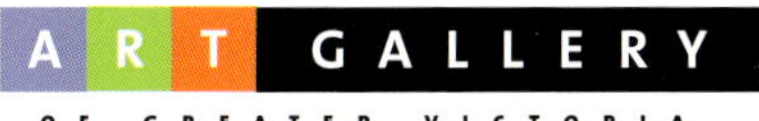

CONTENTS

CATALOGUE ENTRIES BY HAEMA SIVANESAN

FOREWORD

IN THE PRESENT MOMENT: BUDDHISM, CONTEMPORARY ART, AND SOCIAL PRACTICE was initiated by a generous research and exhibition development grant, Re-Envisioning Buddhist Art, funded by the Robert H.N. Ho Family Foundation, Hong Kong. The goal of the grant was to reinvigorate the idea of "Buddhist art" and to expand audience engagement. Drawing on the diverse collections of the Art Gallery of Greater Victoria (AGGV), supplemented by loans and commissioned art projects, *In the Present Moment* makes connections between ideas in contemporary art and their (often unacknowledged or underacknowledged) historical Asian Buddhist antecedents, demonstrating a confluence and continuity of ideas.

In the Present Moment was led by curator Haema Sivanesan, who proposed an innovative curatorial model of exhibition research and development: grounded in scholarly art-historical inquiry, but developed in parallel with community-engaged and artist-centred research that anchors the project in the AGGV's unique Pacific Northwest context. A supportive advisory committee assisted in making community and scholarly connections, providing a range of opportunities for discussion, exchange, and feedback. The committee comprised:

Tzu-I Chung, Curator of History, Royal BC Museum, Victoria;

Shaun Dacey, Director, Richmond Art Gallery;

Katherine Hacker, Emeritus Professor of Art History, University of British Columbia, Vancouver;

Victor Sogen Hori, Associate Professor (retired) in Japanese Religions, School of Religious Studies, McGill University, Montreal;

Jessica Main, Assistant Professor, Robert H.N. Ho Family Foundation Chair in Buddhism and Contemporary Society, University of British Columbia, Vancouver; and

Susanne Ledingham, Elder Seishin, Zenwest; board member, Victoria Multifaith Society; and art educator.

IMAGE OVERLEAF
Charwei Tsai (Taiwan, 1980–)
Driftwood (Heart Sutra), 2019
Performance document: India ink on driftwood
90 min.
Performed on October 27, 2019, as part of *In the Present Moment: A Research Convening*, Visual Arts Building, University of Victoria
Courtesy of the artist / Photo: Laura Gildner

Very special thanks are owing to Lynda Gammon, Marina DiMaio, Jenelle Pasiechnik, Chiaki Ajioka, Marty Gross, Su Yen Chong, Sherry Willing, and Jennifer Van der Pol for their various efforts and contributions towards research support, partnership engagement, and exhibition development.

The development of this book was keenly informed by a weekend-long, artist-centred research convening (October 25–27, 2019) supported by funds from the Andy Warhol Foundation for the Visual Arts, New York. This catalyzing event, comprising keynote presentations, panel discussions, workshops, artists' performances, and installations, fostered a vibrant discursive space for the development of artistic and intellectual ideas while also contributing in important ways to developing public engagement. The research convening was organized by the AGGV in partnership with the University of Victoria's Faculty of Fine Arts, the Centre for Studies in Religion and Society, and Multifaith Services (Interfaith Chapel). Our sincere appreciation is extended to UVic staff and faculty members—Susan Lewis, Paul Bramadat, Paul Walde, Christopher Butterfield, Henri Lock, and Soshin McMurchy.

This publication and exhibition draw on extensive research and, for many artists, reflect lifelong investigations into the relationship between art, life, and Buddhist practice. Sincere thanks are due to the participating artists and to the writers contributing to this volume: Marcus Boon, Oliver Kellhammer, Lydia Kwa, Susan Stewart, Louwrien Wijers, and Mali Wu.

JON TUPPER
Director, Art Gallery of Greater Victoria

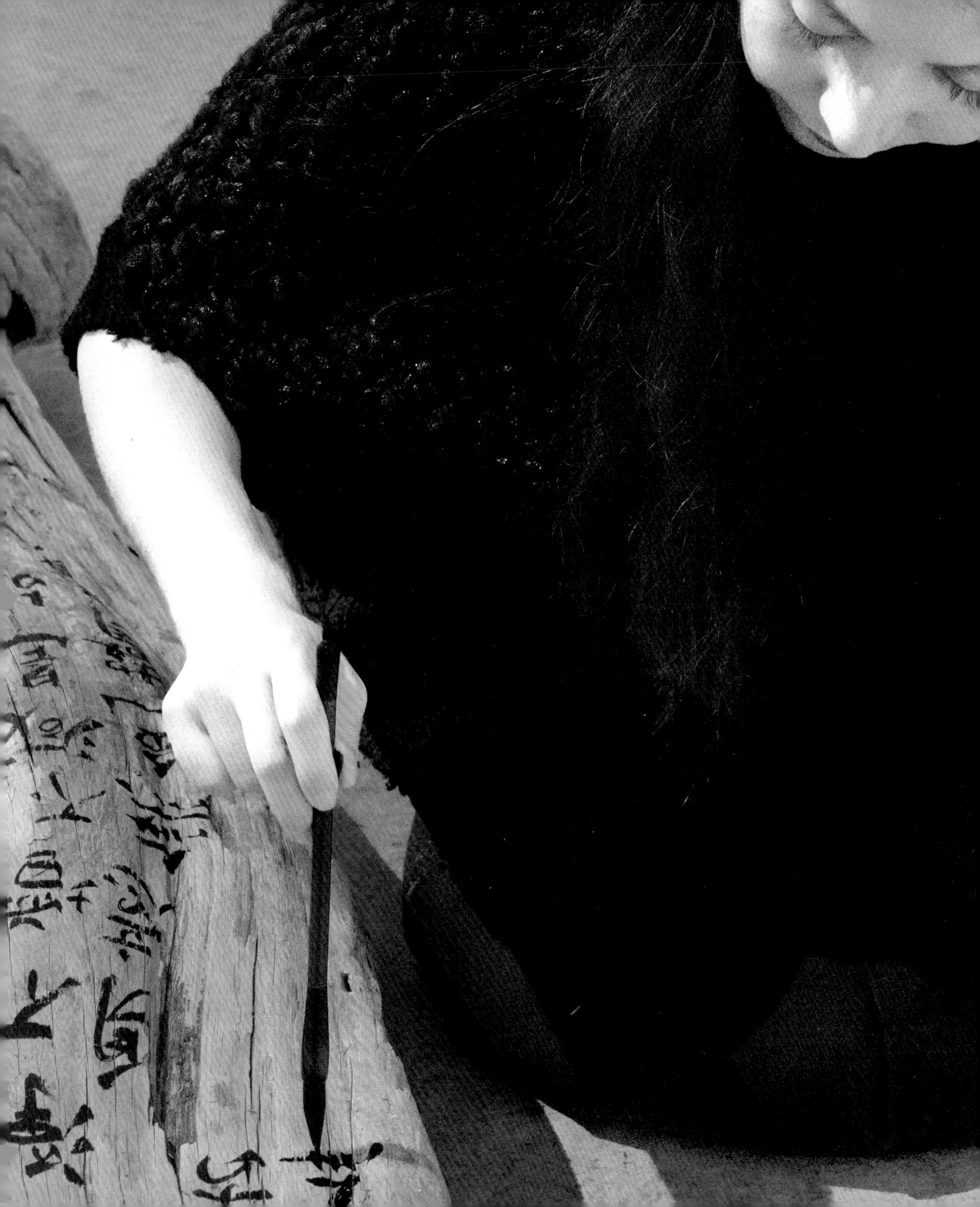

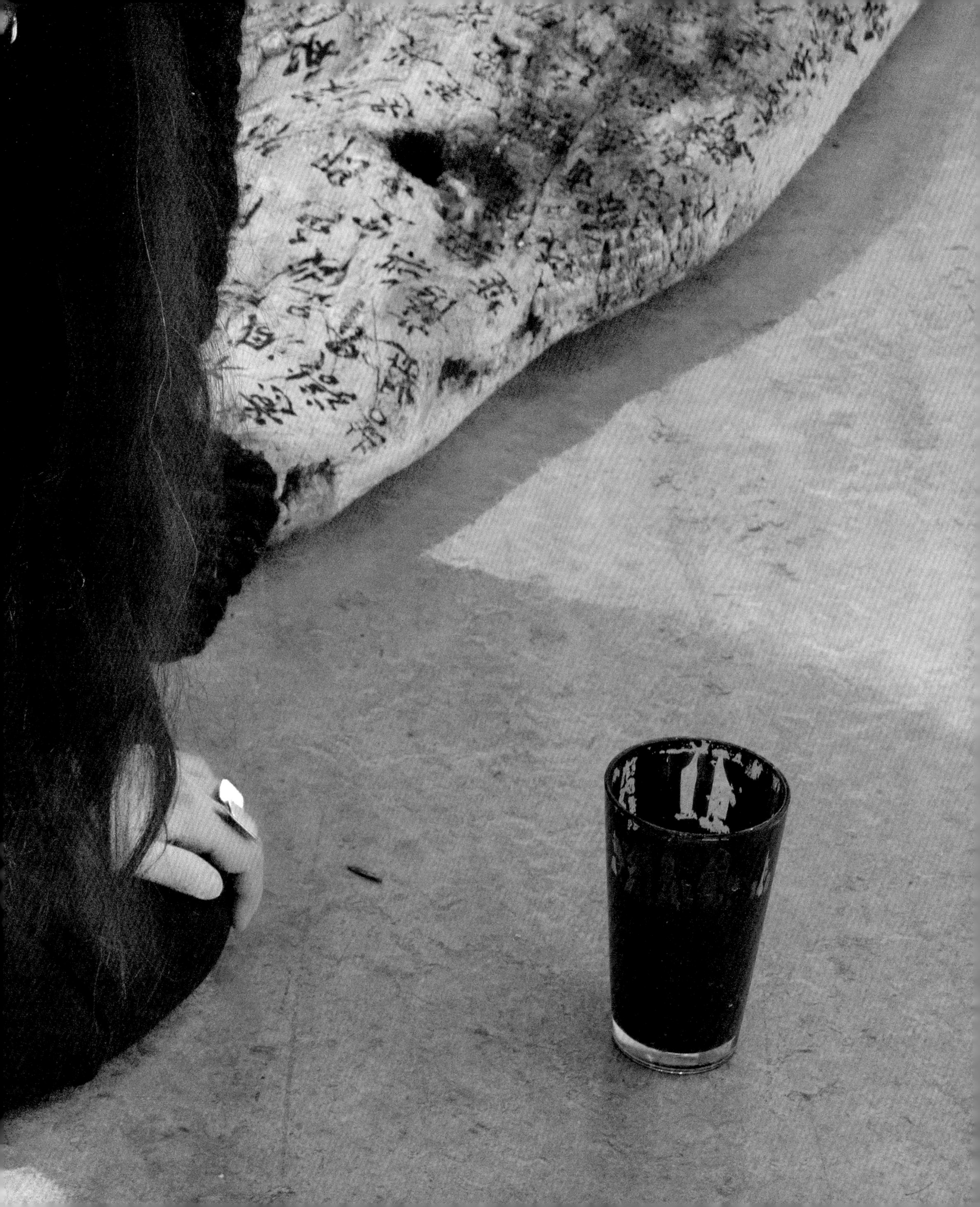

INTRODUCTION

HAEMA SIVANESAN

What is past is left behind.
The future is as yet unreached.
Whatever quality is present
you clearly see right there,
right there.

BHADDEKARATTA SUTTA

The Buddha said that the past is already gone, the future is not yet here; there is only one moment for you to live: that is the present moment.

THICH NHAT HANH

IN BUDDHIST TEACHING, "being in the present moment" refers to a practice of living mindfully with full awareness of the world, including an awareness of the consequences of one's actions. It is a state of active presence combined with profound peace and joyful appreciation, each cumulatively embracing the potential of the eternal now. The reality of the present moment reminds us of the availability of infinite peace and unconditional happiness if we choose—from moment to moment—to access our innate Buddha-nature: the potential of every sentient being to achieve insight into the condition of Emptiness and thereby discover the essential nature of Mind. Being in the present moment provides an approach to experiencing the world; it also provides direction on how to approach the artworks included in this book and the accompanying exhibition.

In the Present Moment: Buddhism, Contemporary Art, and Social Practice explores how artists have grappled with the concept of being in the present moment by using their art practice to explore this deceptively complex concept and to give that inquiry aesthetic form. Tracing a history of the intersection of Buddhist thought and artistic production in North America (United States and Canada) from the mid-20th century to the present, this book explores how Buddhist ideas and philosophy have played an important role in the development of contemporary art. While North America is taken as a provisional geographical starting point, this project effectively traces an international history of cross-cultural encounter and exchange. This book examines the contemporary phenomena of the dissemination and globalization of Buddhism: being adapted by Asian Buddhist scholars and teachers to contexts of colonialism, nationalism, and social and political modernization; being then adopted by North American and European practitioners; and being incorporated by diverse practitioners in the West into their artistic work, sometimes in ways that recirculate to inform avant-garde artistic practices in Asia. Buddhism as a contemporary artistic influence can be shown to flow back and forth between Asia and the West as a dynamic process of artistic inquiry and critique. This spirited exchange and flow of ideas describes Buddhism as "a faith of perpetual evolution and regeneration; one that has no borders, only horizons."[1]

Buddhism as it is known in the West has been significantly shaped by the terms of modernity, where the concept of "modern Buddhism"—that is, Buddhism shaped by the terms of East–West cross-cultural encounters—opens up a new and significant field of inquiry. Modern Buddhism provides an important paradigm by which to consider contemporary artistic work informed by Buddhist ideas and practices. As I argue in my essay "Towards Experiencing Emptiness: Buddhism as an Artistic Methodology" (pages 6–79), the concept of modern Buddhism provides a robust framework for discussions of the role of Buddhism in the development of ideas in the contemporary visual arts. In this context, Buddhism provides artists with new meaning and a new sense of purpose in making art. Surveying a history of artistic engagement, I consider Buddhism as a methodology of art practice, recognizing the significant intertwining of art, life, and Buddhist thought and practice for certain artists in the contemporary North American context. By way of various discussions with artists, I regard art as a site of inquiry into Buddhist ideas and world views, as art is also the site of practices of self- and social actualization.

The remaining essays in this book expand on these concepts. In "The Wheel of Life: From Paradigm to Presence" (pages 80–96), Lydia Kwa examines the work of three Asian Canadian artists who draw on the concepts and symbolism of the Tibetan Wheel of Life and reinterpret the imagery for contemporary times. Howie Tsui, Tomoyo Ihaya, and Haruko Okano each draw on personal experience as well as imagination to create new visual worlds that describe the overcoming of suffering through compassion.

Marcus Boon's essay, "The Sound of the Mandala" (pages 98–123), provides a brief survey of mandala and mandala-like images in Western art. Boon explores their impact on approaches to experimental music and sound art, with an emphasis on mandala-like sound art scores. This rarely discussed association between mandalas and sound provides an important contribution to the broadening of the concept of the mandala in the Western imagination.

In "A Social Vision for Art: Manifesting the Buddha-Nature" (pages 124–140), Louwrien Wijers discusses the impact of a series of transatlantic artistic exchanges that led to a meeting between German artist Joseph Beuys and His Holiness the 14th Dalai Lama. Wijers discusses Beuys's concept of social sculpture—the idea of society and the world as a living sculpture—as it relates to the Tibetan Buddhist notion of art as the expression of one's Buddha-nature. The dovetailing of these two philosophies exhibits the way in which artistic self-inquiry and practice become intertwined with Buddhism, as a methodology. In this context, artists considered themselves as having a role to play in actualizing the creative potential of society, as much as they considered themselves as having an important role to play in *creatively actualizing the potential of society*. Developing on this idea, artists Oliver Kellhammer, Susan Stewart, and Mali Wu discuss the impact of Buddhism on their respective approaches in "Buddhism and Socially Engaged Art Practice" (pages 142–158). Artists such as Kellhammer, Stewart, and Wu consider their art as a platform for social interaction and social change and are part of a larger history of artistic practice that reconsiders the role of the artist in society. Accordingly, for these artists, art is no longer concerned with issues of representation or even visuality but is a relational practice of joy (or Emptiness) and meaning making in life, as life.

Common to all these essays—keeping in mind the attention to being in the present moment—is a concept of art as a multisensory, lived, and embodied relational experience that is attuned to the dynamic nature of the world, rather than as a form of representation. The artists included in this book and exhibition are not looking for ways to visually illustrate Buddhist teachings. Rather, they use their art practice as a site where they can test Buddhist concepts and teachings and verify their truth in an experiential way. It is in this spirit that the reader is invited to consider the works of art assembled in this book.

In the Present Moment is deeply indebted to and builds upon the work of various artists, curators, and scholars who have considered the role of Buddhism in the context of contemporary art. The two most notable projects are Louwrien Wijers's symposium (and accompanying book) *Art meets Science and Spirituality in a changing Economy*, held at the Stedelijk Museum, Amsterdam (1990), and the *Awake: Art, Buddhism and the Dimensions of Consciousness* U.S. national consortium (2001–2003), led by Jacquelynn Baas and Mary Jane Jacob, which resulted in the book *Buddha Mind in Contemporary Art* (2004). The consortium meetings and publication inspired several exhibitions, including *The Invisible Thread: Buddhist Spirit in Contemporary Art* (2003), *The Missing Peace: Artists Consider the Dalai Lama* (2006), *The Third Mind: American Artists Contemplate Asia, 1860–1989* (2009), and *Grain of Emptiness: Buddhism-Inspired Contemporary Art* (2010). I am also indebted to the artists, scholars, and community members who participated in *In the Present Moment: A Research Convening*, co-organized with the University of Victoria (October 25–27, 2019). That conference contributed significantly towards the development of this project.

My intention for *In the Present Moment* is to expand the discussion on the impact of Buddhism on contemporary art in a considered and meaningful way and to provide a glimpse into the broad and deep cultural impacts of Buddhism in the contemporary globalizing world.

HAEMA SIVANESAN
Curator, Art Gallery of Greater Victoria

NOTES

1 Edmund Capon, "Foreword," in Jackie Menzies (ed.), *Buddha: Radiant Awakening* (Sydney: Art Gallery of New South Wales, 2001), p. 10.

TOWARDS EXPERIENCING EMPTINESS

BUDDHISM AS AN ARTISTIC METHODOLOGY

HAEMA SIVANESAN

IN THE MAINSTREAM imagination, the category of "Buddhist art" tends to call up serene images of the gilded Buddhas of historical Asia, or perhaps the swift and elegant ink paintings popularized by Zen monks and nuns (FIGS. 1–2). However, since the mid-20th century, Buddhism has had considerable impact on art in North America, significantly influencing artists of the avant-garde.[1] Buddhism is a philosophy and practice of the mind, concerned with the nature of the self, the problem of human suffering, the potential of human consciousness, and ideas of causality. For artists, especially those working in the 1960s and 1970s, such as John Cage, Yoko Ono, Nam June Paik, Robert Filliou, and Pauline Oliveros, Buddhist thought had considerable impact on art making, and in turn, each had a broad influence on postwar contemporary art, primarily in North America but also on the world stage. These artists engaged variously with Buddhism and Buddhist teachings, whether by way of lectures in English and texts in translation, as in the case of composer John Cage; by way of a socialized cultural understanding, as in the case of Nam June Paik; or by way of formal training with a Buddhist teacher, as in the case of artists Robert Filliou and Pauline Oliveros. Through their engagement with Buddhism, these artists contributed specifically to developments in conceptual art, with ongoing influence and impact for artists working today. As this essay details, these artists grappled with the difficult and often abstract philosophies of Buddhism through processes of art making. In turn, they participated in and contributed to the dissemination of Buddhism in the West, becoming conduits for processes of East–West exchange and demonstrating how Buddhism could find cultural expression in North America. The experimental and conceptual (rather than representational) nature of their artworks suggests how art functions as a site of inquiry into Buddhist thought.

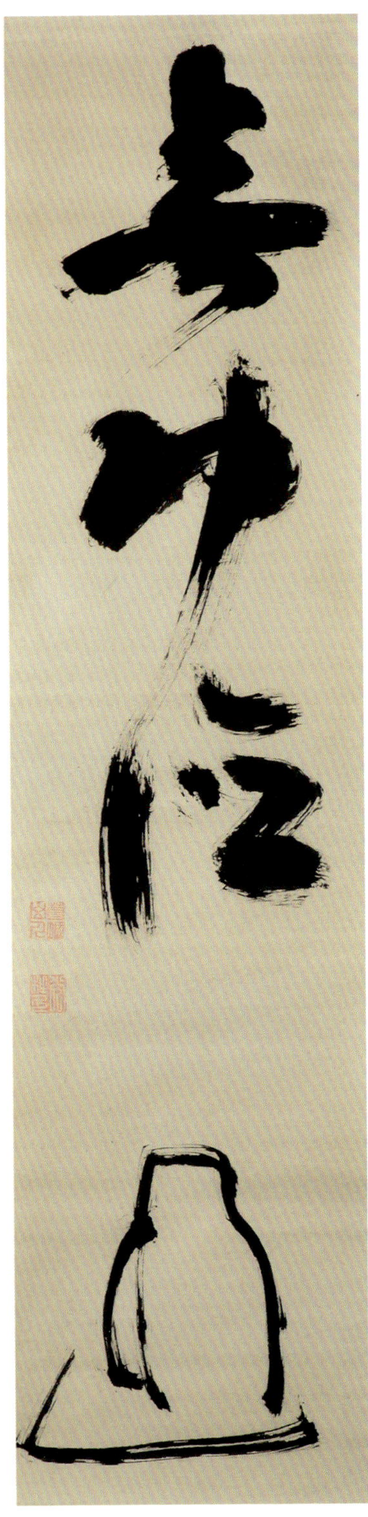

FIG. 1
Jiun Kozuki (Japan, 1718–1804)
Daruma, 1775
Ink on paper
109.8 × 27.2 cm
Inscription: "The place without effort (or merit)"
Gift of Mr. and Mrs. R.W. Finlayson, Toronto
Art Gallery of Greater Victoria 1977.116.001
Photo: Stephen Topfer

Zen was the form of Buddhism first introduced to North America in the late 19th century by Japanese teachers who served immigrant communities. It became popularized among non-Asian Americans after World War II. The single most important influence was the scholar Daisetz T. Suzuki, who lectured on Buddhism at Columbia University (1952–1957). Derived from the Sanskrit word *dhyana*, *Zen* literally means "meditation." This monochrome ink painting depicts the figure of Daruma, a semi-legendary Buddhist monk who lived during the 5th or 6th century. According to legend, Daruma is said to have lived in a cave, meditating on a wall for nine years, not speaking to anyone. His teaching and practice formed the foundation of Zen, which teaches that enlightenment is achieved through the profound realization that one is already an enlightened being. This awakening can happen gradually or in a flash of insight.

FIG. 2 (FACING)
Toyo Sesshu (Japan, 1420–1506)
Untitled Landscape, 15th century
Two-panel hanging scrolls: ink on silk
48.5 × 22 cm
Gift of Anand Pandarinath in Loving Memory of Dr. Pandarinath
Art Gallery of Greater Victoria 2002.021.009 and 2002.021.010
Photo: Stephen Topfer

A Zen monk and master of the rapidly painted *sumi-e*, or "flung ink," style of painting, Sesshu captured in his paintings a deep experience of—and feeling for—nature as significant to Zen practice.

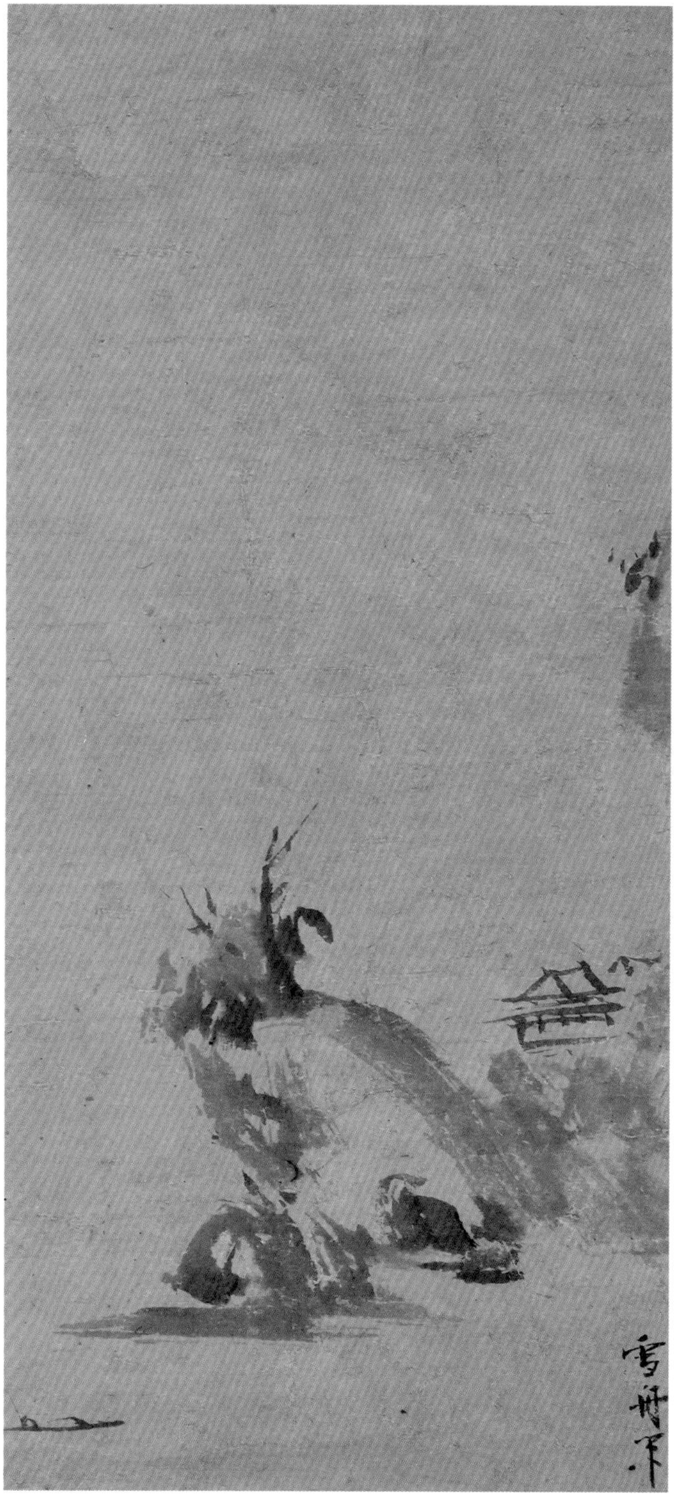

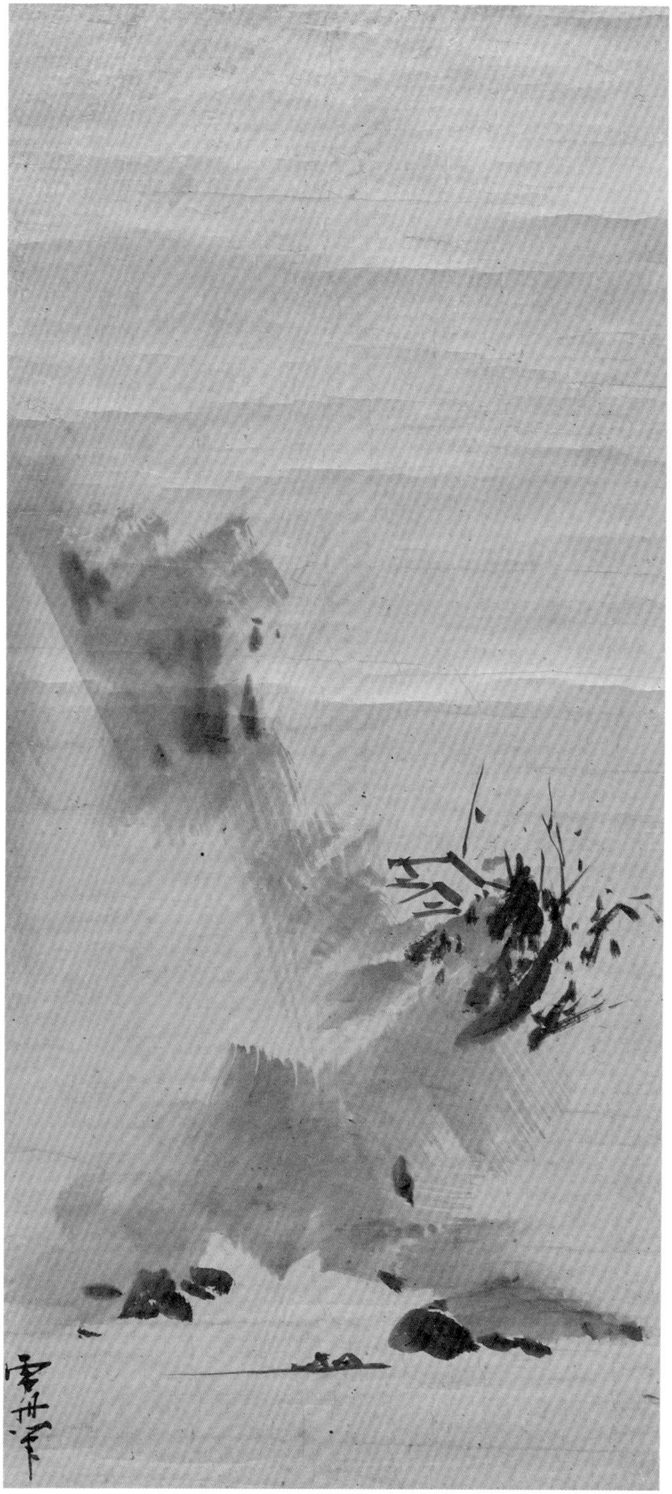

AN APPROPRIATE STATE OF MIND

On December 25, 1932, a short article appeared in the *New York Times* declaring that "American seekers after the 'Light of Asia' [could] now study Zen or meditative Buddhism at a hostel... specially built for foreign comfort and dedicated in the name of world peace to foreigners in search of the wisdom of the East" (FIG. 3).[2] The hostel was attached to the Enpuku-ji Temple in Yawata, not far from Kyoto, which had been established by Kozuki Tesshu Roshi with the assistance of the Japanese scholar and translator of Buddhism Daisetz Teitaro Suzuki. Two years after the founding of the hostel, the Seattle-based painter Mark Tobey travelled to Asia—to Hong Kong, Shanghai, Tokyo, and Kyoto—with his friend the noted potter Bernard Leach. Tobey had a deep interest in the expression or representation of the spiritual in art.[3] In Japan, he spent a month at the zendo (Zen monastery) of the Enpuku-ji Temple. He was the first American artist known to have spent time at a zendo, and his experiences were recorded in his notebooks, letters, and other writings.

Almost twenty-five years later, Tobey was invited to present a paper at the 6th National Conference of the U.S. Commission for the United Nations Educational, Scientific and Cultural Organization (UNESCO). In his paper "Japanese Traditions and American Art," he reflected on the impact that his stay at the zendo had on his approach to painting:

> When I resided at the Zen monastery I was given a sumi-ink painting of a large free brush circle to meditate upon. What was it? Day after day I would look at it. Was it selflessness? Was it the universe—where I could lose my identity? Perhaps I didn't see its aesthetic and missed the fine points of the brush which to a trained oriental eye would reveal much about the character of the man who painted it. But after my visit I found I had new eyes and that which seemed of little importance became magnified in words, and considerations not based on my former vision...[4] (FIG. 4)

Most of Tobey's time at the monastery was spent meditating, but he also practised sumi-ink painting, wrote haiku poetry, and learned Japanese syllabaries. This experience of contemplative and creative solitude affected him deeply, and taught him how to see a work of art in new ways. He continued,

FIG. 3
"Japanese Provide for Study of Buddhism by Foreigners," *The New York Times*, December 25, 1932

Japanese Provide for Study Of Buddhism by Foreigners

Special Correspondence, THE NEW YORK TIMES.

TOKYO, Dec. 5.—American seekers after the "Light of Asia" can now study Zen, or meditative Buddhism, at a hostel which has been specially built for foreign comfort and dedicated in the name of world peace to foreigners in search of the wisdom of the East. It is attached to the Empuku Temple in Yawata, not far from Kyoto.

The building, as described in the vernacular newspapers, is externally in pure Japanese style but is fitted with electric heaters, running water and foreign plumbing. The accommodation includes a chapel, private rooms for the students, bathrooms, kitchen and a meditation hall, all in Western style.

Students must pay 15 yen a month as room rent, the equivalent at present exchange of $3, and pay for their food in addition. They will be guided in their meditations by Chief Priest Kotsuki and his sermons will be interpreted once a week by Dr. Daisetsu Suzuki, who has lived in the United States and has an American wife.

FIG. 4

Nakahara Nantembo
(Japan, 1839–1925)
Enso, 1925
Ink on paper
126 × 31.8 cm
Gift of Judith Patt
Art Gallery of Greater Victoria 2012.023.020
Photo: Stephen Topfer

The *enso* symbolizes the Buddhist concept of Emptiness and exemplifies various qualities of Japanese aesthetics. For the Zen monk Nantembo, as for other Zen monks and nuns, calligraphy and painting were a form of Zen practice. The calligraphic mark is a trace of the artist's meditative flow of energy.

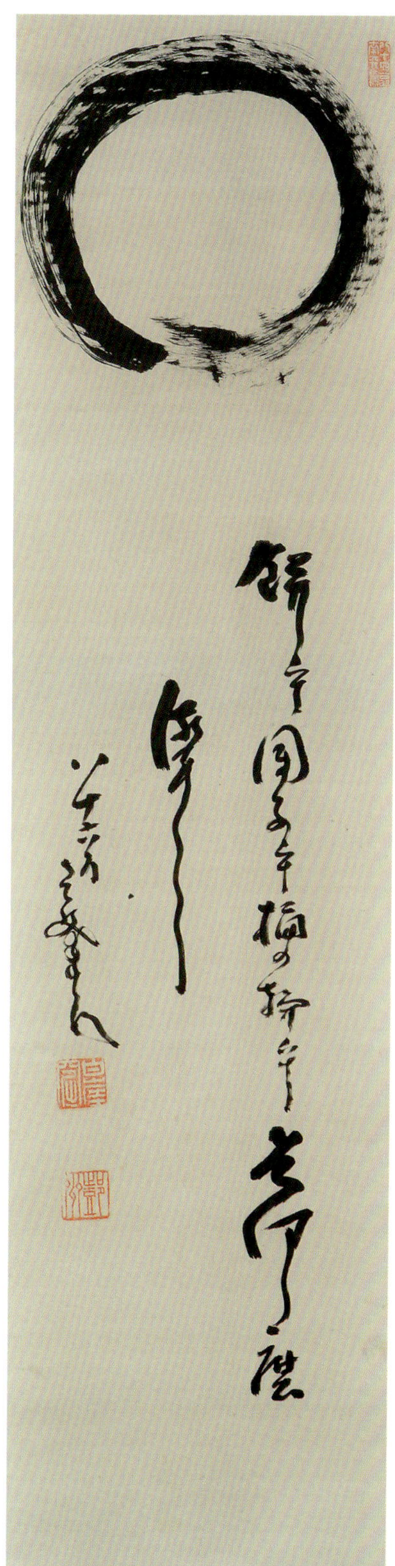

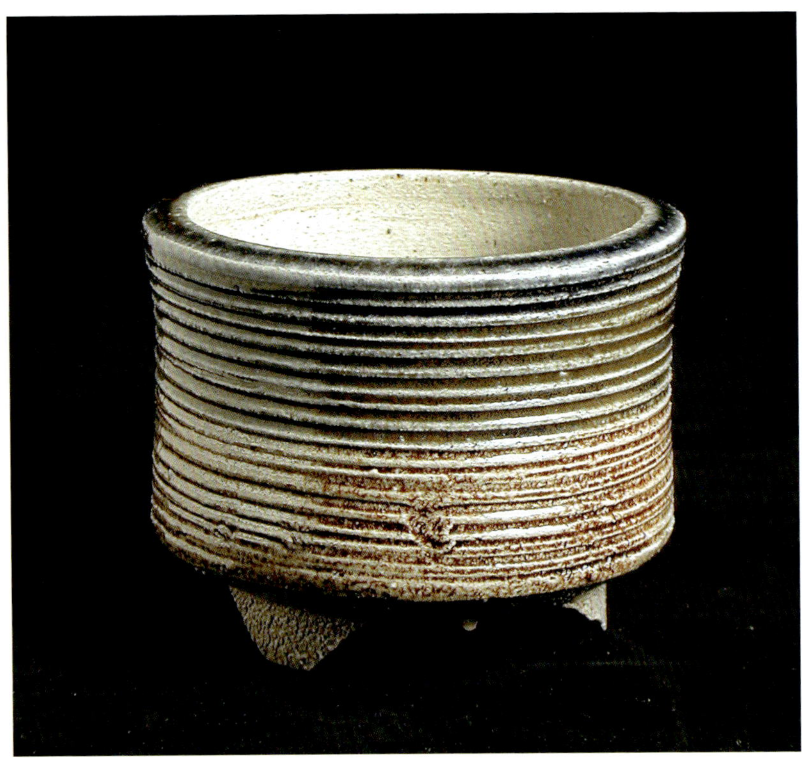

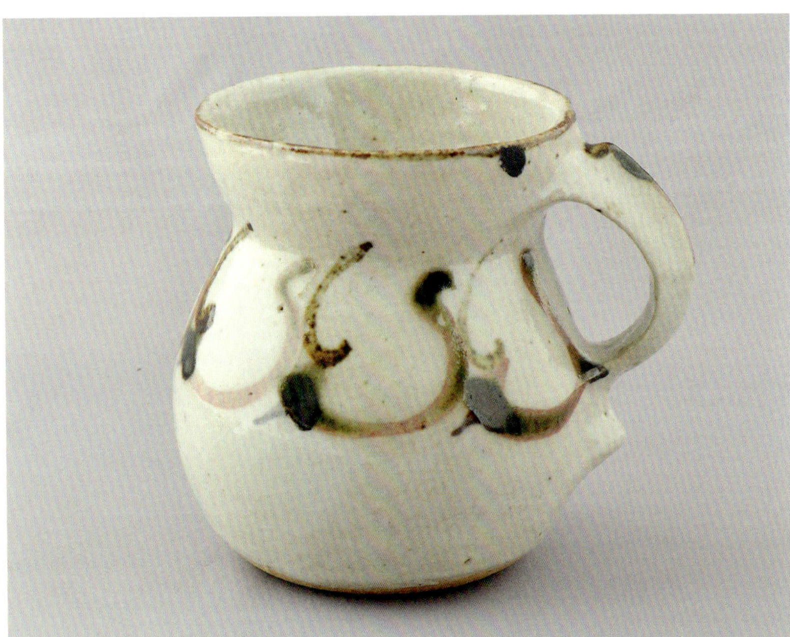

FIG. 5 (TOP)
Shoji Hamada (Japan, 1894–1978)
Incense burner, mid-20th century
Stoneware with salt glaze
8.5 × 10.8 cm
Fred and Isabel Pollard Collection
Art Gallery of Greater Victoria 1968.003.001
© Tomoo Hamada
Photo: Stephen Topfer

FIG. 6 (BOTTOM)
Kanjiro Kawai (Japan, 1890–1966)
Jug, c. 1940
Stoneware
12.5 × 14.5 × 10 cm
Gift of the Family of Aiko Suzuki
Art Gallery of Greater Victoria 2014.023.001
© Estate of Kawai Kanjiro; Courtesy of the Kawai Kanjiro Memorial Museum, Kyoto, Japan.
Photo: Stephen Topfer

FIG. 7 (TOP)
Shoji Hamada (Japan, 1894–1978)
Bottle, mid-20th century
Glazed stoneware
22.4 × 15.6 × 8 cm
Collection of Jessie Isobel Binning
Courtesy of UBC Museum of Anthropology, Vancouver 2695/18
© Tomoo Hamada
Photo: Kyla Bailey

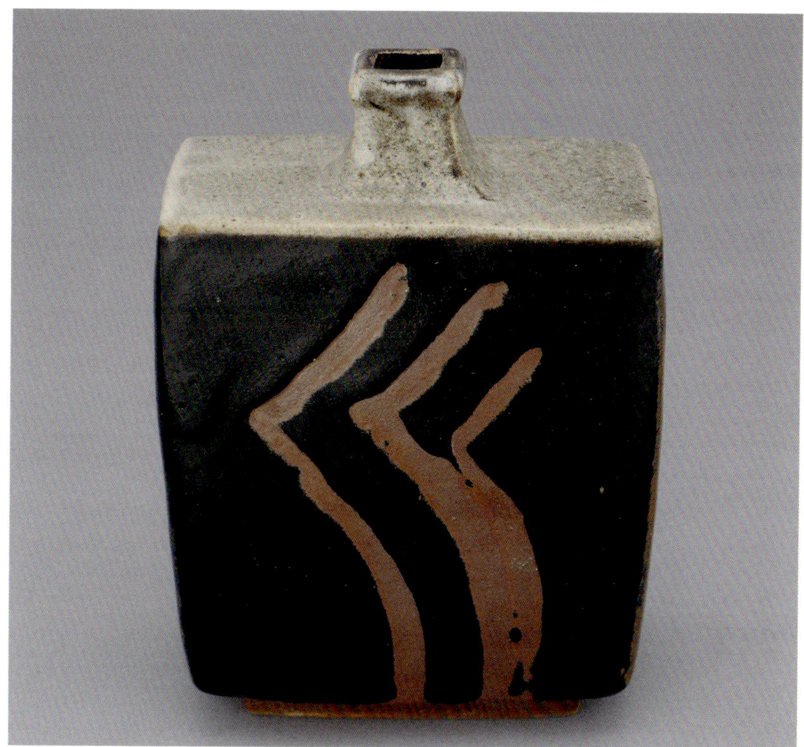

The Japanese Mingei "folk art" movement was part of a wider cultural and intellectual exchange in the early part of the 20th century. Just as Eastern philosophy and aesthetics were being introduced to the West, Western ideas of art and design were also entering Japan.

Suzuki was a central figure in this exchange and had an important influence on Soetsu Yanagi, the art critic and philosopher who, along with potters Shoji Hamada and Kanjiro Kawai, founded the Mingei movement. Informed by Buddhist ideas, Mingei promoted a concept of beauty as the inherent condition and expression of a thing, the transcendence of the dualism of beauty and ugliness.

FIG. 8 (BOTTOM)
Kanjiro Kawai (Japan, 1890–1966)
Suzuri (Inkstone), c. 1936
Stoneware with iron glaze
5.5 × 11.4 × 22.2 cm
Fred and Isabel Pollard Collection
Art Gallery of Greater Victoria 1968.004.001
© Estate of Kawai Kanjiro; Courtesy of the Kawai Kanjiro Memorial Museum, Kyoto, Japan
Photo: Stephen Topfer

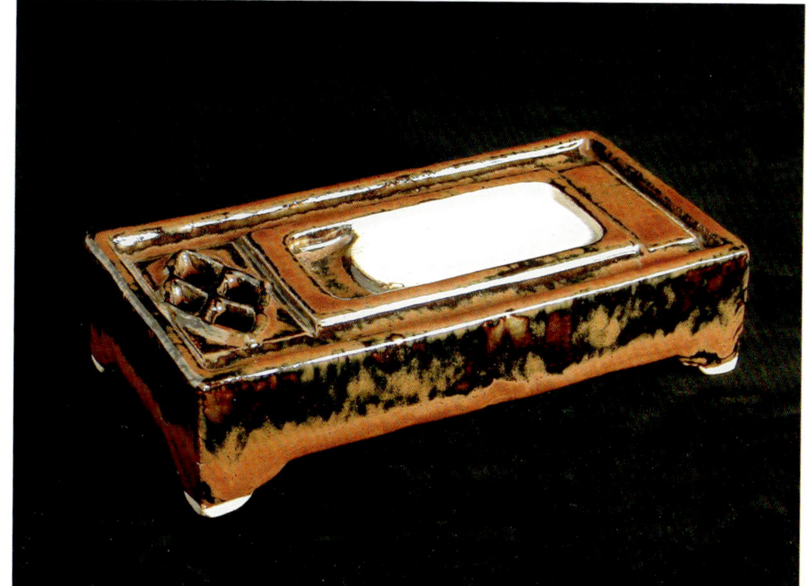

We hear some artists speak today of the act of painting... But a State of Mind is the first preparation and from this the action proceeds. Peace of Mind is another ideal, perhaps the ideal state to be sought for in the painting, and certainly preparatory to the act.[5]

Tobey's study of Zen continued informally in Seattle after the Second World War. In the late 1950s, he began a friendship with a Zen master and kendo instructor, Tomatsu Takizaki,[6] who in turn introduced him to a circle of accomplished Japanese American artists, including George Tsutakawa, Paul Horiuchi, and John Matsudaira, artists who were leading figures in the Pacific Northwest's Asian American art community. As art historian Barbara Johns notes, "Tobey... and Takizaki had intense discussions several days a week, sometimes extending into the night... At the same time that the discussions of Zen were underway, Tobey began some new work in sumi. A medium traditionally valued in Zen influenced art..."[7] (FIGS. 11–15). George Tsutakawa later commented, "Very few people could handle the sumi ink like Tobey. It was a great period for him."[8]

What Tobey learned from his study of Zen was the value of the preparation and cultivation of an appropriate state of mind as being foundational to art and aesthetic experience. His study of Zen nurtured a contemplative methodology that informed his

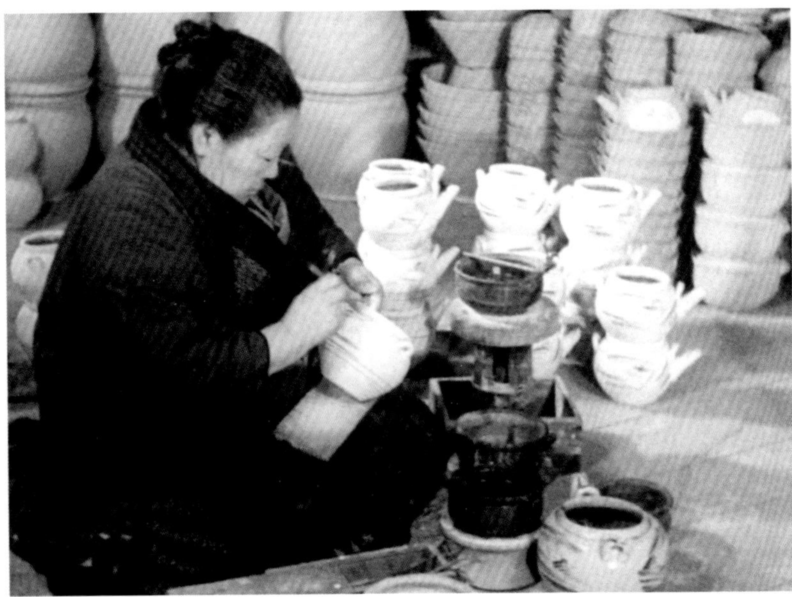

FIG. 9 (BELOW)
Masu Minagawa decorating Mashiko sansui teapots
Film still from *Mashiko Village Potter* (Japan, 1937)
32 min.
Produced by Kokusai Bunka Shinkokai
© The Mingei Film Archive/Marty Gross Film Productions, Inc., Toronto.

After spending a month at a Zen monastery, Mark Tobey travelled to Tokyo to meet up with a friend, the potter Bernard Leach, to visit the pottery village of Mashiko and witness the first firing of the now famous Mingei pottery kilns. Leach wrote, "It was only possible to fit in meetings with Mark in Tokyo and Mashiko... When Mark and I met, we talked endlessly, and I have a pictorial record on film of him watching Minagawa... decorating pots."*

FIG. 10 (FACING)
Mark Tobey
(USA/Switzerland, 1890–1976)
Untitled, 1940
Tempera on paper
22.2 × 14.3 cm
Gift of Dr. Pierre Dow
Art Gallery of Greater Victoria 1980.093.001
© Mark Tobey Estate/Seattle Art Museum
Photo: Stephen Topfer

Seattle-based artist Mark Tobey travelled to Japan in 1934 and spent a month at the zendo at the Enpuku-ji Temple, Yawata. He was the first American artist known to have spent time at a Zen monastery. The experience affected him deeply and shaped his approach to painting in significant ways. Although the priests at the Zen temple advised him that *satori*, or "sudden awakening," was impossible for a Westerner, Tobey championed the potential of Zen and contemplative practices for modern artists in the West.

* Bernard Leach, *Beyond East and West: Memoirs, Portraits and Essays* (London: Faber & Faber, 2012), n.p.

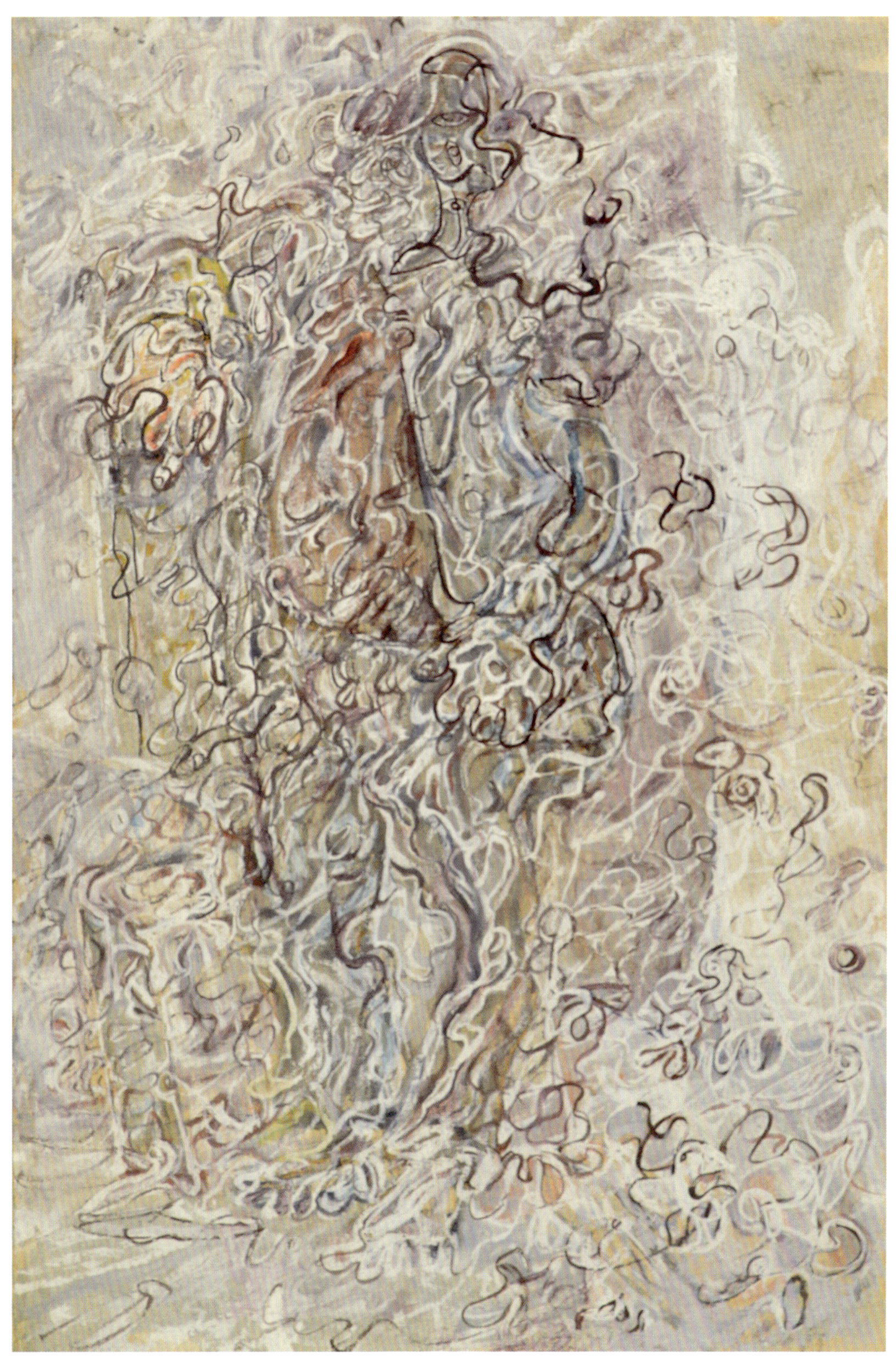

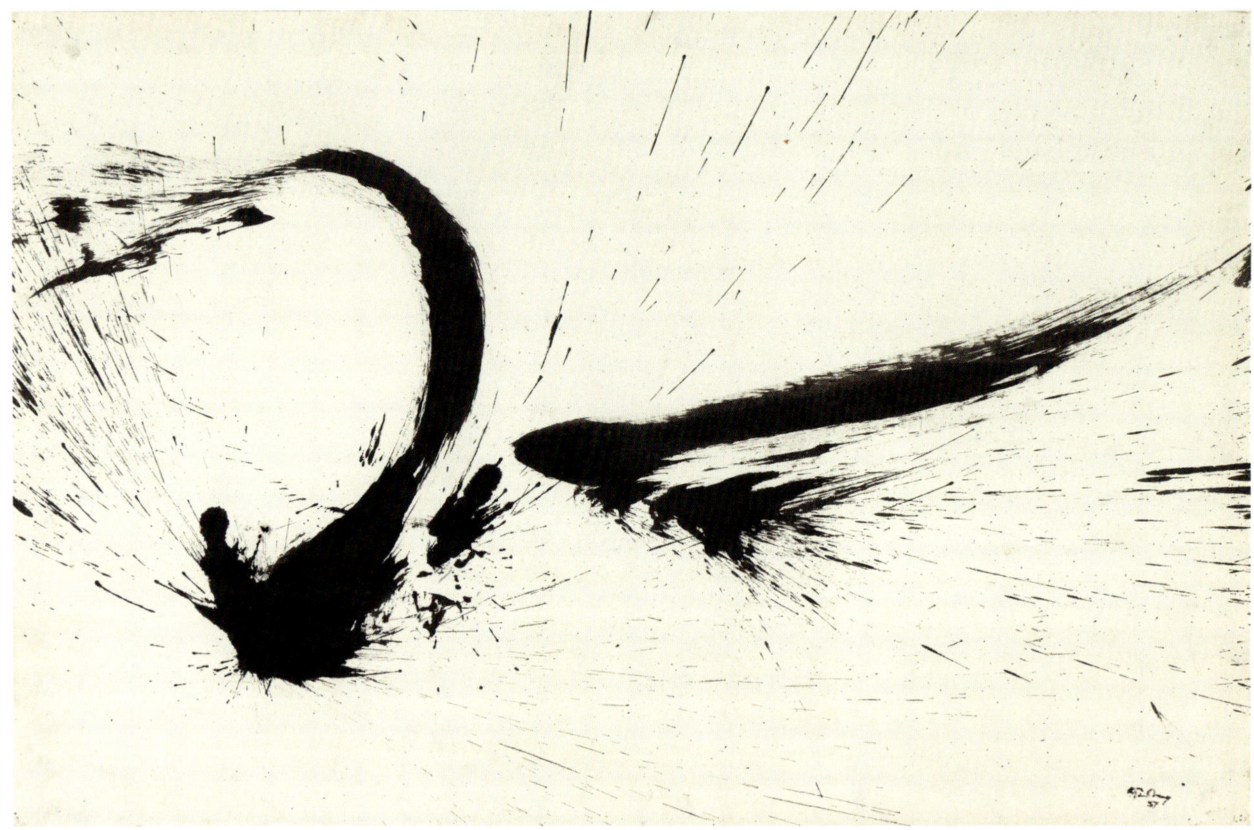

FIG. 11
Mark Tobey
(USA/Switzerland, 1890–1976)
Space Ritual #18, 1957
Sumi ink on wove paper,
mounted on board, 59.2 × 88.3 cm
Gift of the Estate of Mark Tobey / Seattle Art Museum 87.20 / © Mark Tobey Estate/Seattle Art Museum Photo: Elizabeth Mann

In the mid-1950s, Tobey began experimenting with sumi (Chinese ink), working in a "flung ink" style popularized by Zen masters such as Sesshu in the 15th century. Irene Namkung, the daughter of photographer Johsel Namkung, recalls visiting Tobey's studio:

> [I] remember very clearly the sunny day at about age 14, when my parents were sitting around with George Tsutakawa and Paul Horiuchi and Ayame. One of them said, "Where's Mark?"... my parents and Paul and George and myself... piled into cars and went to Mark's studio... We climbed a bunch of stairs to the front door and knocked. Mark, or maybe it was first his friend Pehr, led us into a huge room with a very high ceiling, which was filled with row upon row of long tables, end to end, covered with sumi-e paper. Black ink was splashed everywhere: on the walls, ceiling, floor, and of course, incredible art on the tables. We were all silent and overwhelmed. The first comment from George and Paul was that Mark had created a new, energetic Western form of painting with sumi ink.*

* Irene Namkung, email correspondence with the author, January 28, 2021.

FIG. 12
Mark Tobey
(USA/Switzerland, 1890–1976)
Untitled, 1957
Sumi ink on wove paper, 40.2 × 28.5 cm
Gift of Mr. and Mrs. C.D. Graham in recognition of the artist's 85th birthday / Art Gallery of Greater Victoria 1975.060.001 / © Mark Tobey Estate/Seattle Art Museum / Photo: Stephen Topfer

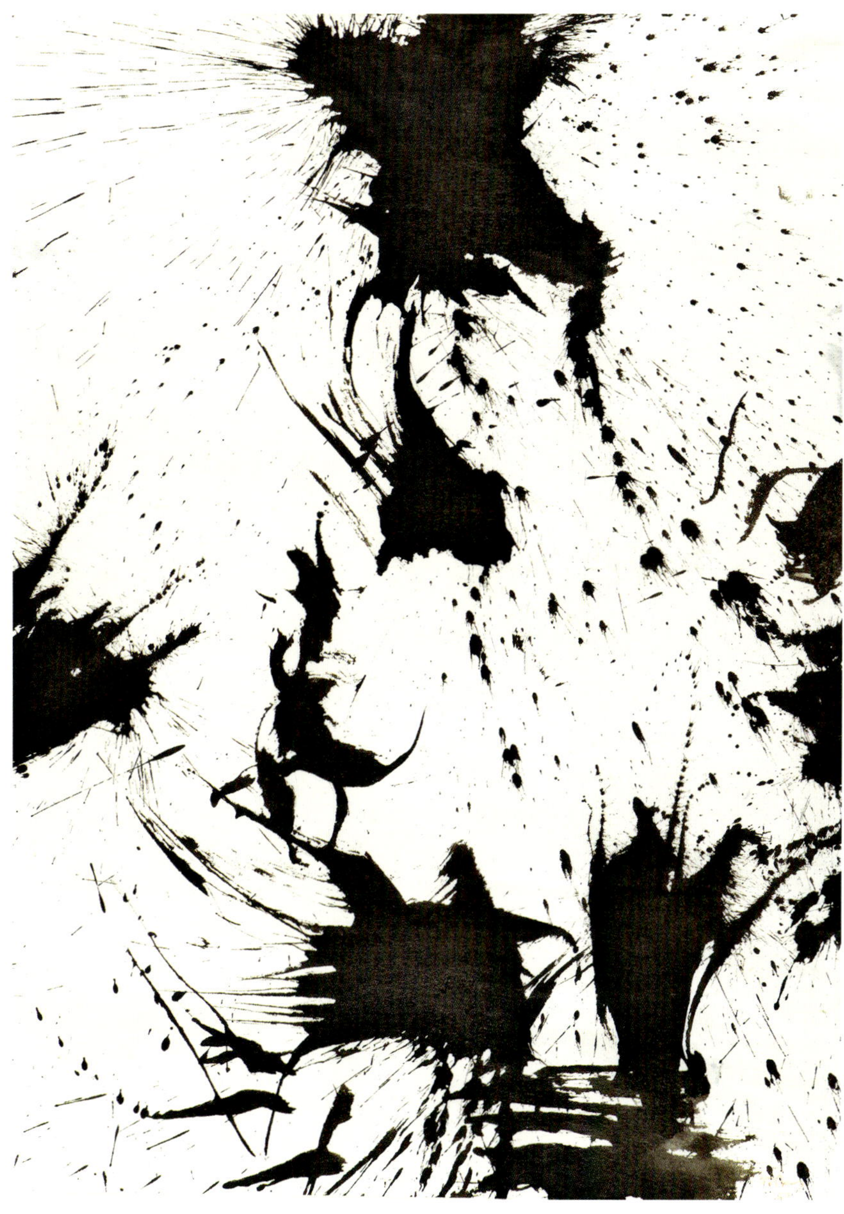

Tobey's approach to sumi-e has been described as "a new, energetic Western form of painting," at once informed by his study of Chinese calligraphy and Zen. The post–World War II period, following the signing of the Treaty of Peace with Japan (1951), restimulated Tobey's interest in Zen and its aesthetic values, particularly the Japanese concept of *shibui*. *Shibui* referred to a subtle and unobtrusive notion of beauty which Tobey sought to convey in his work. The Japanese art critic Michiaki Kawakita wrote that in 1958 Tobey took him to the Willard Gallery, New York, to show him his work. Kawakita murmured in response to what he saw, "Oh, this is *shibui*," to which Tobey responded, "Yes, *shibui*, *shibui*! That's the effect I want!" and continued that only those who can understand *shibui* can understand his work.* But Tobey lamented that it was rare. Kawakita regarded Tobey's preoccupation with *shibui* as a search for "depth" in his work.

* Michiaki Kawakita, "'Shibusa' to gendai bijutsu" [Shibusa and Contemporary Art], in *Geijutsu Shincho*, vol. 11, no. 11 (1960), pp. 64–74. I am grateful to Dr Chiaki Ajioka for drawing my attention to this essay, and for her translation.

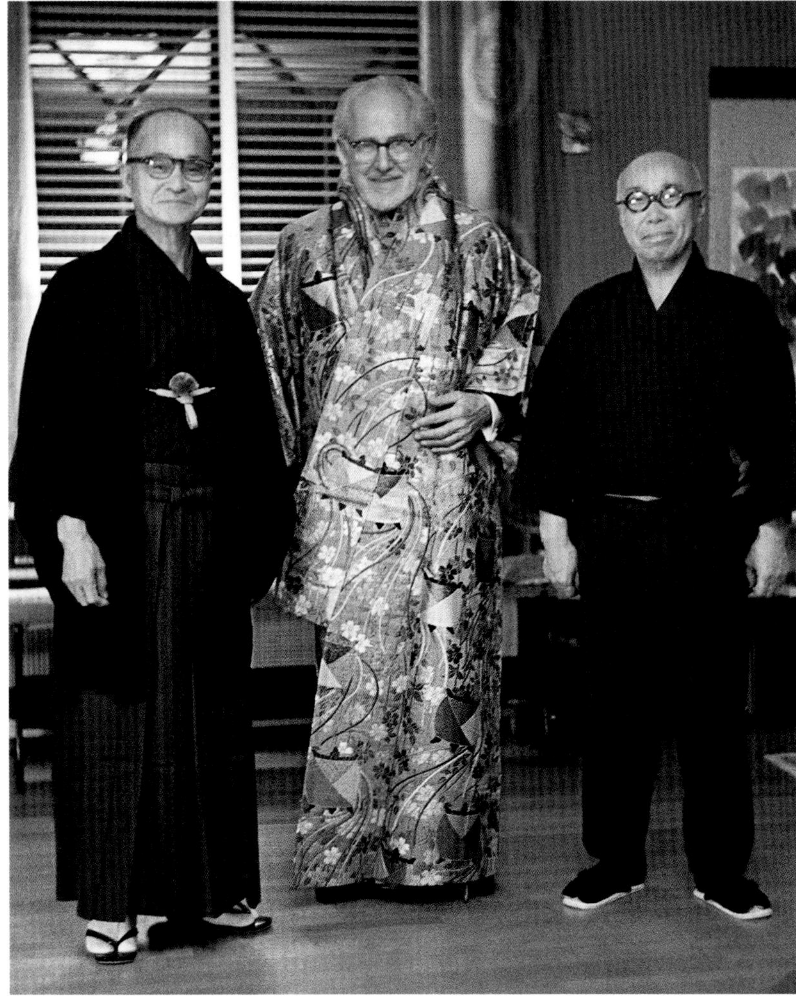

FIG. 13 (LEFT)
Johsel Namkung
(Korea/USA, 1919–2013)
Manzo Nomura, Mark Tobey and Shoji Hamada at the home of George Tsutakawa, 1963
Gelatin silver print, digitized
Courtesy of Irene Namkung, Seattle
© Estate of Johsel Namkung

FIG. 14 (FACING TOP)
Johsel Namkung
(Korea/USA, 1919–2013)
Paul Horiuchi, George Tsutakawa, Mark Tobey and Mineko Namkung painting with sumi in the home of George Tsutakawa, 1960
Gelatin silver print, digitized
Courtesy of Irene Namkung, Seattle
© Estate of Johsel Namkung

FIG. 15 (FACING BOTTOM)
Tomatsu Takizaki, Paul Horiuchi and Mark Tobey, critiquing a painting at Tobey's studio, late 1950s–early 1960s
University of Washington Libraries, Special Collections, Neg UW26955z
Photo: George Uchida

unique approach to painting. The circle of Japanese American artists that Takizaki had introduced him to was encouraged by Tobey's championing of Zen to further explore Zen approaches in their own artistic practices. What these artists shared, as Johns notes, was not the influence of Asian art filtered through Western experience, "but—from the outset—a fundamentally different perspective on the relationship between nature, the individual, and art."[9] Tobey's influence across a wide network of artist peers and friends contributed to developments in contemporary art that reverberated throughout the 20th century.

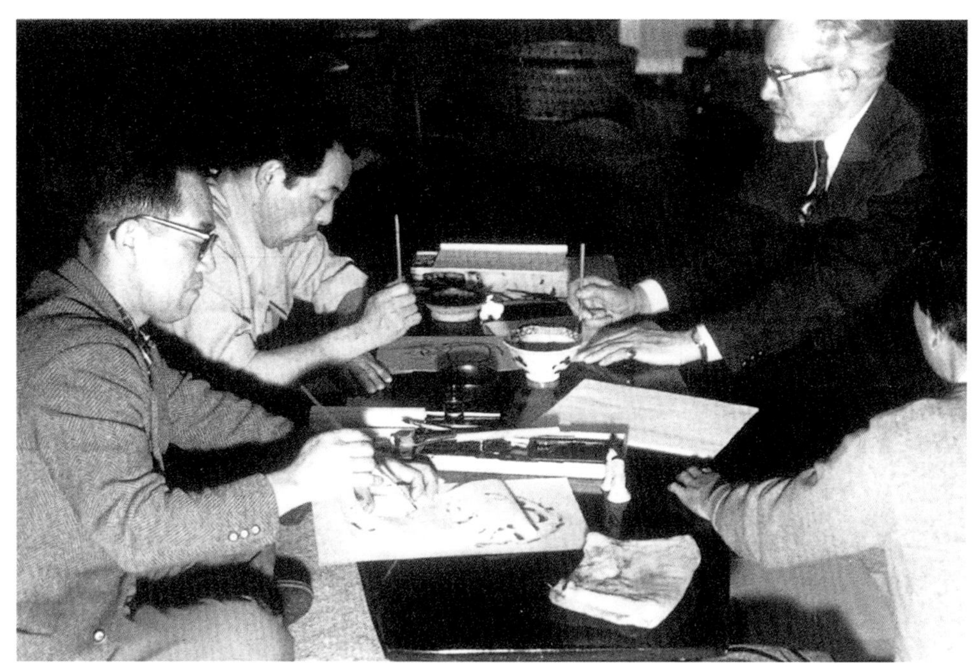

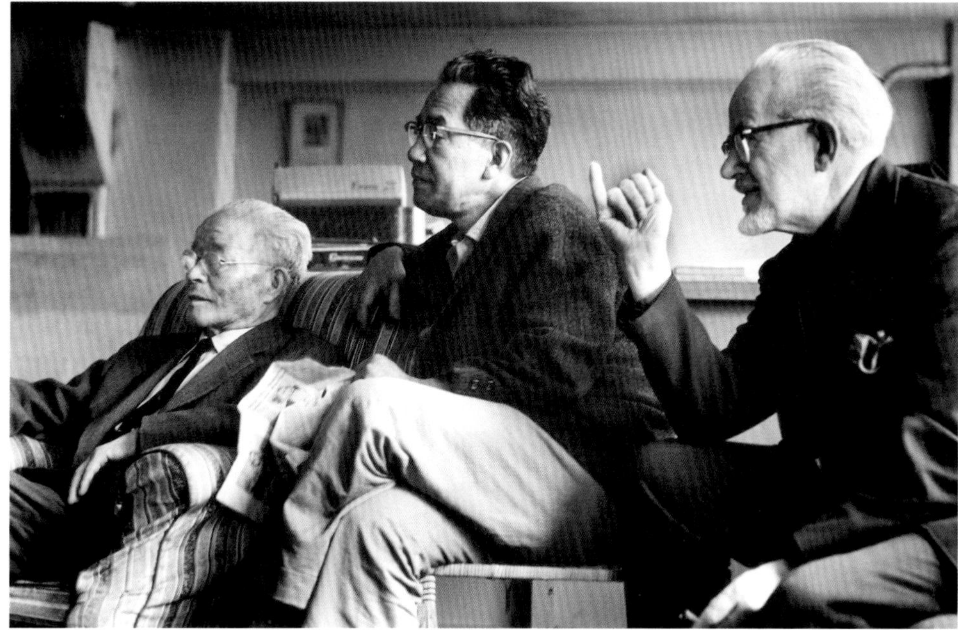

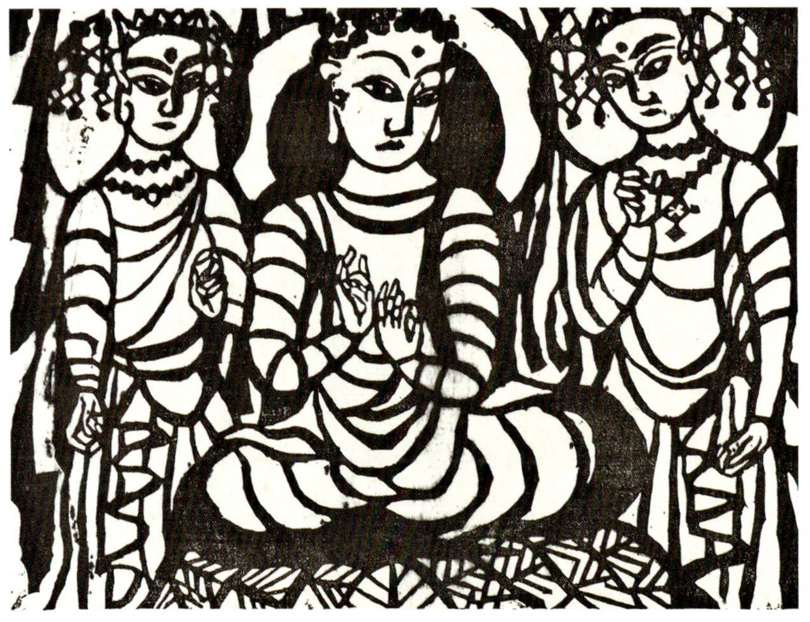

FIG. 16 (TOP)
Shiko Munakata
(Japan, 1903–1975)
Shaka Nyorai (Shakyamuni Buddha), 1936
From a series of 23 prints, *Kegonkyo (Avatamsaka Sutra)*
Woodcut print on paper
30.2 × 39.2 cm
Gift of Fred and Isabel Pollard
Art Gallery of Greater Victoria 1971.007.001

Photo: Stephen Topfer

Shiko Munakata was a Japanese printmaker associated with the Mingei movement. The religious imagery of Buddhist temples often inspired his work. Munakata won the Grand Prize at the Venice Biennale in 1956 and exchanged letters with Mark Tobey in 1959 prior to his tour of the United States. He was among a select group of Japanese artists, mainly printmakers, who were invited to the United States to improve cultural relations between the two nations after World War II.

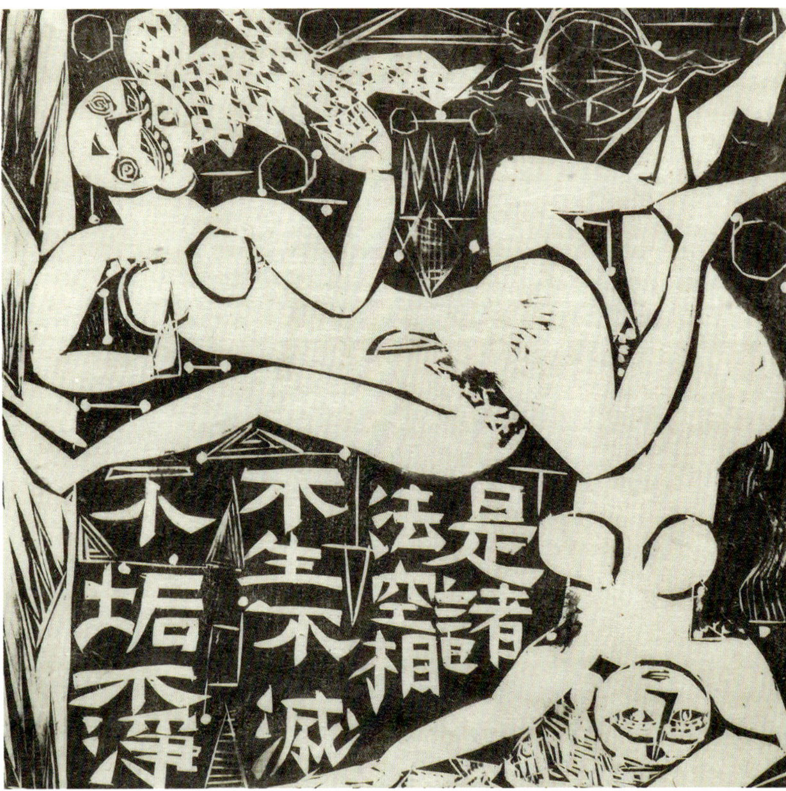

FIG. 17 (BOTTOM)
Shiko Munakata
(Japan, 1903–1975)
Fu Sho Nosaku, 1957
From the series of 16 prints
Re-opening Prajnaparamita: Unborn
Woodcut on paper
22 × 21.9 cm
Inscription: "All Dharmas are empty and have no characteristic. They are unborn and unceasing, undefiled and unpurified."
Fred and Isabel Pollard Collection
Art Gallery of Greater Victoria 1968.018.001

Photo: Stephen Topfer

FIG. 18 (TOP)
Kiyoshi Saito (Japan, 1907–1997)
Stone Garden, Kyoto, 1965
Woodcut print on paper
153.5 × 97 cm
Gift of Fred and Isabel Pollard
Art Gallery of Greater Victoria 1967.030.001

Photo: Stephen Topfer

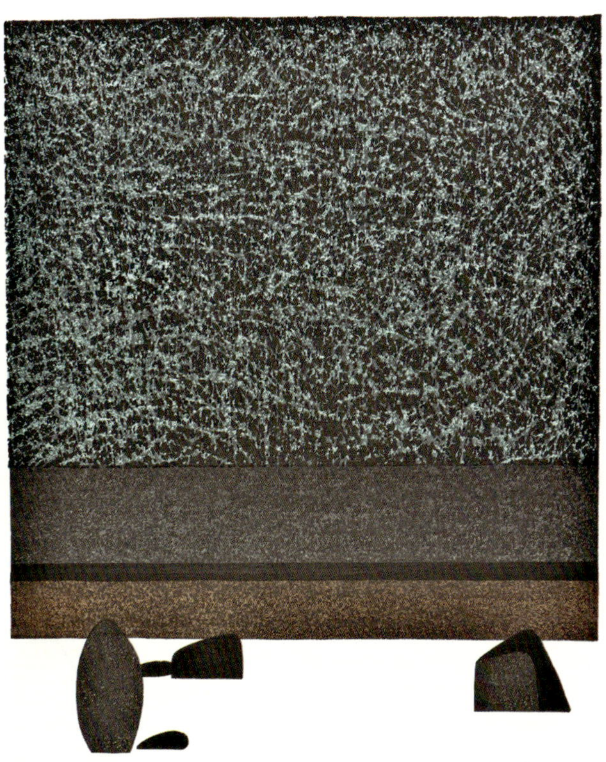

Kiyoshi Saito was one of the most popular Japanese artists among Americans in the postwar period. He was the first Japanese artist to be invited to the United States to foster cultural exchange between the two nations, in 1956. In Seattle, Saito was welcomed at the home of artist George Tsutakawa and introduced to artists including Mark Tobey and Paul Horiuchi. These exchanges were significant in forming lasting relationships between artists in Japan and artists in America, suggesting how new ideas in art were fostered by cross-cultural interpersonal relationships.

FIG. 19 (BOTTOM)
Kiyoshi Saito (Japan, 1907–1997)
Stone Garden, Ryoan-ji, 1955
Woodcut print with colours on paper
97 × 153.5 cm
Gift of Fred and Isabel Pollard
Art Gallery of Greater Victoria 1968.263.001

Photo: Stephen Topfer

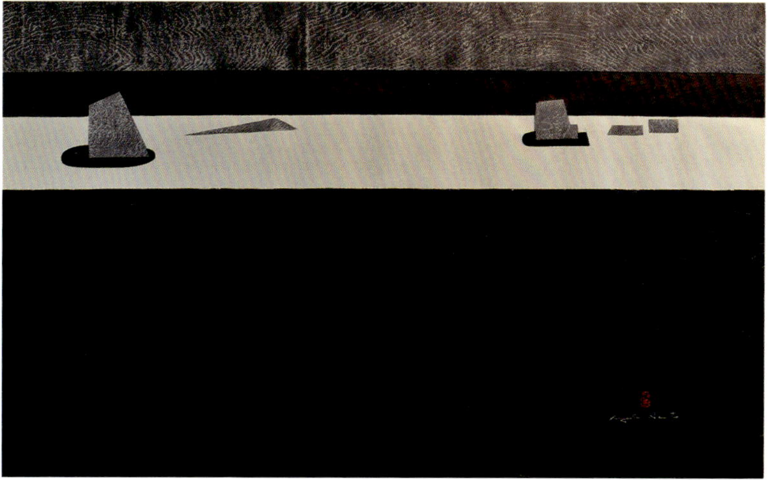

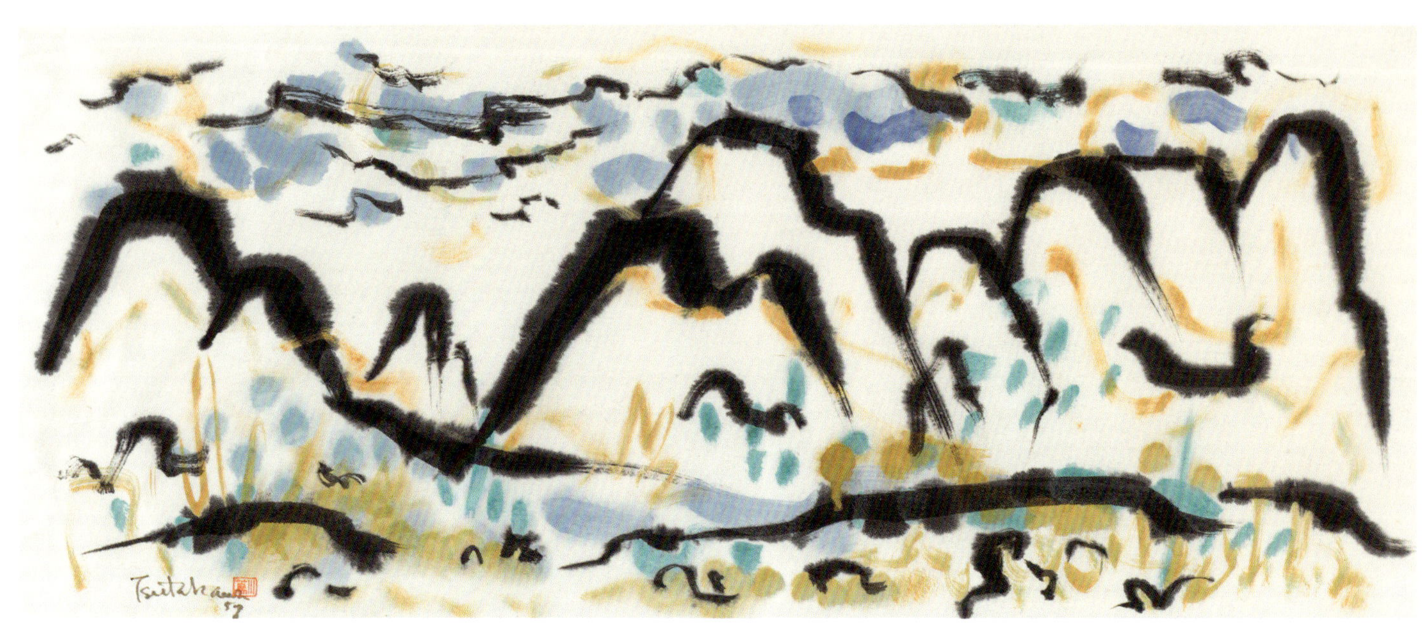

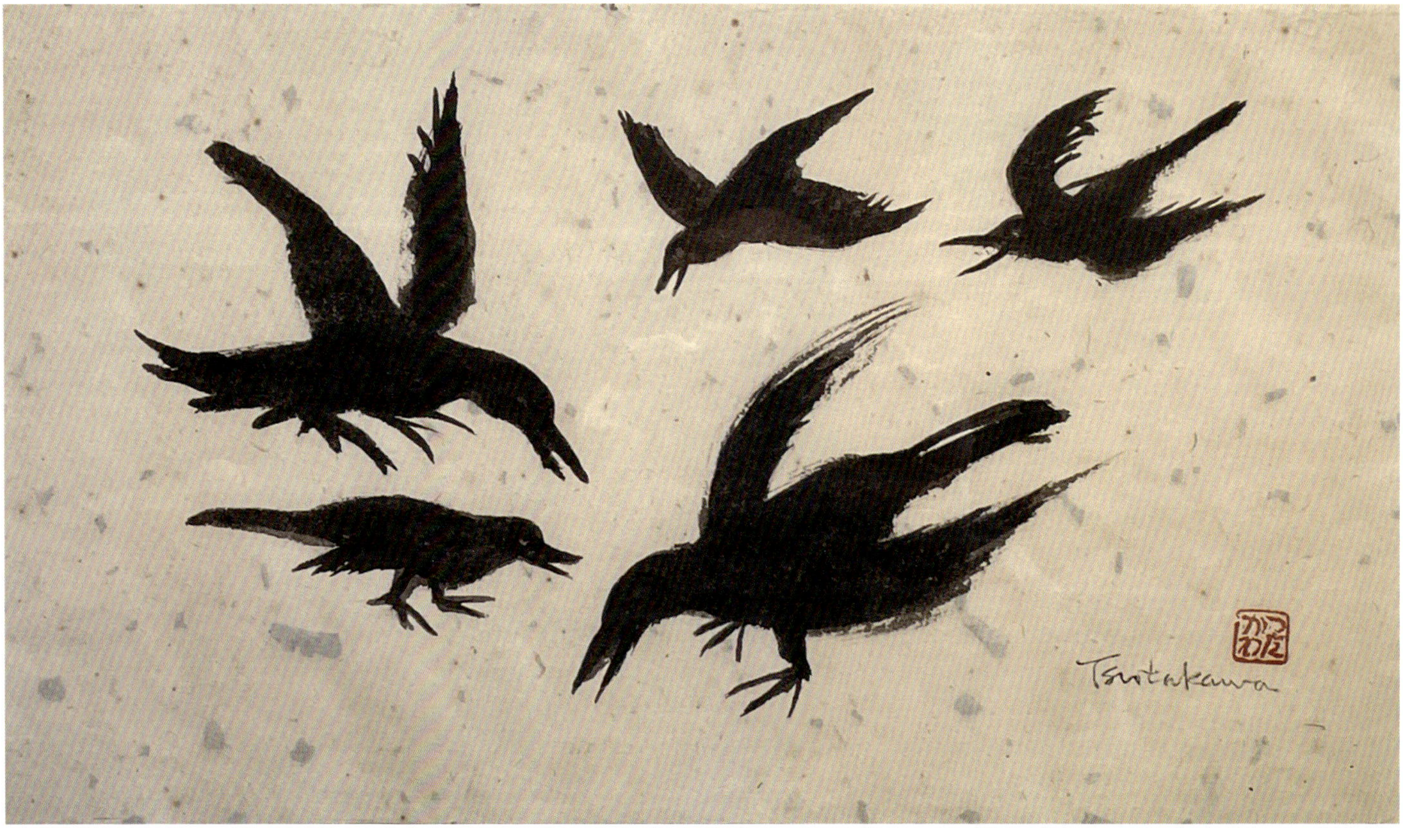

FIG. 20 (TOP)
George Tsutakawa (USA, 1910–1997)
Mountain Landscape, 1957
Ink and watercolour on Japanese sumi paper
27.94 × 63.5 cm
Gift of Robert Kaplan and Jane Kaplan from the collection of Charles and Lillian Kaplan
Seattle Art Museum 2010.32.2
© Tsutakawa Art Legacy LLC; Courtesy of the Tsutakawa Family / Photo: Elizabeth Mann

George Tsutakawa is best known as a sculptor, and although born and raised in the United States, spent time in the 1920s, during his early childhood, in Japan with his grandparents. He recalled in an oral history interview that during the time that he lived in Japan, his grandmother would send him to a Zen master: "We were told to sit and first listen to his lecture, stories, and then he would make tea or go through tea ceremony, and make all of us kids—small class, maybe eight or ten—drink this bitter tea, have a small piece of candy, and then we'll all go to his small kiln and make things with clay... a small pottery class."* Tsutakawa attributes his decision to become an artist to the influence of his grandparents in Japan.

FIG. 21 (BOTTOM)
George Tsutakawa (USA, 1910–1997)
Blackbird Study, 1975
Sumi ink on mulberry paper
26 × 48.9 cm
Estate of the artist, Seattle
© Tsutakawa Art Legacy LLC; Courtesy of the Tsutakawa Family / Photo: Gerard Tsutakawa

* Martha Kingsbury, interview with George Tsutakawa, September 8, 1983, Seattle, WA (Smithsonian Institute, Archives of American Art). Available at www.aaa.si.edu/collections/interviews/oral-history-interview-george-tsutakawa-11913#transcript.

BUDDHISM AS A METHODOLOGY OF CONTEMPORARY ART PRACTICE

For artists such as Mark Tobey or his New York–based friend and peer Charmion Von Wiegand (FIGS. 78–81, PAGES 102–104), the study of Asian art provided an antidote to the culture of materialism and individualism characterizing modern art in the mid-century in North America. Artists such as Tobey and Von Wiegand regarded painting as a site of spiritual inquiry and expression. For Von Wiegand, drawing initially on her study of theosophy and later on her practice of Tibetan Buddhism in New York, painting provided a context within which to explore esoteric spiritual and metaphysical ideas—of the relationship between the body and the cosmos, of sacred space and colour, of cycles of life, and ultimately, the transcendent experience of Tibetan Buddhist religious practice.

Von Wiegand, an art critic and curator as well as an accomplished painter and collagist, embraced Tibetan Buddhism in New York in 1967 after meeting and building close relationships with the Tibetan refugee community. Her late paintings, in particular, reveal the impact and potential of Buddhism as it coincided with the Western imagination. Works such as *Untitled* (1964) (FIG. 80, PAGE 103) or *Invocation to the Adi-Buddha* (1968–1970) (FIG. 81, PAGE 104) visualize the *experience* of Tibetan Buddhist ritual and meditation as sound, form, and colour, synthesizing Tibetan Buddhist colour symbolisms and tantric geometries with esoteric visual theories drawn from her deep study of Neo-plasticism. Von Wiegand's late paintings provide a visual expression of Tibetan Buddhist practice and its experiential effects. These paintings could be regarded as a form of "modern Buddhist art," constituted through the encounter between East and West and demonstrating Buddhism's relevance to the modern West.[10]

Artists such as Tobey and Von Wiegand drew on Buddhism not simply as a source of artistic inspiration but as a *methodology* of art practice, where Buddhism contributed a framework of thinking and system of methods for the creation of works of art. In other words, artists were interpreting Buddhist ideas and doctrines to infer a new artistic methodology to counteract the prevailing commodification of art. For these artists, and numerous others in their extended circle, art making was not simply the pursuit of creative self-expression but a practice of contemplative, experiential, and philosophical inquiry, directed towards the goal of self- and social transformation. Considering

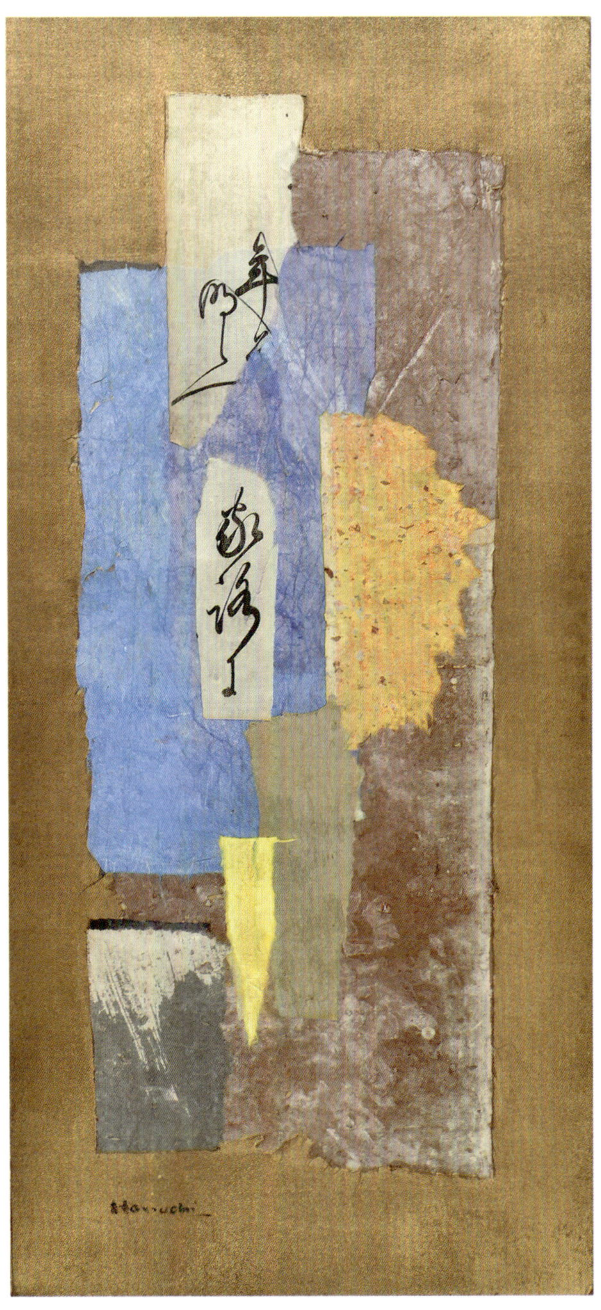

FIG. 22
Paul Horiuchi (Japan/USA, 1906–1999)
Ancient Colors and Words #2, c. 1965
Paper collage with ink and gold leaf
91.6 × 41.5 cm
Fred and Isabel Pollard Collection
Art Gallery of Greater Victoria 1970.018.001
Photo: Stephen Topfer

Paul Horiuchi studied calligraphy and sumi painting as a child in Japan, but it was not until mid-life that he focused on painting, going on to develop his signature collage style. Horiuchi typically painted landscape and nature themes with references to Japanese culture. By their mutual connection to Zen master Tomatsu Takizaki, Horiuchi became friends with Mark Tobey, who encouraged him to look to his Japanese heritage to develop his unique modernist style.

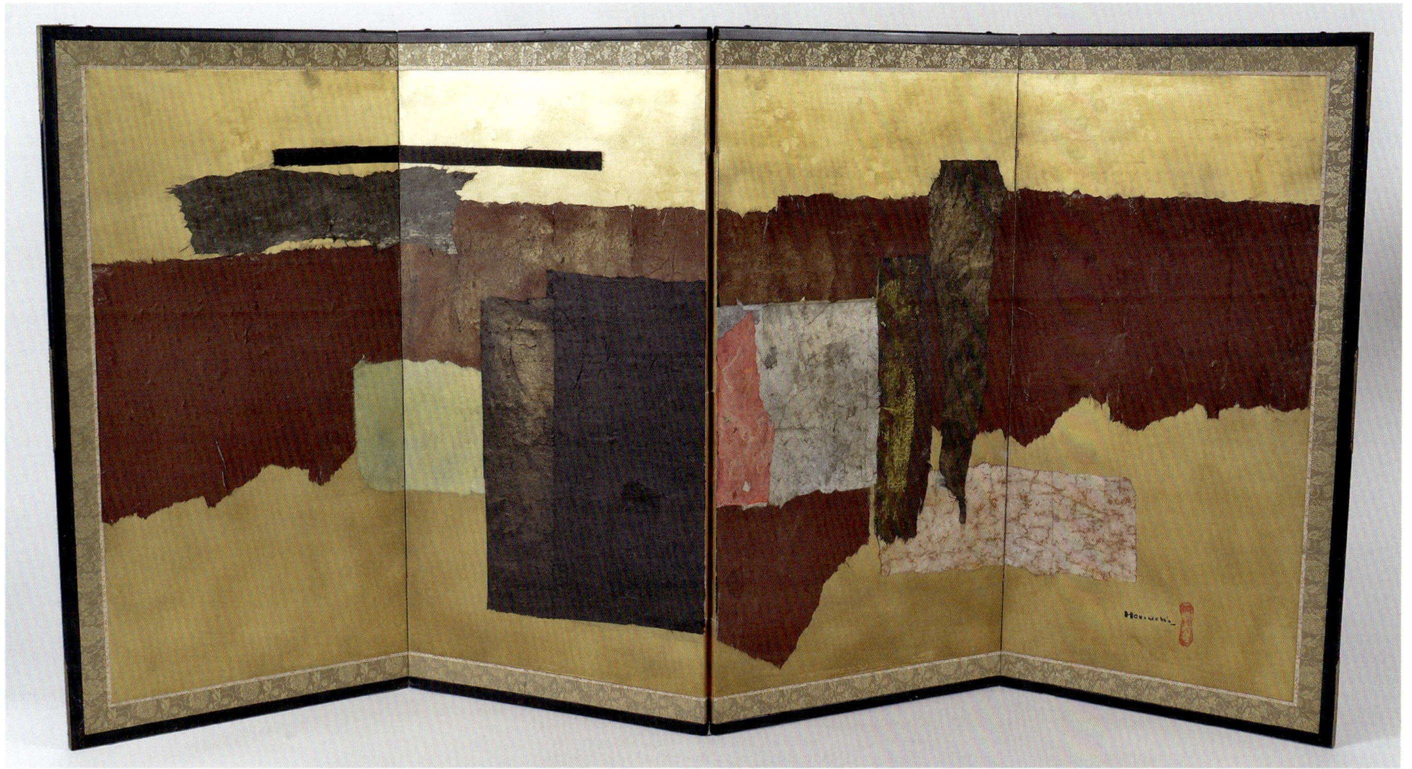

FIG. 23
Paul Horiuchi (Japan/USA, 1906–1999)
Esthetics of the Past, c. 1965
Four-fold screen: paint and collaged paper
81 × 176 cm
Art Gallery of Greater Victoria 1968.090.001
Photo: Stephen Topfer

Buddhism as a methodology of art practice encompasses a range of intellectual, meditational, experiential, and interpersonal methods, directed not only towards the generation of creative outcomes but at deepening an artist's understanding of Buddhist concepts and teachings. Art making provides a context wherein Buddhist ideas can be independently examined, activated, performed, tested, and actualized in such a way that the practice of art and the practice of Buddhism are intertwined. Understanding how Buddhism functions as a methodology of contemporary art practice, however, shifts the focus of inquiry from the formal and stylistic qualities of an art object to the processes of artistic creation. In turn, the highly subjective, experimental, and sometimes iconoclastic nature of these artistic inquiries has contributed to the making different of the visual culture of Buddhism in the contemporary context. These artistic experiments have contributed to the cultural redefinition of Buddhism as suggested by the term "modern Buddhism."

MODERN BUDDHISM

In his influential book *The Making of Buddhist Modernism*, Buddhist studies scholar David McMahan charts the development of modern Buddhism, which he identifies as

> a new form of Buddhism that is a result of [a] process of modernization, westernization, reinterpretation, image-making, revitalization, and reform that has been taking place not only in the West but also in Asian countries for over a century. This new form of Buddhism has been fashioned by modernizing Asian Buddhists and western enthusiasts deeply engaged in creating Buddhist responses to the dominant problems and questions of modernity...[11]

McMahan outlines a range of features that characterize modern Buddhism, including the influence of Protestant and Enlightenment values; the tendency to secularism; the de-emphasis of ritual and metaphysical elements, including concepts of reincarnation; de-traditionalization; and the opening up of monastic practices to lay communities. His tracing of the sociopolitical, philosophical, and cultural developments that have contributed to the development of modern Buddhism pose questions, not only of adaptation and authenticity, but of Buddhism's capacity to provide solutions to the problems of modernity in largely secular, materially driven, Western cultural contexts.

Another distinguished scholar of Buddhism, Donald Lopez Jr., writes,

> It seems clear that much of what we regard as Buddhism today is, in fact, modern Buddhism. And modern Buddhism seems to have begun, at least in part, as a response to the threat of modernity, as perceived by certain Asian Buddhists, especially those who had encountered colonialism. Yet these modern Buddhists were very much products of modernity, with the rise of the middle class, the power of the printing press, the ease of international travel. Many of these leaders were deeply involved in independence movements and identified Buddhism with the interests of the state... Yet together they forged an international Buddhism that transcends cultural and national boundaries, creating... a cosmopolitan network of intellectuals, writing most often in English.[12]

As Lopez and McMahan both point out, modern Buddhism has been concerned with the redefinition of Buddhism in accordance with what were considered its essential teachings by modern proponents, particularly those that encountered colonialism. These scholars and teachers—including prominent figures such as Anagarika Dharmapala, Daisetz T. Suzuki, Alan Watts, Thich Nhat Hanh, Chogyam Trungpa, and the 14th Dalai Lama—participated in a process of separating what was considered essential to Buddhism from what was considered cultural, each contributing to a concept of Buddhism as a universal religion.[13] It is interesting to note that in North America, the arrival and influence of Buddhist teachers mirrored U.S. foreign policy relations with Asia, hence the preference in the West for certain forms of Buddhism over others, with impact on developments in the visual arts.

As the artist and writer Ellen Pearlman has noted, in the United States, "Buddhism's emphasis on pacifism, non-theism, anti-materialism ... attracted many forward-thinking individuals," including artists and intellectuals.[14] But unlike the context of Buddhism in Asia, where practitioners are largely socialized into forms of Buddhism by way of long-standing religious and cultural institutions, traditions, and practices, Buddhists in North America arrive at a commitment to practice by way of an intellectual engagement with Buddhist thought and philosophy, often as an individual spiritual and/or meditational practice, outside the conventions of an established religious community. Criticisms of modern Buddhism, therefore, centre on its privileging of a private spirituality, which "selectively places those elements that are consistent with modern sensibilities at the core of the tradition and dismisses all else,"[15] thereby oversimplifying and distorting a complex religion.

But while these criticisms provide us with reasonable caution, various Buddhist studies scholars also contend that the ongoing globalization of Buddhism suggests the need for new paradigms to better explain and examine its modernization. These scholars argue that "Buddhist transformations in Asia and in the West are not seen as distinct but as related, taking place in communication across multiple nodes that cross East–West lines."[16] The implications of this for the visual arts is to rethink the historicization and orientalization of Buddhism and Buddhist art as an area-specific, geographically bound field of practice and therefore to consider the relationship between Buddhism and art more expansively, accounting for it as a living, global religion with ongoing contemporary relevance and cultural impact. In this regard, contemporary artists working with Buddhism as a methodology provide us with insight into both the risks and opportunities of such cross-cultural engagement. What follows in this essay, then, is a survey of how contemporary artists working in North America have engaged with Buddhism and Buddhist ideas, reflecting on the impact that Buddhism has had on art in the 20th and 21st centuries.

AWARENESS PRACTICE

In 1945, the experimental composer and pioneering music theorist John Cage purchased a painting by Mark Tobey at the artist's first solo exhibition at the Willard Gallery, New York. The painting, titled *Crystallizations* (1944) (FIG. 24), consisted of all-over, closely worked line, producing a dense, energetic, netlike quality of the figure ground and conveying a modulated and vibrating quality of light. The success of the work relies on the quality of the line. The varied strokes move in different directions, and the line work possesses a quality of inscription—having the appearance of being cut or etched into the surface of the painting with a fine brush or stylus, which referenced Tobey's interest in Asian calligraphy.

Cage reflected,

> [I]t was Tobey who had a great effect on my way of seeing, which is to say my involvement with painting, or my involvement with life even ... I remember a particular walk with Mark Tobey from the area of Seattle around the Cornish School downhill and through the town toward a Japanese restaurant—a walk that would not normally take more than 45 minutes, but on this occasion it must have taken several hours, because he was constantly stopping and pointing out things to see, opening my eyes in other words ... Just seeing what there was to see ... Only if you move from understanding to actual experience can you really begin to see.[17]

Tobey's awareness of nature—of vastness contained within the smallest detail—as expressed through his painting introduced Cage to the Buddhist principle of interpenetration. Cage's experience of Tobey's painting held an analogy with Chan and Zen approaches to experiencing the world, recognizing the primacy of experience over theory. Cage described *Crystallizations* as having the quality of the North Star, guiding him in his own work. It was a reminder of the Zen attention to awareness and interconnectedness, of vastness encompassed by microcosmic detail. He wrote,

> It was a canvas that had been utterly painted. But it [was not] the geometrical abstraction that interested me, so it brought about a change. And also that walk to the Japanese restaurant brought about a change in my eyes and in my relation to art such that when I left the Willard Gallery exhibition, I was standing at a corner on Madison Avenue and waiting for a bus and I happened to look at the pavement and I noticed that the experience of looking at the pavement was the same as the experience of looking at the Tobey. Exactly the same. The aesthetic enjoyment was just as high.... So, you have a change then in my view.[18]

The impact of Tobey's work on Cage was to change or expand his perspective of the world. But more importantly, the painting demonstrated to Cage how a work of art could have the capacity to reveal meaning in everyday life. Rather than taking a didactic approach to the interpretation of Tobey's painting, whereby he would have determined the meaning or impact of the work of art by way of pictorial analysis, Cage was disarmed and affected by the capacity of the painting to expand his perception and experience of the mundane world. Cage did not respond to *Crystallizations* in terms of formalism or the artwork's painterly qualities; instead, he was interested in how this painting situated an experience of a higher order, heightening the viewer's capacity for perception. In this sense, *Crystallizations* functioned for Cage as the *enso* calligraphy had for Tobey at the Enpuku-ji zendo—as a "visual koan," we could say, or as a visual provocation that required one to suspend analytical or representational explanation in order to effect a truth.

The American Zen teacher Charlotte Joko Beck writes that the goal of Zen meditation is to regulate attention. The heart of Zen practice, she states, is careful attention to or awareness of the mundane or trivial actions of one's day-to-day life to cultivate a broad scope of attention without focusing on any one specific object or end, thereby allowing space for awareness to arise. She writes,

FIG. 24
Mark Tobey (USA/Switzerland, 1890–1976)
Crystallizations, 1944
Tempura on board
45.7 × 33 cm
Mabel Ashley Kizer Fund, Gift of Melitta and Rex Vaughan, and Modern and Contemporary Acquisitions Fund / Stanford University, Cantor Arts Centre 2000.29

Informed by Asian calligraphy and the artist's experience of Zen monastic life, this painting relies on the quality of line to convey a sense of modulated, vibrating light. This painting was purchased in 1945 by the avant-garde composer John Cage, for whom it stood as a reminder of the Zen attention to awareness and interconnectedness.

> In awareness practice, we notice our thoughts and the contraction in our body, taking it all in and returning to the present moment. That's the hardest practice... Every moment in life is the absolute in itself... That's all there is. There is nothing other than this present moment...[19]

In this practice of just experiencing, Beck suggests, there is no space for self-centred thoughts. Thus, Zen is a practice of opening the mind by refocusing attention away from the ego-self, as a method of mental regulation designed to reorient one's relationship to the material world.

For Cage, Zen awareness or "bare attention"—that is, moment-to-moment awareness without reactivity—when applied to the appreciation of an artwork such as Tobey's painting, shifted the experience of looking from a totalizing approach that essentializes an image to one that considers a work within an expanded, experiential context. As the art critic and writer Kay Larson puts it, "Cage... learned from Tobey—and from Tobey's painting—that art could implicitly move beyond the frame into the ordinary world."[20] This approach to the experience of a work of art that prioritized noticing over formalist aesthetics impacted Cage's approach to artistic creation, privileging attention or awareness in the everyday. Cage's study of Buddhism resulted in the *decentring* of the artistic self in order to propose an egoless approach to the production of art. This in turn resulted in the *dematerialization* of the art object,[21] which radicalized art production in the mid-20th century.

INTERPENETRATION

Cage's famous "silent" composition *4′33″* (1952) (FIG. 25)—during which a performer walks onto the stage, sits at the piano, sets out a stopwatch, closes the lid of the keyboard, sits quietly for thirty seconds, raises the lid, looks at the stopwatch before closing the lid and so on, raising and lowering the keyboard lid to mark time in accordance with the score—was significantly informed by the composer's study of Buddhism with Suzuki, the Japanese scholar and promoter of Buddhism. Cage was particularly inspired by Suzuki's interpretation of the Flower Garland Sutra (Avatamsaka Sutra) (FIG. 26), a teaching variously translated as "interpenetration," "interdependence," or "dependent origination," a key doctrine of Buddhist philosophy that states that all phenomena arise in dependence upon other phenomena.[22]

Larson's summation of this difficult Buddhist text is useful:

> The Flower Garland Sutra is a hypnotically detailed compilation of oral teachings. It's a notoriously difficult text based on a fundamentally simple observation: Mind... is the universe. Ego creates the appearance of separation, but the seeming divisibility of "me" and "others" is a fiction born of the self. Everything exists in mutually unobstructed interpenetration. All things and all beings are mutually dependent and co-arising... The Flower Garland Sutra describes a powerful interlinking of all beings in a web of relations... [23]

Cage identified the concept of interpenetration as being of particular significance to his approach to this composition:

> Interpenetration means that each one of these most honoured ones of all is moving out in all directions penetrating and being penetrated by every other one no matter what the time or what the space. So that when one says that there is no cause and effect, what is meant is that there are an incalculable infinity of causes and effects, that in fact each and every thing in all of time and space is related to each other and every other thing in all of time and space. This being so there is no need to proceed in dualistic terms of success and failure or the beautiful and the ugly or good and evil but rather simply to walk on... [24]

Accordingly, *4′33″* can be regarded as a creative expression of Cage's engagement with this Buddhist doctrine[25] in that the composition artistically interprets the concept of interpenetration as moment-to-moment awareness. It requires the listener to experience and regard music "not as a communication from the artist to an audience, but rather as an activity of sound in which the artist found a way to let sounds be themselves."[26]

A decade later, a related score, *0′00″ for Yoko Ono and Toshi Ichiyanagi* (1962) (FIGS. 29–30), expanded on this creative interpretation. The score consists of a simple sentence: "In a situation having maximum amplification, or none (or both), perform a disciplined action." Whereas *4′33″* was given form by way of the titular time structure of the score, indicated in the performance

FIG. 25
John Cage (USA, 1919–1992)
4′33″ [Tacet Score], 1960
Experimental music score: ink on paper
29 × 21.5 cm
Music Division, The New York Public Library for the Performing Arts

John Cage's famous "silent" score is a creative exploration and expression of the Buddhist concept of interpenetration (dependent origination), as found in the Flower Garland Sutra. This doctrine states that all phenomena arise in dependence upon other phenomena. Cage's experimental composition suspends conventional concepts of music to create a context for the experience of the interpenetration of all things as infinite and perpetual sounds. Several versions of the *4′33″* score were made. The first version of the so-called Tacet Score is typewritten and lists the three movements of the piece in Roman numerals with the word *tacet* written underneath each. In music, *tacet* instructs the performer that the voice or instrument should be silent.

I

TACET

II

TACET

III

TACET

NOTE: The title of this work is the total length in minutes and seconds of its performance. At Woodstock, N.Y., August 29, 1952, the title was 4' 33" and the three parts were 33", 2' 40", and 1' 20". It was performed by David Tudor, pianist, who indicated the beginnings of parts by closing, the endings by opening, the keyboard lid. However, the work may be performed by any instrumentalist or combination of instrumentalists and last any lengths of time.

THE MOVEMENTS MAY

AFTER THE WOODSTOCK PERFORMANCE A COPY IN PROPORTIONAL NOTATION WAS MADE FOR IRWIN KREMEN. IN IT THE TIMELENGTHS

FOR IRWIN KREMEN JOHN CAGE

OF THE MOVEMENTS WERE 30" 2'23" and 1'40". H

30"

223

1 40

112

112

2/24

6777

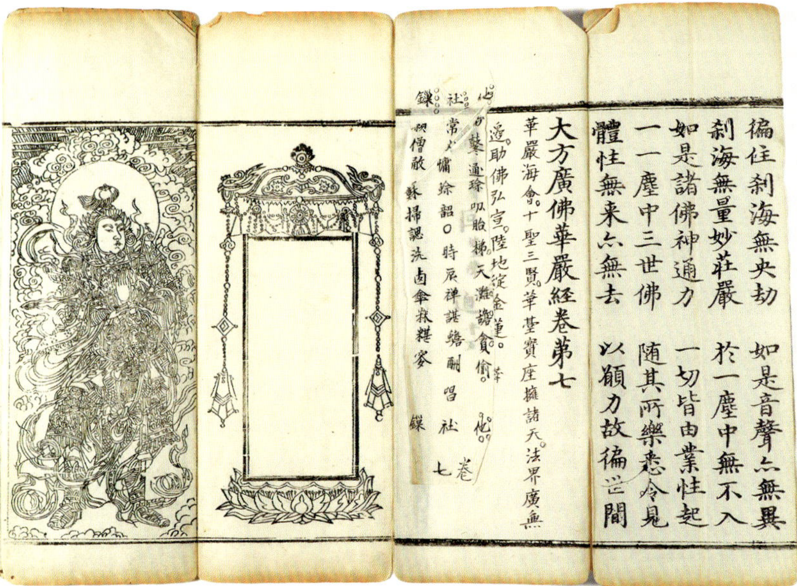

FIG. 26 (LEFT)
Hua Yan Jing Zhuan
(Avatamsaka Sutra)
China, 13th or 14th century
Folded book, woodcut on wove paper
35.5 × 12 cm
From the Rev. Dr. James M. Menzies Collection, given by his son, Arthur R. Menzies
Art Gallery of Greater Victoria 1982.075.007-009
Photo: Stephen Topfer

FIG. 27 (FACING TOP)
Paul Walde (UK/Canada, 1968–)
The Nature of Silence, 2012
Single channel HD video with stereo sound
5.12 min.
© Courtesy of the artist

The Nature of Silence is a tribute to John Cage's most famous work, *4′33″*. Shot on location at Maverick Concert Hall near Woodstock, New York, it documents the environment in which the work was presented on the occasion of the sixtieth anniversary of its premiere.

FIG. 28 (FACING BOTTOM)
Nam June Paik (Korea/USA, 1932–2006)
A Tribute to John Cage, 2008
Video installation: single channel video, colour, with sound
29.02 min.
Collection SFMOMA
Camille W. and William S. Broadbent Fund purchase
© Nam June Paik Estate
Courtesy Electronic Arts Intermix (EAI), New York

by the opening and closing of the keyboard, *o′oo″ for Yoko Ono and Toshi Ichiyanagi* does away with this structure, to acknowledge the omnipresence of the concept of interpenetration. The avant-garde artist and songwriter Yoko Ono toured Japan with Cage in 1962 (FIG. 33). Ono recalled that they argued about why *4′33″* had to last a specific period of time. "Why did it have to be four minutes and 33 seconds? He [Cage] talked about how in the West you had to have a frame, so he dedicated a work to me called '*o′oo*,'"[27] an open-ended composition.

Cage subsequently grasped the profound meaning of these so-called silent scores: "I don't sit down to do it; I turn my attention toward it. I realize that it's going on continuously..."[28] This realization indicates the significance and impact that *4′33″* and the subsequent silent scores had in shaping and developing Cage's world view in accordance with Buddhist philosophies.

Decades later, Ichiyanagi reflected on his experience of touring with Cage in Japan. He remarked that the American composer "acted like a Buddhist monk. That was very striking for us. In Japan, Buddhist monks and ordinary people are very separated. But Americans can bring the same ideas to their lives and their professions."[29] Ichiyanagi's observation suggests that for Cage, art and Buddhism coincided *as practice*, so that what Cage was trying to achieve through music and composition was not the *representation* of Buddhist ideas in aesthetic form but

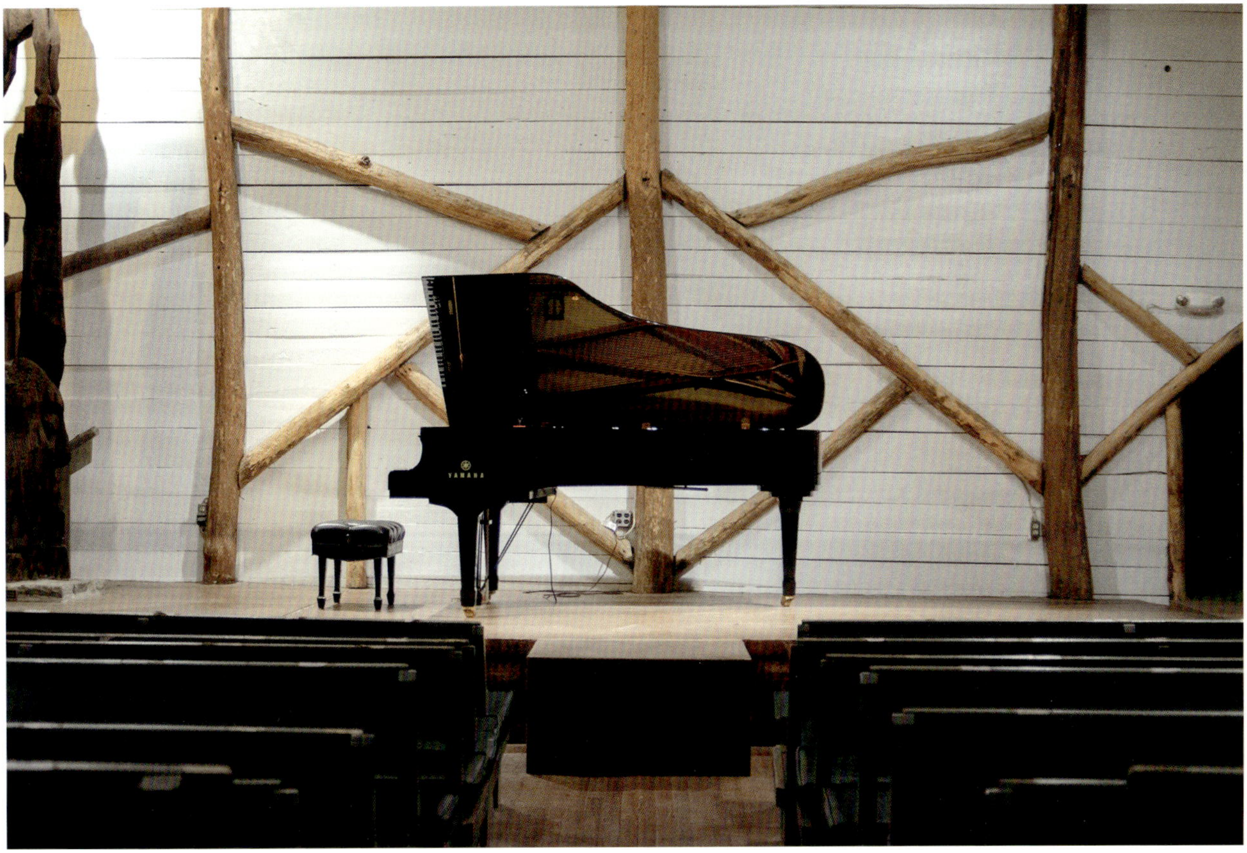

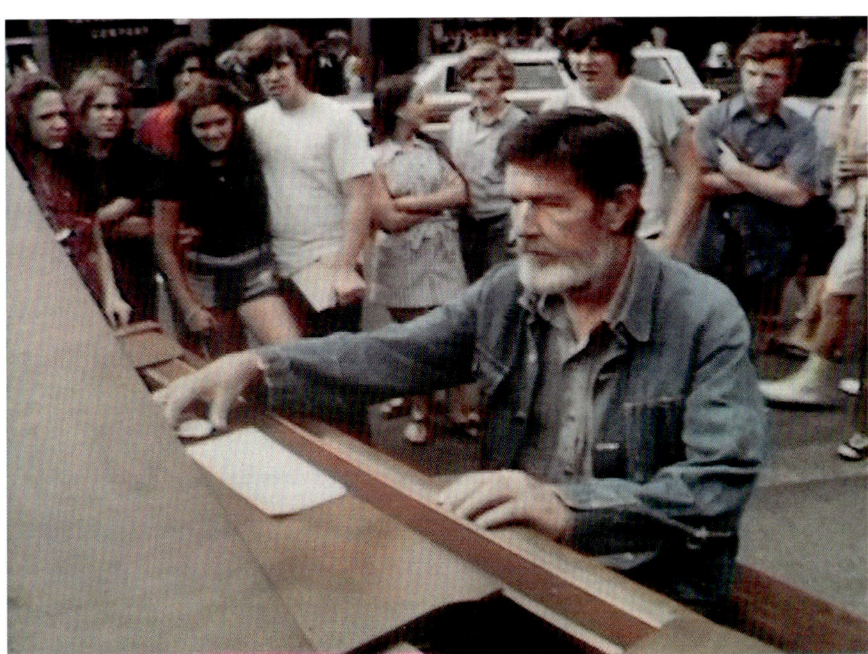

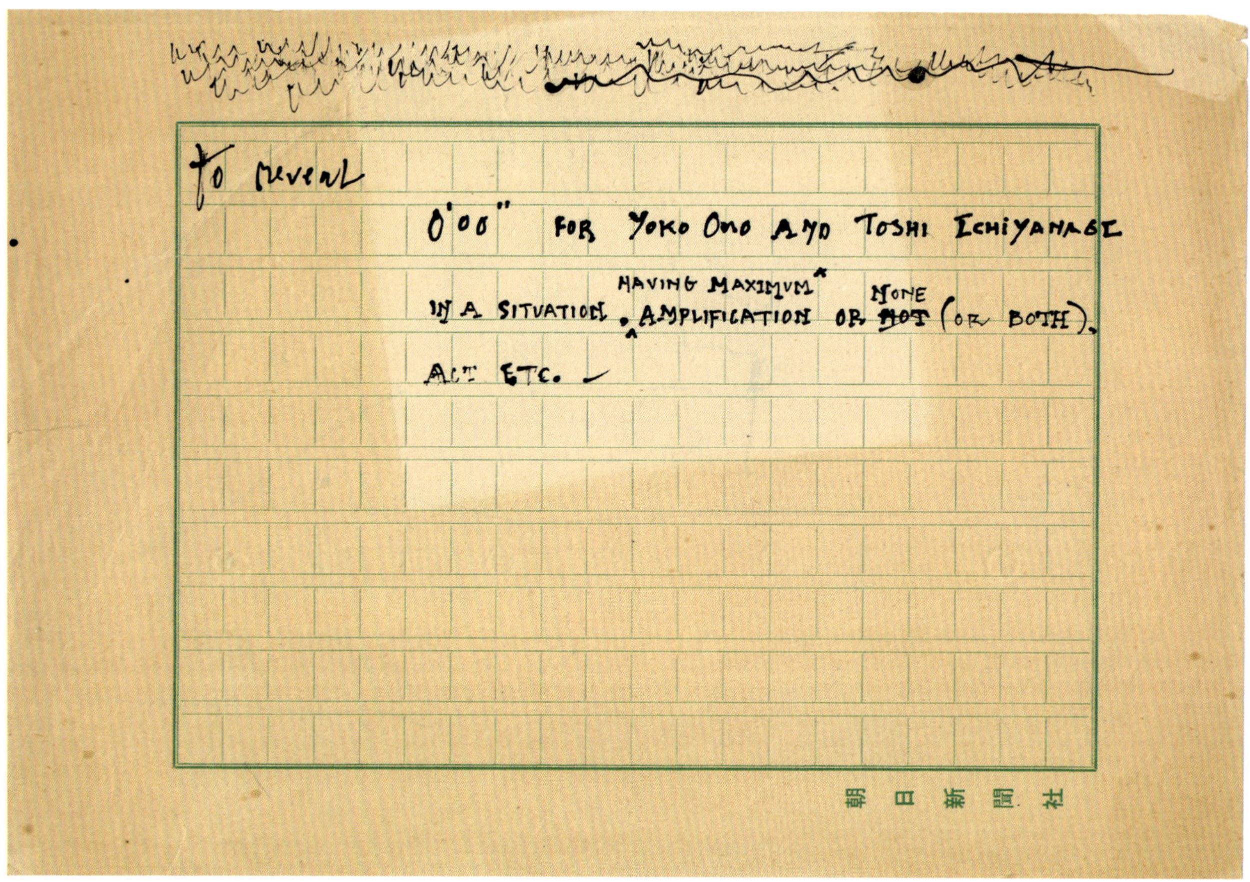

FIG. 29 (ABOVE)
John Cage (USA, 1919–1992)
0'00" for Yoko Ono and Toshi Ichiyanagi, 1962
Notes for score: ink on paper
18 × 25.6 cm
Music Division, The New York Public Library for the Performing Arts / © 1962 by Henmar Press Inc. Used by permission of C.F. Peters Corporation. All rights reserved.

FIG. 30 (FACING)
John Cage (USA, 1919–1992)
Notes for score, *0'00" for Yoko Ono and Toshi Ichiyanagi*, 1962
Ink on paper
22 × 15 cm
Music Division, The New York Public Library for the Performing Arts / © 1962 by Henmar Press Inc. Used by permission of C.F. Peters Corporation. All rights reserved.

the *interpenetration* of Zen through art, so that each informs the other in comprehending the experience of the world. What Cage appears to have been grappling with in these silent scores was the way in which art could produce a loss of one's sense of self approximate to the loss of a sense of self in Buddhist meditation. For Cage, these experimental compositions were a means of exploring both the meaning of Zen and the higher potential of music as related or equivalent experiences.

Between 1956 and 1960, Cage taught a course on experimental composition at The New School, New York, which brought these concepts of Zen awareness to a new generation of avant-garde artists. Ichiyanagi attended these classes, and Ono, Ichiyanagi's wife at the time, sat in to audit.[30] As the art historian David Doris has noted, "though certainly not a Zen missionary, [Cage] was one of the most important conduits of Eastern thought to the Western world."[31] In turn, as Ichiyanagi

provided (or not) with

In a situation ~~having~~ maximum

~~but~~ no without

amplification, (~~not~~ ~~melu~~ ~~no~~ feedback)

perform a disciplined

~~or none (or b~~ , action having no

attention to the situation (electronic, musical,

theatrical), ~~to fulfill or~~ wholly or

~~in such a way that "here" precedes "composition"~~

~~partially, an obligation to another~~

~~or to oneself.~~

No stop-watch is to be used.

Tokyo, Oct 24, 1962

This lecture was printed in Incontri Musicali, *August 1959. There are four measures in each line and twelve lines in each unit of the rhythmic structure. There are forty-eight such units, each having forty-eight measures. The whole is divided into five large parts, in the proportion 7, 6, 14, 14, 7. The forty-eight measures of each unit are likewise so divided. The text is printed in four columns to facilitate a rhythmic reading. Each line is to be read across the page from left to right, not down the columns in sequence. This should not be done in an artificial manner (which might result from an attempt to be too strictly faithful to the position of the words on the page), but with the* rubato *which one uses in everyday speech.*

LECTURE ON NOTHING

I am here , and there is nothing to say .
If among you are
those who wish to get somewhere , let them leave at
any moment . What we re–quire is
silence ; but what silence requires
is that I go on talking .
Give any one thought
a push : it falls down easily .
; but the pusher and the pushed pro–duce that enter–
tainment called a dis–cussion .
Shall we have one later ?

♍

Or , we could simply de–cide not to have a dis–
cussion . What ever you like . But
now there are silences and the
words make help make the
silences .

I have nothing to say
and I am saying it and that is
poetry as I need it .

This space of time is organized
. We need not fear these silences, —

♍

we may love them .
This is a composed
talk , for I am making it
just as I make a piece of music. It is like a glass
of milk . We need the glass
and we need the milk . Or again it is like an
empty glass into which at any
moment anything may be poured
. As we go along , (who knows?)
an i–dea may occur in this talk .
I have no idea whether one will
or not. If one does, let it. Re–

♍

gard it as something seen momentarily , as
though from a window while traveling .
If across Kansas , then, of course, Kansas
. Arizona is more interesting,
almost too interesting , especially for a New–Yorker who is
being interested in spite of himself in everything. Now he knows he
needs the Kansas in him . Kansas is like
nothing on earth , and for a New Yorker very refreshing.
It is like an empty glass , nothing but wheat , or
is it corn ? Does it matter which ?
Kansas has this about it: at any instant, one may leave it,
and whenever one wishes one may return to it .

♍

Or you may leave it forever and never return to it ,
for we pos–sess nothing . Our poetry now
is the reali–zation that we possess nothing
. Anything therefore is a delight
(since we do not pos–sess it) and thus need not fear its loss
. We need not destroy the past: it is gone;
at any moment, it might reappear and seem to be and be the present
. Would it be a repetition? Only if we thought we
owned it, but since we don't, it is free and so are we

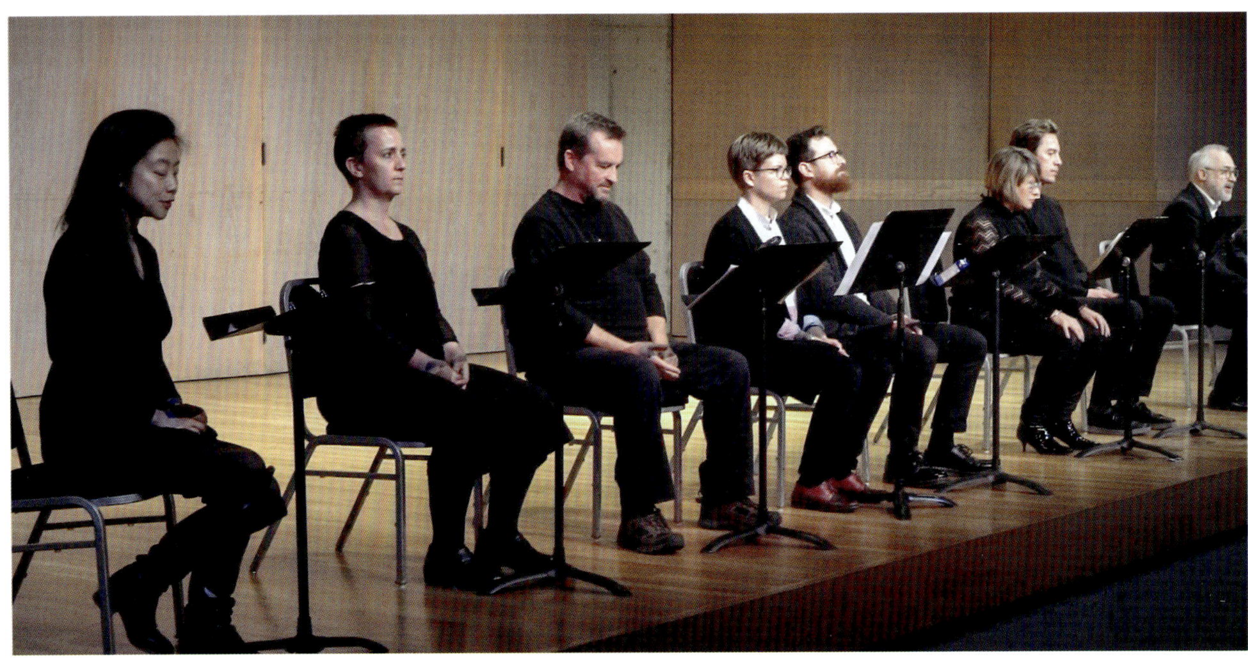

FIG. 31 (PREVIOUS SPREAD)
John Cage (USA, 1919–1992)
Lecture on Nothing, 1950
Excerpt from the book *Silence: Lectures and Writings*, pp. 109–110

The subject of "nothing" is given extended attention in Cage's composition. The composition functions as both a text to be read and a score to be performed. The piece has a formal and visual time structure denoted by a series of "empty" time intervals. The central statement of the lecture, "there is nothing to say . . . and I am saying it," reveals Cage's inquiry into Zen: the idea that no thing is permanent and no thing is independent of everything else, a paraphrasing of the essential teaching of the Heart Sutra: "Emptiness is form and form is emptiness."

FIG. 32 (ABOVE)
John Cage (USA, 1919–1992)
Lecture on Nothing, 1950
Performance document,
Philip T. Young Recital Hall, University of Victoria, 2019

Scored by Kay Larson, directed by Christopher Butterfield

Readers: Daniel Brandes, Laura Brandes, Christopher Butterfield, Cissie Fu, Laura Giffen, Peter Hatch, Gwen Jamieson, Cathy Lewis, Kegan McFadden, Christine Walde

Musicians: Nathan Friedman, Julien Haynes, Alex Jang, Hollas Longton, Tiess Mackenzie, Emily Morse, Tina Pearson, Christopher Reiche, George Tzanetakis, Paul Walde

Photo: Laura Gildner

The writer and art critic Kay Larson proposes that in *Lecture on Nothing*, Cage resolves to embody Buddhist concepts of enlightenment as action, deliberately invoking a process that goes nowhere.* Cage makes the first consciously driven, Buddhist-inspired process art. Larson explains that the text-score evokes the turning line of the Heart Sutra: "No path, no wisdom, and no gain." Nowhere to go. Nothing to achieve. In that case, just be here now.

Larson's interpretation of Cage's score, performed at the University of Victoria in October 2019, drew on Cage-inspired "chance operations" to establish the parameters of the performance. She included musicians playing a variety of instruments (bass guitar, clarinet, violin, accordion, ping-pong balls) scattered throughout the theatre, alongside spoken-word artists, to create a fulsome and lively interpretation of this seminal work.

* Kay Larson, *Lecture on Nothing*, Orion Keynote Lecture, *In the Present Moment: A Research Convening*, organized by the Art Gallery of Greater Victoria with the University of Victoria, October 25, 2019.

FIG. 33 (TOP)
John Cage and Yoko Ono in Japan, 1962
© Courtesy of Kumiko Yoshioka
Photo: Yasuhiro Yoshioka

FIG. 34 (BOTTOM)
Yoko Ono (Japan/USA, 1933–)
Secret Piece, 1953
From the book *Grapefruit*
(Tokyo: Wunternaum Press, 1964)
Artist's book; offset
14 × 13.8 × 3.2 cm (closed)
© Yoko Ono
Digital Image © The Museum of Modern Art/
Licensed by SCALA/Art Resource, NY

Secret Piece was written in 1953, indicating how Ono's independent experiments with sound and composition intersected with ideas of artists such as Cage. The simplicity of Ono's composition suggested that any person could be a composer or performer, just as long as they paid enough attention to the beauty of the everyday sounds around them. Ono said: "Art is not a special thing. Anyone can do it. Making art does not have to be so unusual. What I mean is that middle-aged men and housewives, your neighbors can also do it . . . If everybody were to become an artist, what we call "Art" would disappear. I think it would be fine if this were to happen and [what I have envisioned] becomes a reality."*

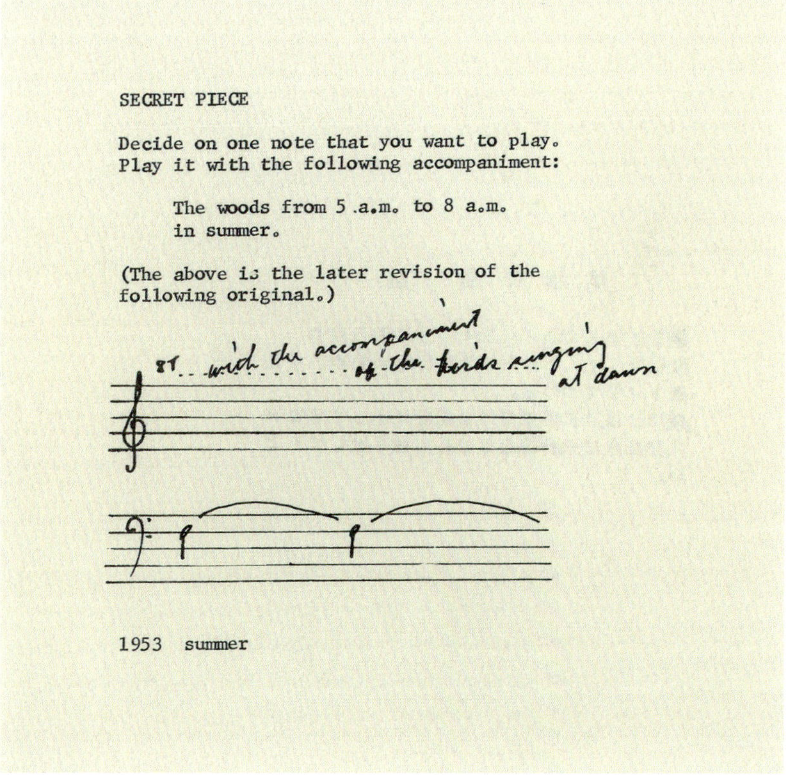

SECRET PIECE

Decide on one note that you want to play.
Play it with the following accompaniment:

The woods from 5 a.m. to 8 a.m.
in summer.

(The above is the later revision of the following original.)

1953 summer

* Yoko Ono in 1964, in Midori Yoshimoto (transcribed and translated), "Some Young People – From Nonfiction Theater," *Review of Japanese Culture and Society*, December 2005.

has commented, Cage demonstrated to Asian artists that traditional ideas and art forms "could be approached from a contemporary point of view and the other way around too."[32] This example suggests how conceptual art emerged at the interface between Eastern ideas and Western methods of interpretation.

FIG. 35
Alison Knowles (USA, 1933–)
#2 Proposition (Make a Salad), 1962
Published score in *By Alison Knowles. A Great Bear Pamphlet* (New York: Something Else Press, 1965)
Artist's book: offset printing on buff paper, staple bound, 16 pages
21.59 × 13.97 cm
University of British Columbia, Morris/Trasov Archive (M/T 098.24)

CULTURALLY BUDDHIST

From the early 1960s, Zen as a method of artistic production found currency among a group of New York artists, including visual artists, poets, designers, and musicians, many of whom took Cage's course at The New School. These avant-garde artists formed a loosely organized group named Fluxus, eventually becoming an international network that prioritized process over product. These artists experimented with alternate approaches to art making in order to challenge the increasing commodification of art and its attendant elitism. Fluxus proposed an alternate significance of art in the everyday, seeking to challenge the notion of "artistic genius," destabilizing traditional ideas of the artist as an inimitable producer of unique objects, and proposing a relational approach to the creation of a work. Fluxus works depended on the active participation of the viewer and were concerned with the production of disarming aesthetic experiences: experiences that would focus attention on the noticing of mundane phenomena, facilitating—with regards to the Western point of view, at least—a new kind of perception of the world. Their objective was to encourage the viewer-participant to perceive the details of everyday life as extraordinary.

For example, the Fluxus artist Alison Knowles's participatory score *Make a Salad* (1962) (FIGS. 35–36), which consisted of a single-line instruction, "Make a salad," drew on the Zen concept of "bare attention"[33] to consider practices in daily life as encompassing the experience of art. When the artist first performed this work at the Institute of Contemporary Arts, London, the quotidian actions of making a salad were undertaken with deliberate attention to the moment of each action, as a practice of mindfulness. The intention of the work was to disrupt the art/non-art binary by considering the everyday action of making a salad as extraordinary. Knowles explained,

> I think that many of the pieces are just simple refreshment pieces done for whatever day's work you have to do,

IMAGE BANK
303 EAST 8th AVENUE
VANCOUVER, B.C. V5T 1S1

by Alison Knowles

#1 —

Shuffle (1961)

The performer or performers shuffle into the performance area and away from it, above, behind, around, or through the audience. They perform as a group or solo: but quietly.

Premiered August 1963 at National Association of Chemists and Perfumers in New York at the Advertisers' Club.

#2 —

Proposition (October, 1962)

Make a salad.

Premiered October 21st, 1962 at Institute for Contemporary Arts in London.

2

by Alison Knowles

#2a —

Variation #1 on Proposition (October, 1964)

Make a soup.

Premiered November 9th, 1964 at Cafe au Go Go in New York.

#3 —

Nivea Cream Piece (November, 1962) — for Oscar Williams

First performer comes on stage with a bottle of hand cream, labeled "Nivea Cream" if none is available. He pours the cream onto his hands, and massages them in front of the microphone. Other performers enter, one by one, and do the same thing. Then they join together in front of the microphone to make a mass of massaging hands. They leave in the reverse of the order they entered, on a signal from the first performer.

Premiered November 25th, 1962 at Alle Scenen Theater, Copenhagen, at Fluxus Festival.

#3a —

Variation #1 on Nivea Cream Piece (no date, evolved through many performances from the above)

Large quantities of Nivea Cream must be available, at least one large jar per person. The performers enter and each lathers up his arms and face, then his colleagues, in a fragrant pig-pile.

3

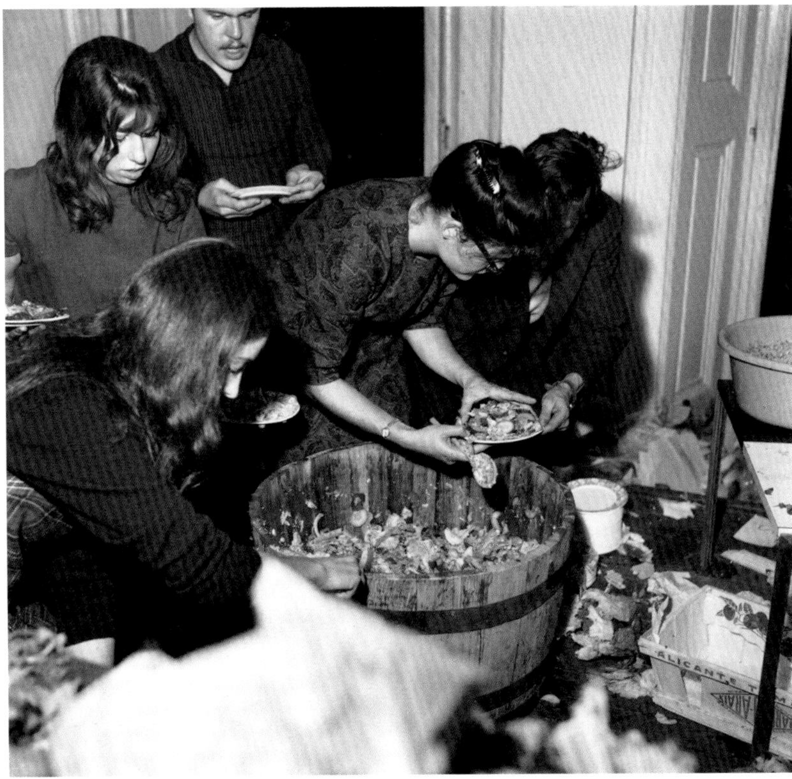

FIG. 36
Alison Knowles (USA, 1933–)
#2 Proposition (Make a Salad), 1962
Performance document: Festival of Misfits, ICA, London, October 24, 1962
Gelatin silver print
sheet: 25.4 × 20.3 cm
The Gilbert and Lila Silverman Fluxus Collection Gift
The Museum of Modern Art, New York, NY, USA
Digital Image © The Museum of Modern Art / Licensed by SCALA / Art Resource, NY
© Alison Knowles

> supporting occurrences in life... Whatever it is you have to touch and work with, you can make a kind of performance of it, but it has to be stripped of the hangings and accoutrements of theater. What happens is that a kind of revelation, no an emptiness, opens up...[34]

The intended effect was to render the art/life binary as superfluous, resulting in a form of revelation, or awareness, that is "empty awareness": awareness without reactivity in the everyday, as everyday life. *Make a Salad* was an experiment in investigating and sustaining a state of mindful awareness *as* a form of aesthetics. In turn, the participatory nature of this work encouraged the viewer-participant to also become engaged with, or immersed in, the flow of the mindfulness practice. Relational performance pieces such as this one transformed abstract Buddhist concepts, as introduced to the United States by scholars such as Suzuki, into aesthetic experiences. They stand as cultural expressions of an engagement with Buddhism as defined by the American imagination.

The Buddhist studies scholar Melissa Anne-Marie Curley argues that Fluxus produced a generational subculture of artists that could be regarded as culturally Buddhist. Curley notes that the work of these artists describes the expression of Buddhist ideas and values as they were being interpreted and taking hold "outside the precincts of an orthoprax Zen centre."[35] This would not be the first time in the history of Buddhism that its visual and cultural forms shifted and adapted in accordance with the values and expressions of its adoptive culture. Buddhism's relevance and resilience throughout the history of its dissemination across Asia, and around the world, owes much to its capacity to adapt to the cultural norms and expressions of its host culture. But the Fluxus engagement with Zen is distinct from the development of Buddhist art in Asia, because in the Fluxus context, Buddhism was made an *object* of artistic inquiry, whereas up to this point, Buddhism had been the *subject* of representation, where artworks were typically made for the purpose of religious ritual, dissemination, and merit-making. Accordingly, the Fluxus approach to art was highly subjective, experimental, and secular in nature, taking place outside of religious conventions. Fluxus practices described an intellectual engagement with Zen, consonant with how Buddhism was introduced to America, by way of scholarly lectures in English and texts in translation, rather than by way of immersion into a religio-cultural community. Accordingly, these creative experiments, inquiring into Buddhist concepts, were idiosyncratic, even iconoclastic, and not regulated by religious or ritual prescriptions. They resulted in a making strange of Zen, which, Curley argues, paved a way for new discourses and cultural approaches to Buddhism.[36]

The Korean-born Fluxus artist Nam June Paik, who spent his youth in Japan, was familiar with the language and aesthetics of Zen and traditional East Asian art. Setting his work in conversation with Cage, Paik drew on the language of Zen, as interpreted by Fluxus, to critique Zen orthodoxy while at the same time reflecting on Zen meaning.[37] A famous example is *Zen for Head* (1962) (FIG. 37), a performance artwork in which the artist dipped his head in a bucket of ink mixed with tomato juice and drew a line with his head on a strip of paper on the floor. This performance constituted his interpretation of a Fluxus score by composer La Monte Young, *Composition 1960 #10 (to Bob Morris)* (1960), which read, "Draw a straight line and follow it." But it also referenced the single-stroke calligraphic line or staff made famous by the late-19th-century Zen monk Nantembo (FIG. 38). Once, when asked if he were a Buddhist, Paik replied, "No, I am an artist... Because I am a friend of John Cage, people tend to see me as a Zen monk... I am not a follower of Zen, but I react to Zen in the same way that I react to Johann Sebastian Bach."[38] Paik was as interested in questioning and challenging the conventions of orthodox Zen as he was in challenging the conventions of Western classical music. His response to Zen stands as an equivocal response to Cage's intellectualized and somewhat idealized understanding of Zen in New York, where a methodology of Zen in the arts meant something quite different from its cultural meaning in Japan. As Paik famously stated, "Zen is anti-avant-garde, anti-frontier spirit, anti-Kennedy. Zen is responsible of Asian poverty. How can I justify Zen, without justifying Asian poverty??"[39] The art historian Tae-seung Lim suggests that Paik's seemingly iconoclastic approach to Zen is in keeping with the East Asian aesthetic concept of *yi*, translated as "unconventional naturalness," and as a paramount aesthetic in Zen that refers to the transgression of worldly and social conventions to communicate a spontaneous and heightened state of awareness and to "destroy illusion," that is, the illusion of truth or propriety created by social forms and conventions.[40]

Lim, alongside Asian art historian Walter Smith, points out that Paik's work is usually discussed with reference to Western ideas in contemporary art with only brief reference to Asian ideas and aesthetics. However, both Lim and Smith argue that Paik's work represents a modernization of East Asian ideas expressed as contemporary art,[41] requiring interpreters and critics who can read the work from both Eastern and Western perspectives in order to fully account for the content of the work.

Another well-known work by Paik, *TV Buddha* (1974) (FIG. 42), which exists in several variations, takes the form of a video art installation where a statue of a Buddha in meditation is placed before a TV monitor. A camera is placed behind the monitor creating a closed-circuit image loop so that an image of the statue of the Buddha appears on the TV screen. The hallmark of the television image and of video art is that the image is continuously moving and does not represent a static scene. But in this work, although the TV image is continuously moving in time, the focus is on the unmoving image of the Buddha, as though observing itself in motionless contemplation, creating a paradoxical video image. Reading *TV Buddha* from the perspective of East Asian aesthetics, Lim suggests that this work expresses a concept of "stillness in movement and movement in stillness," where the static form of the Buddha statue represents stillness and self and the continuous stream of the video image represents movement and nature.[42] Lim points out that images representing this concept have a long history in East Asian painting, referring to practices of the contemplation of one's true Buddha-nature to obtain wisdom or insight. In other words, the practice of beholding the Buddha-nature within oneself is regarded as a condition of becoming a Buddha. Accordingly, *TV Buddha*—variously read by Western interpreters as an image of self-confrontation, or the play of illusion and reality, or non-closure, or even narcissism—when considered from an Asian perspective could also be read as an image of samadhi or oneness, where there is no distinction between the act of meditation and the object/support of meditation.[43] Smith notes that Paik remained silent on the matter of the interpretation of his work, enjoying its ambiguity. However, this ambiguity or ambivalence—this doubling of meaning by a manner of working between cultural traditions in ways that acknowledged history and iconographic convention without conforming to it—provided Paik with a means by which to reveal the "other" of Zen: its avant-garde potential.

Artists of Asian background were visible and prominent protagonists of the Fluxus avant-garde. A key figure and important organizer of early Fluxus events in New York was the conceptual artist Yoko Ono, who introduced a number of avant-garde Japanese artists to the Fluxus network.[44] In the early 1960s, Ono was known for her "instruction pieces," characterized by the use of ordinary language to immediately bring a visual image to mind, as "mind art," or conceptual art. Ono's concise and disarming use of language recalled the poetic form and simplicity of the haiku, but the instruction form grappled with the Buddhist notion that all phenomena are phenomena of the mind. These instruction pieces did away with the need for the art object and encouraged the viewer to perceive the artwork for themselves, in their own mind, so that the viewer would become a participant in the work by way of their own imagination. But as disarmingly simple and direct as these instruction pieces appeared to be, Ono was deeply engaged with questions regarding the nature of the mind, the nature of reality, and the conflict or paradox between

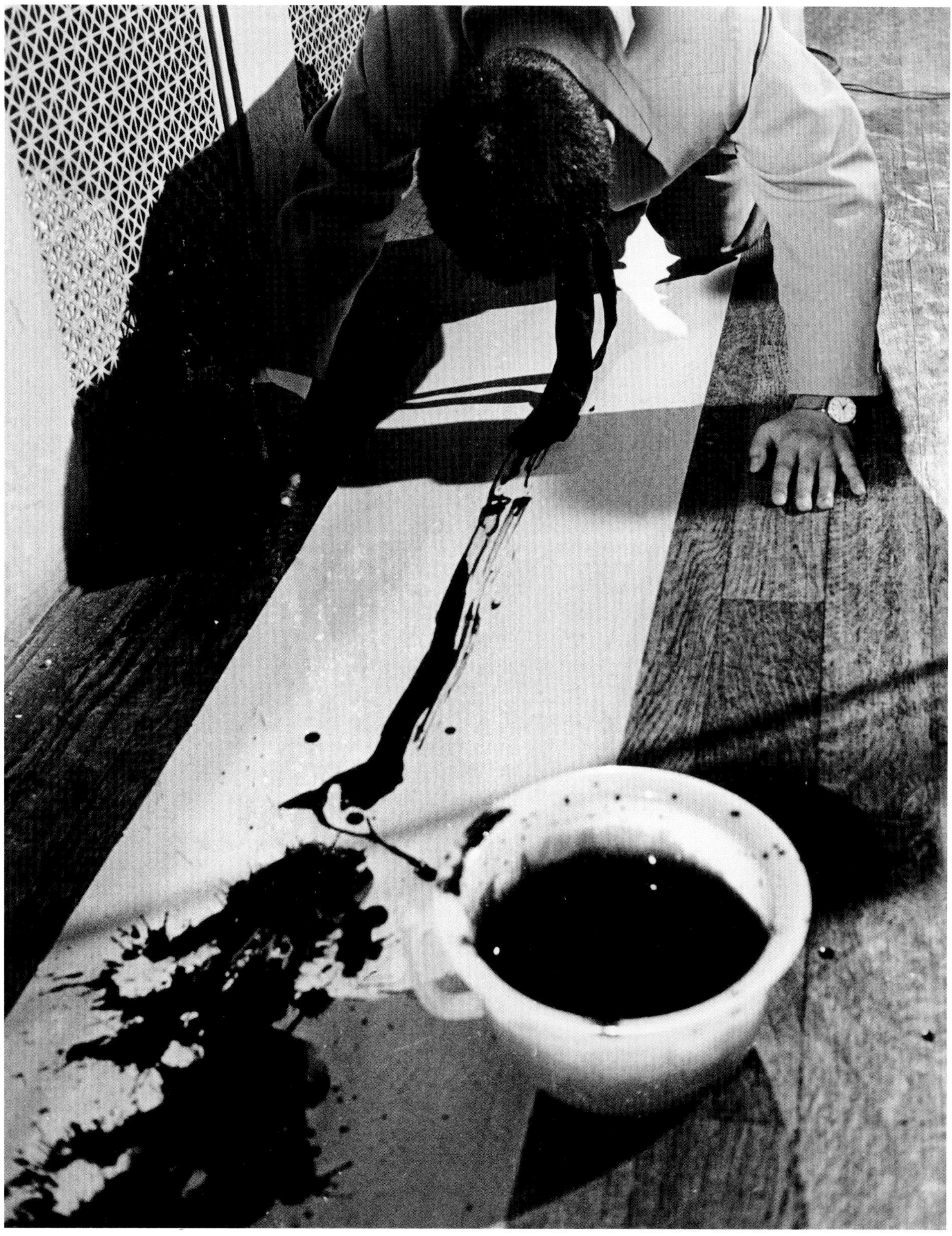

FIG. 37 (FACING)
Nam June Paik
(Korea/USA, 1932–2006)
Zen for Head, 1962
Performance document: La Monte Young's *Composition 1960 #10 (to Bob Morris)* performed by Nam June Paik at Fluxus Internationale Festspiele Neuester Musik, Stadtisches Museum, Wiesbaden, September 1–23, 1962
The Museum of Modern Art, New York, NY, USA

La Monte Young's evocative series *Compositions 1960* proposed a radical and poetic approach to sound as an extra-musical action. *Composition 1960 #10*, which read, "Draw a straight line and follow it," was famously interpreted by Nam June Paik in the performance titled *Zen for Head*. Paik took the idea of the calligraphic line or staff, as made famous by the Zen monk Nantembo, and literally turned the image on its head in a way that produced the concept of calligraphic or painterly mark making as both iconoclastic and enduring.

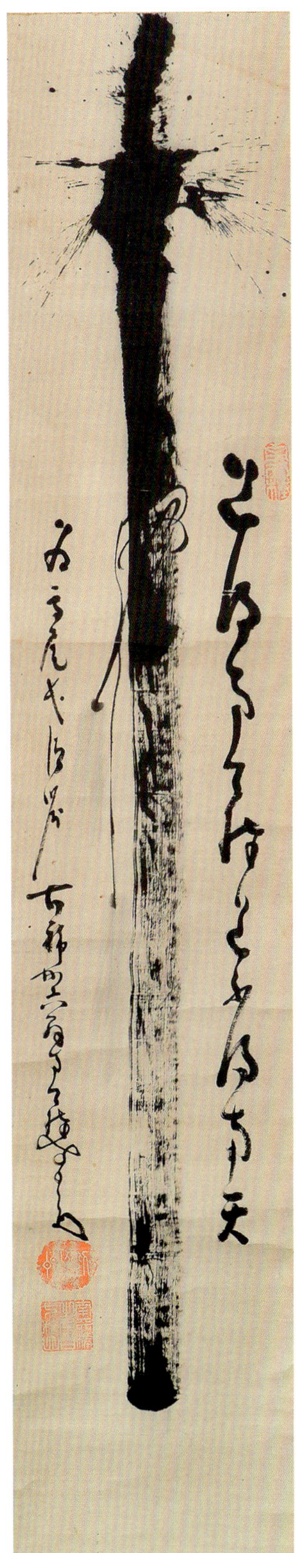

FIG. 38 (RIGHT)
Nakahara Nantembo
(Japan, 1839–1925)
Nanten staff, late 19th century to early 20th century
Mounted scroll: ink on paper
118 × 22 cm
L Wright Collection, Vancouver / Photo: Stephen Topfer

A disciplined Zen monk and teacher and prolific painter, Nantembo learned to use painting and calligraphy as a means of expressing the Zen spirit that lies beyond words. He created most of his paintings and calligraphies when he was in his late seventies and early eighties. The most intriguing subject of all was the staff or stick cut from a nanten tree, used to discipline students at the monastery. The stick became the monk's namesake and emblem, which he depicted by one powerful calligraphic brushstroke. The spirit of Zen, captured by this single, powerful calligraphic line, provided inspiration for numerous conceptual works of art in the mid-20th century.

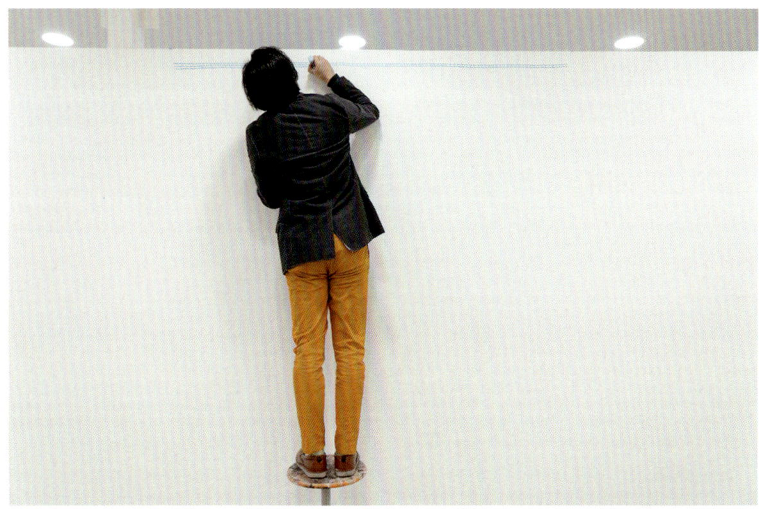

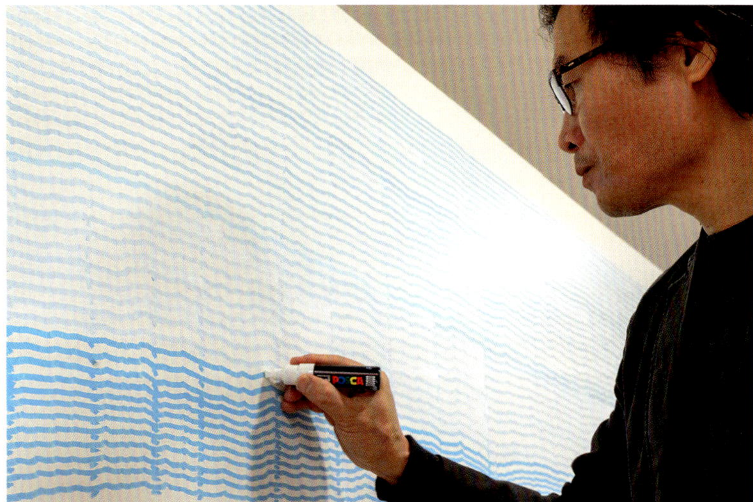

FIG. 39 (TOP LEFT)
Michael Zheng 郑济忠
(China/USA, 1965–)
Mindwaves, 2019
Meditation wall drawing:
markers on drywall
243.84 × 365.76 cm
Document of performance presented in conjunction with *In the Present Moment: A Research Convening*, Visual Arts Building, University of Victoria, October 26 and 27, 2019
Courtesy of the artist
Photo: Laura Gildner

FIG. 40 (BOTTOM LEFT)
Michael Zheng 郑济忠
(China/USA, 1965–)
Mindwaves, 2019
Meditation wall drawing:
markers on drywall
243.84 × 365.76 cm
Document of performance presented in conjunction with *In the Present Moment: A Research Convening*, Visual Arts Building, University of Victoria, October 26 and 27, 2019
Courtesy of the artist
Photo: Laura Gildner

FIG. 41 (FACING)
Michael Zheng 郑济忠
(China/USA, 1965–)
Draw a Line and Follow It #14, 2020
Pen and ink on paper
22.5 × 30 cm
Courtesy of the artist

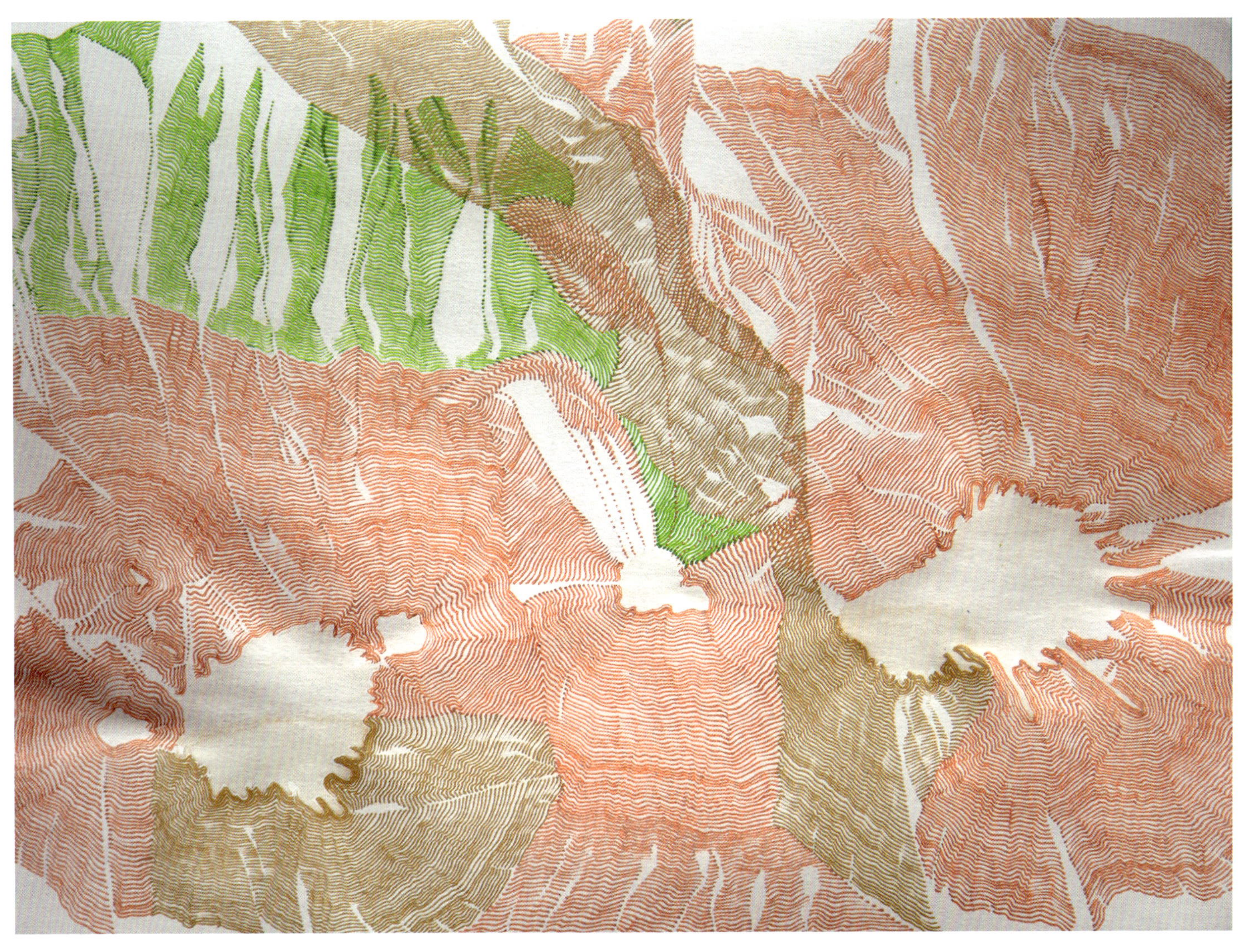

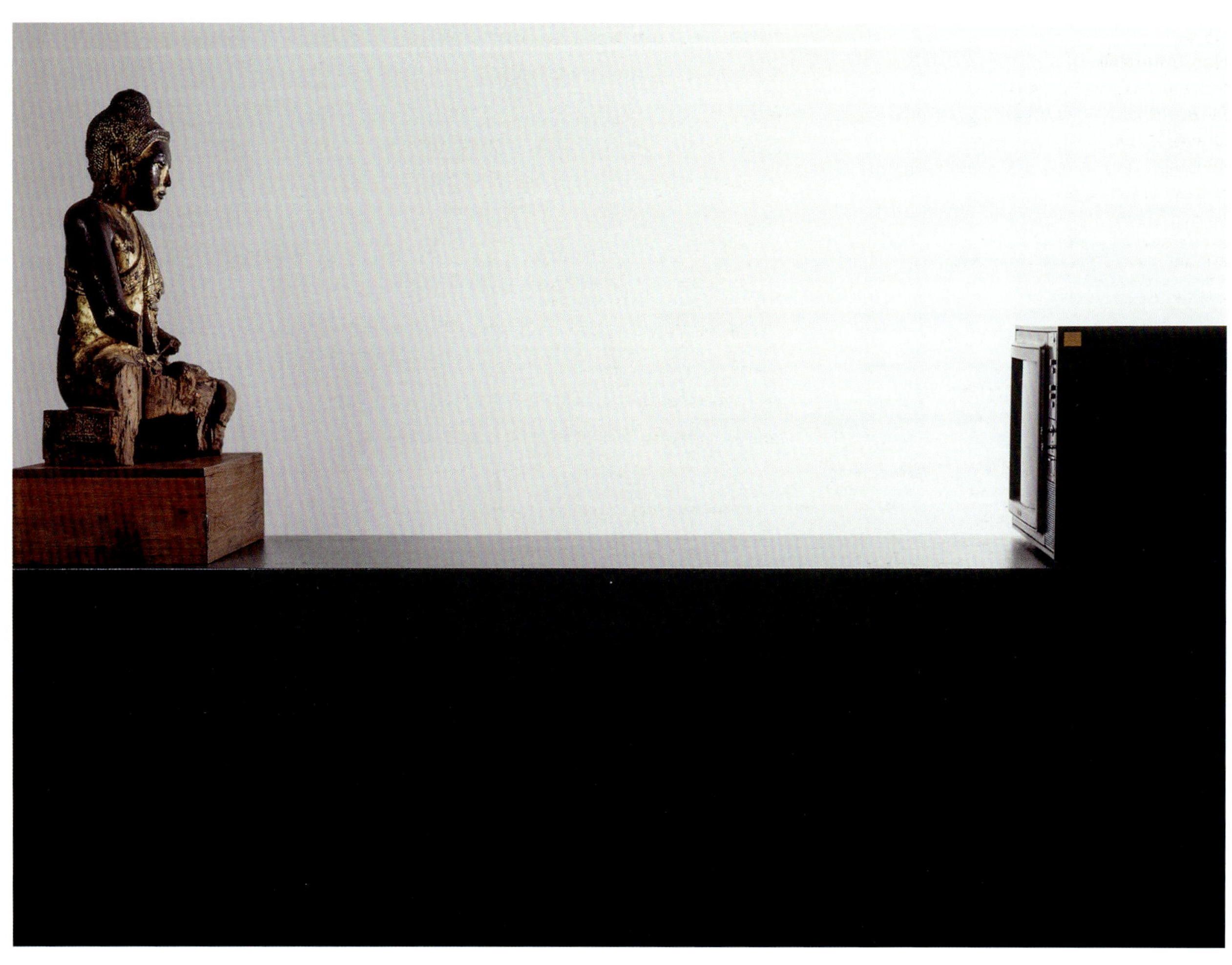

FIG. 42
Nam June Paik
(Korea/USA, 1932–2006)
TV Buddha III: McLuhan's Grave, 1984
Antique Buddha, television monitor and two videotapes with sound
30 min. (each); 135 × 246.6 × 61 cm
Gift of Esperanza and Mark Schwartz
Collection Musée d'Art Contemporain de Montreal

Photo: Ron Diamond

This version of Paik's well-known *TV Buddha* installations connects the artist's interest in Zen with Marshall McLuhan's theories on media and technology, as a tribute to the Canadian philosopher. If when read from a Buddhist perspective, *TV Buddha* refers to a concept of samadhi, or "oneness"—the idea that there is no distinction between the act of meditation and the object/support of meditation—then this version of *TV Buddha* draws a striking yet somewhat absurd analogy between this concept in Buddhism and McLuhan's adage "The medium is the message."

consciousness, mind, perception, and reality—questions that find their lineage in Buddhism. One of Ono's most provocative works developing from these instruction pieces was *The Strip-Tease Show* (1964), conceived as a striptease of the mind, "not to reveal to others, but for the audience to see something hidden in humans."[45]

The Strip-Tease Show was intended to demonstrate that the audience could imagine what they wanted to see in their minds, rather than depending solely on visuality, and to trouble the truth of the object. Ono was referencing the Buddhist idea that the mind distorts reality and projects it as reality in itself. In other words, the piece was intended as a stripping of the mind.

A key work in *The Strip-Tease Show* was *Cut Piece* (1964) (FIG. 45), based on the Jataka story of Prince Mahasattva, the historical Buddha in a previous life, who offers himself up to a hungry tigress. The story is depicted on one of the panels of the Tamamushi Shrine at the temple of Horyu-ji and is essentially a story of self-sacrifice, illustrating the overcoming of fear for compassion[46] (FIGS. 43–44). Ono explained, "According to legend, Buddha renounced his privileged position to go out into the world and to give whatever was requested of him ..." The relationship between the Buddha's giving and the artist's giving intrigued Ono.[47] Ono discussed the work in the British underground magazine *Unit*: "Traditionally, the artist's ego is in the artist's work. In other words, the artist must give the artist's ego to the audience. I had always wanted to produce a work without ego in it. I was thinking of this motif more and more, and the result was *Cut Piece*."[48]

In form and method, *Cut Piece* drew considerably on ideas in Buddhism. Realizing the piece as a staged performance in a concert format, Ono wears her best clothes and assumes a formal, kneeling *seiza* posture, a posture of humility in Zen meditation. She sits silently, not moving, the staging amplifying the quality of sparseness. The audience is also quiet. The artist's invitation for audience members to come up, one by one, and cut off the artist's clothing is a renouncing of the artist's ego and a provocation to the audience, setting in motion a dialectical relationship between artist and audience. The artist sacrifices herself to the audience. Ono reflected on the intention of the work:

> It was a form of giving, giving and taking. It was a kind of criticism against artists, who are always giving what they

want to give. I wanted people to take whatever they wanted to, so it was very important to say you can cut wherever you want to. It is a form of giving that has a lot to do with Buddhism. There's a small allegorical story about Buddha. He left his castle with his wife and children and was walking towards a mountain to go into meditation. As he was walking along, a man said that he wanted Buddha's children because he wanted to sell them or something. So Buddha gave him his children. Then someone said he wanted Buddha's wife and he gave him his wife. Someone calls that he is cold, so Buddha gives him his clothes. Finally a tiger comes along and says he wants to eat him and Buddha lets the tiger eat him. And in the moment the tiger eats him, it became enlightened or something. That's a form of total giving as opposed to reasonable giving like "logically you deserve this" or I think this is good therefore I am giving this to you.[49]

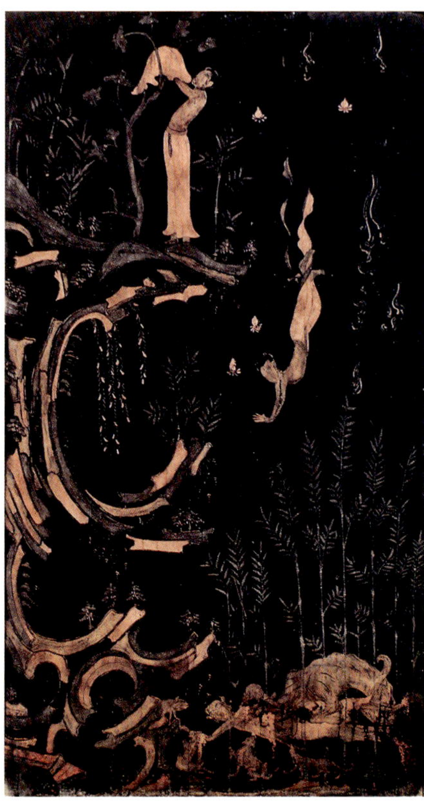

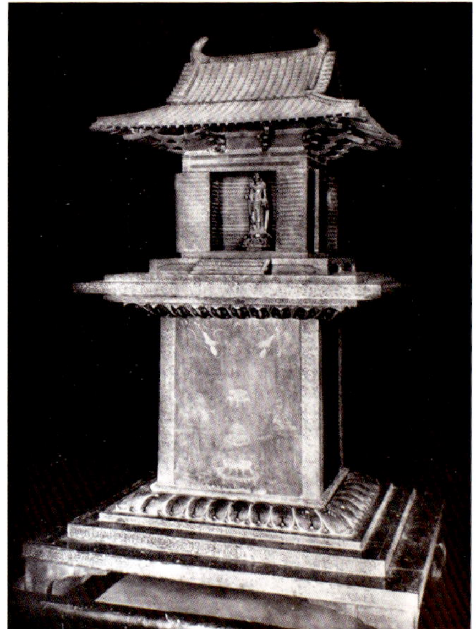

In a Western context, *Cut Piece* is often read as a canonical work of feminist art. But Ono's initial intention was to examine the idea of self-sacrifice as a means of pacifism—the dynamics of giving something up for a higher purpose, or greater good, and thereby transforming the value of a thing by way of selfless giving.[50] However, Ono's avant-garde interpretation of Zen was perplexing to mainstream Japanese audiences and ridiculed or ignored by Japanese critics. For Japanese audiences, her Zen-informed Fluxus works represented a defamiliarization of Zen ideas and imagery, whereby concepts commonly understood in everyday Japanese cultural life were made strange by way of their artistic interpretation. Yet this breaking with the iconographic orthodoxy of Zen visual culture by Fluxus artists established important precedents. During this period, Ono introduced artists such as Takehisa Kosugi, Shigeko Kubota, and Mieko (Chieko) Shiomi to the Fluxus network.[51] Kubota's infamous *Vagina Painting* (1965) (FIG. 46), a performance during which the artist attached a brush dipped in red paint to her underwear and squatted down to make a painting, referenced and critiqued the Asian calligraphic approach to mark making. It echoed Nam June Paik's performance *Zen for Head*, while also commenting on—or speaking back to—the masculinist concept of New York action painting. Among this Fluxus circle, the Asian body took a prominent role on the performance stage, unsettling both Asian

FIG. 43 (FACING TOP)
Panel depicting the Jataka story of the Hungry Tigress, Tamamushi Shrine, Horyu-ji Temple
Nara, Japan; Asuka period, mid-7th century
Photo: unknown, public domain, Wikimedia Commons

FIG. 44 (FACING BOTTOM)
Tamamushi Shrine, Horyu-ji Temple
Nara, Japan; Asuka period, mid-7th century
Photo: unknown, public domain, Wikimedia Commons

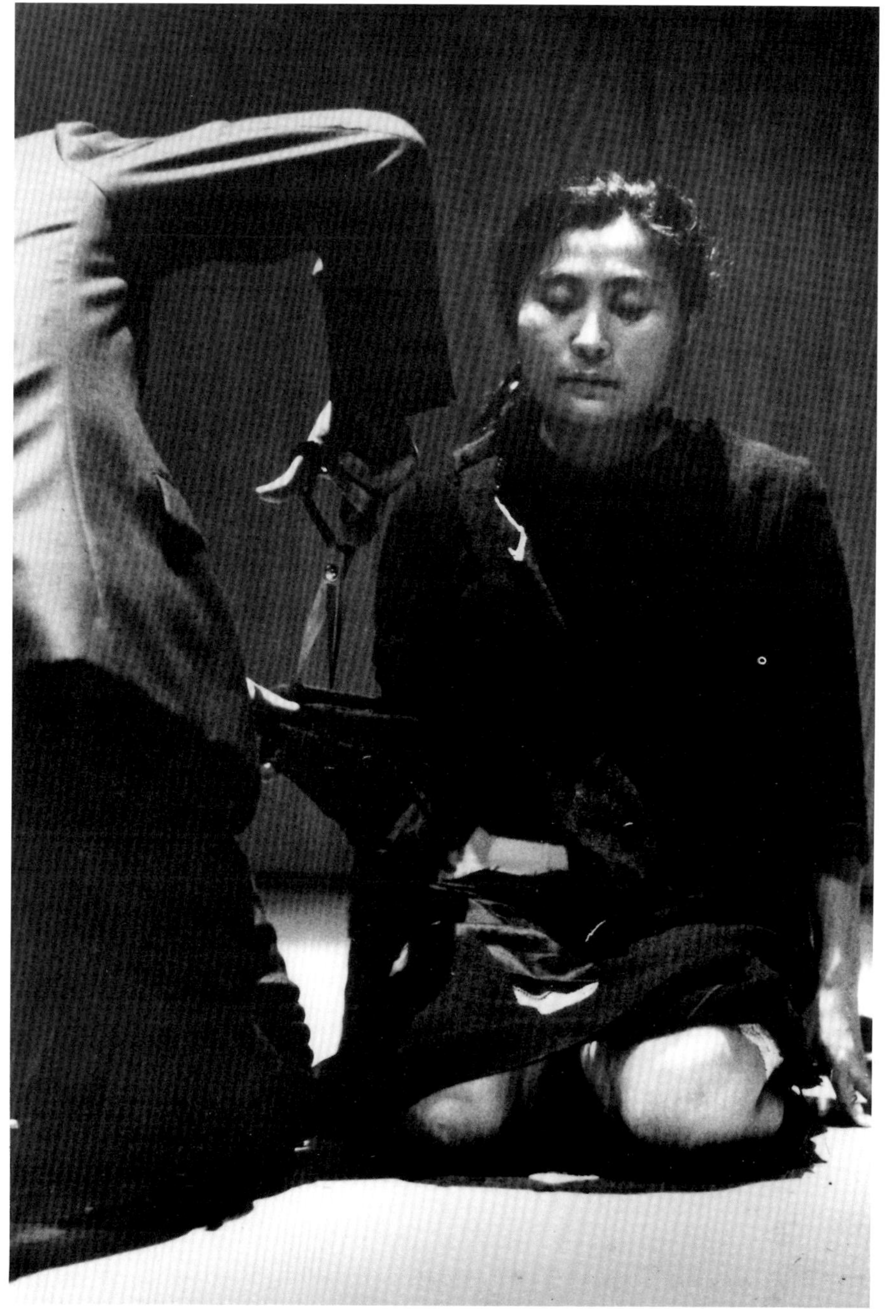

FIG. 45 (RIGHT)
Yoko Ono (Japan/USA, 1933–)
Cut Piece, 1964
Performance document from *Yoko Ono Farewell Concert: Strip-Tease Show*
Sogetsu Art Center, Sogetsu Kaikan Hall, Tokyo, Japan, August 11, 1964

Photo: Minoru Hirata

Ono's well-known performance and score was based on the Jataka story of Prince Mahasattva, the historical Buddha in a previous life, who offers himself up to a hungry tigress. The story is depicted on one of the panels of the Tamamushi Shrine at the temple of Horyu-ji, Nara, and is essentially a story of self-sacrifice, illustrating the overcoming of fear for compassion. The artist has explained that the performance was intended as a form of giving, examining the idea of self-sacrifice as a means of pacifism.

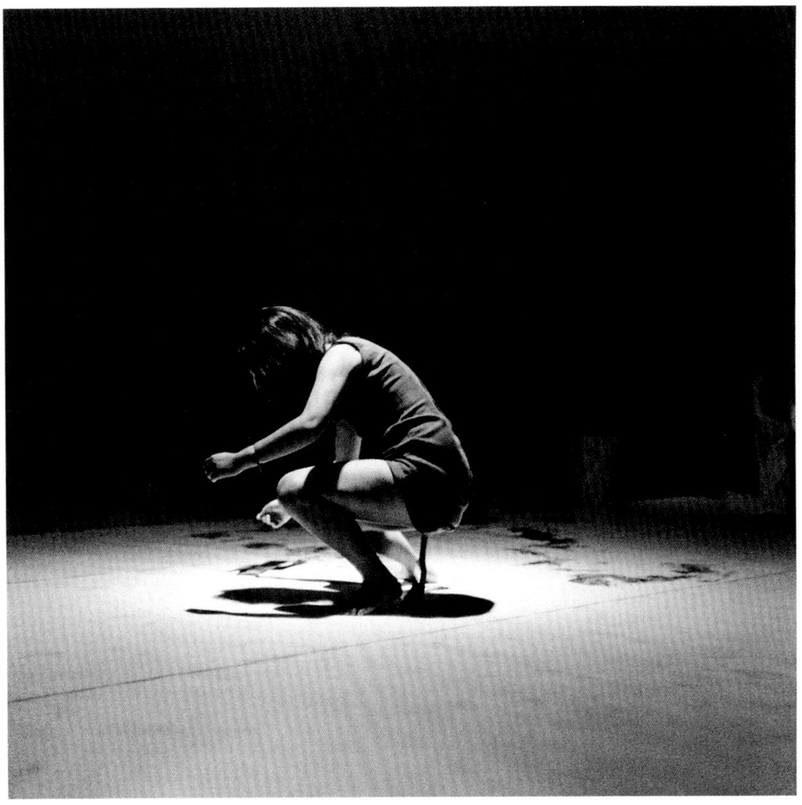

FIG. 46
Shigeko Kubota
(Japan/USA, 1937–2015)
Vagina Painting, 1965
Performance document:
Perpetual Fluxfest, Cinematheque,
New York, July 4, 1965
Gelatin silver print
image: 35.6 × 35.5 cm
sheet: 50.2 × 40.4 cm
The Gilbert and Lila Silverman Fluxus Collection Gift, 2008 / Museum of Modern Art, New York.

orthodoxies and Western conventions and opening up new spaces of artistic and critical discourse.

This Fluxus legacy continues to be important for Asian diasporic artists critically considering their own subject positions in a globalized contemporary art context. For example, the Vancouver-based performance artist David Khang draws on Fluxus, in particular the Fluxus recasting of the Asian calligraphic mark, to contend with the intersectional subject position of the Asian American body as it is represented in contemporary art. His work grapples with how the racialized Asian body is constructed by language (as symbolized by calligraphy), contemporary theory, and the Western gaze. Khang addresses both Asian and Western biases of heteronormativity, patriarchy, class privilege, and various forms of cultural orthodoxy in relation to contemporary art and questions of Asian-ness (FIGS. 47–48). Khang asks: Who attributes contemporary work to the category of Asian-ness, and on what terms? And who determines its meaning? How are these images of Asian bodies in the context of contemporary performance art susceptible to being read by way of either

FIG. 47
David Khang (Canada, 1964–)
Draw a straight line/Zen for Mouth, 2003
Endurance performance
approx. 25 min.
Performed at Track 16 Gallery, Los Angeles
Courtesy of the artist, Vancouver
Photo: Yerin Mok

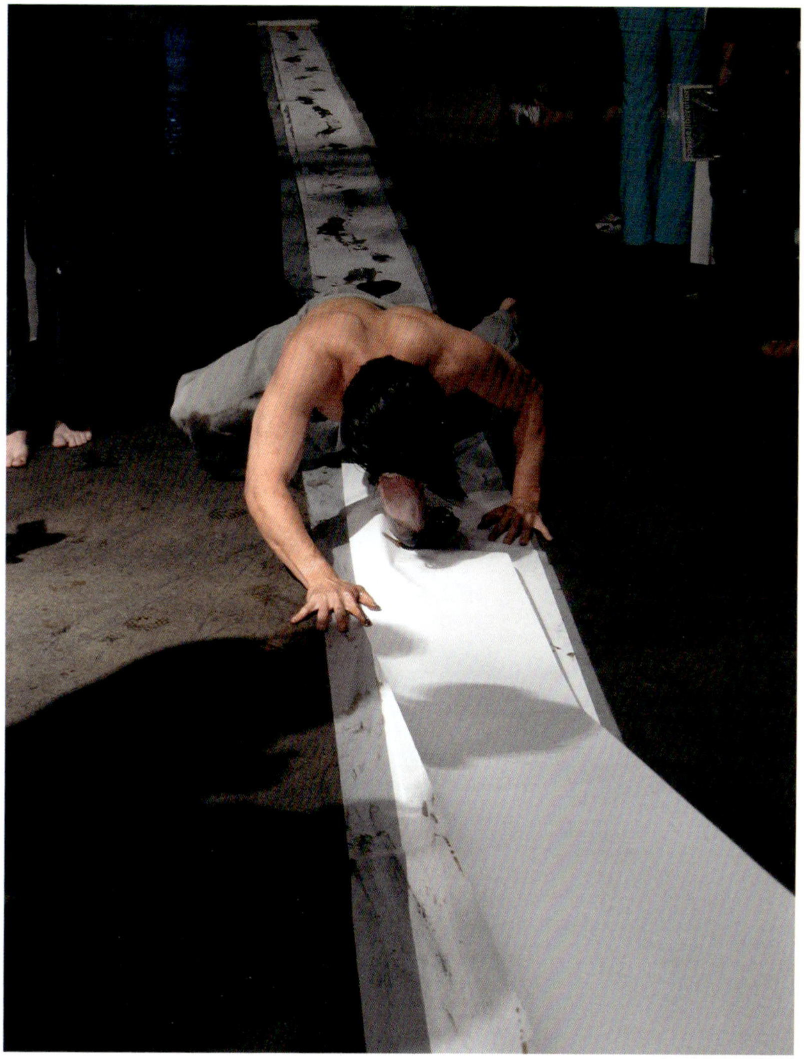

an orientalizing trope or an occidentalizing one, without consideration of a third term of ambiguity or ambivalence? What is at stake when certain cultural taxonomies—in this case, the conventions of Asian art and iconography—are broken down, destabilizing the meanings of well-understood visual forms? What gets lost in the process? On the other hand, what opportunities—what agency—are created?

If critics of modern Buddhism offer a perspective on this conundrum relating to contemporary or avant-garde creative expressions of Buddhism, they cite the risks of the loss of tradition, the loss of cultural communities, issues of Western exceptionalism, and the negative impacts of the emphasis on

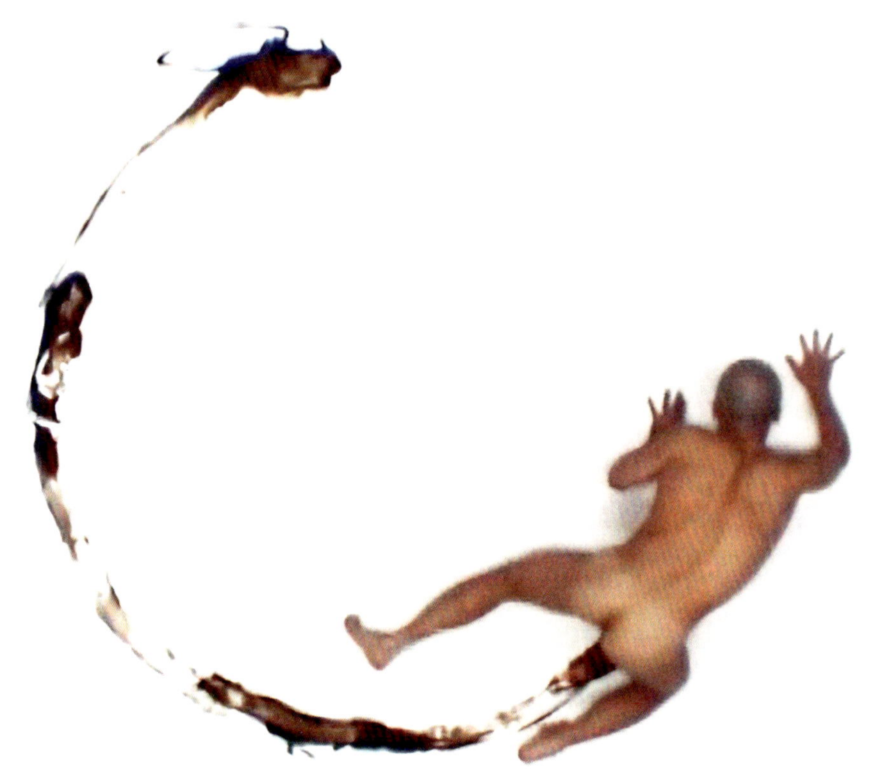

FIG. 48 (FACING)
David Khang (Canada, 1964–)
Linea Lingua, 2004
Video loop
5.00 min.
Courtesy of the artist, Vancouver

FIG. 49 (RIGHT)
Nobuo Kubota (Canada, 1932–), W. Mark Sutherland (Canada, 1955–)
Slowpokes, 2007
Sound poem: video
5.12 min.
Courtesy of the artists
Photo: W. Mark Sutherland

Nobuo Kubota is an intermedia artist working between and across sound, video, text, and sculptural installation. In the 1970s he was awarded a Canada Council grant to travel to Japan to spend time in a Zen monastery in Kyoto. As a child, interned at the Slocan internment camp in interior British Columbia, Canada, Kubota learned to chant the Buddhist sutras in Japanese, even though he could neither speak the language nor comprehend the words. His enjoyment was in the experience of the qualities of embodied sound and "mouth mechanics." Kubota began collaborating with W. Mark Sutherland in the early 1990s, producing dynamic, improvised sound poems and videos. Sutherland describes their close friendship and collaboration as based on "shared sensibilities and interests in Zen Buddhism, John Cage, Ornette Coleman, free jazz, Nam June Paik, Gagaku orchestra music, sound poetry, visual poetry, noise, etc."*

* W. Mark Sutherland, email correspondence with the author, January 17, 2021.

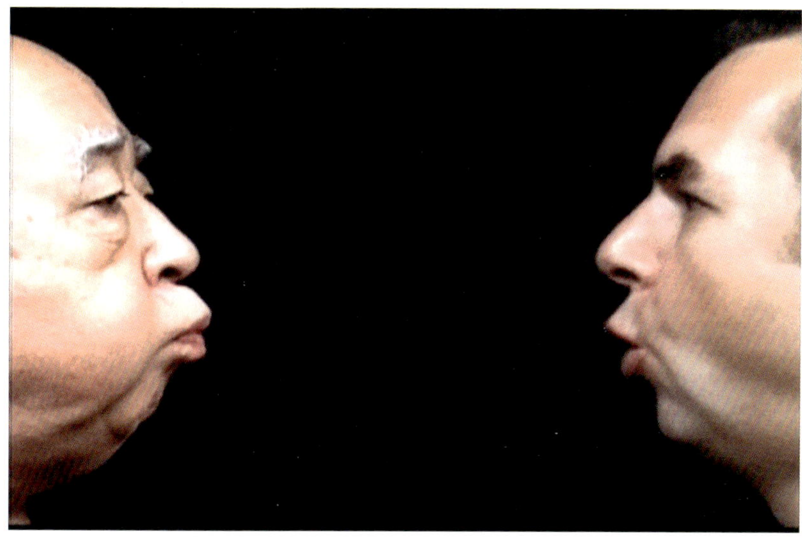

individuality and individual experience at the expense of religious institutions, among other criticisms.[52] But what I believe artists are trying to do by way of their inquiry into Buddhism is to counteract the conservative and dogmatic or entrenched cultural aspects of Asian Buddhisms—as, for example, Paik's rebuff to Zen orthodoxy or Ono's critique of Zen patriarchy—precisely to respond to issues in the modern world, and thereby to imagine and create new forms of community with the potential to address contemporary problems and social injustices.

ETERNAL NETWORK

In 1967, the French Fluxus artist Robert Filliou, who had a significant impact on Canadian artists, conceived of an artistic project called La Fête Permanente, or the Eternal Network (FIG. 50), defined as follows:

> There is always someone asleep and
> Someone awake
> Someone dreaming asleep someone
> Dreaming awake
> Someone eating someone hungry
> Someone fighting someone loving
> Someone making money someone broke
> Someone travelling someone staying put
> Someone helping someone hindering

Someone enjoying someone suffering
Someone indifferent
Someone starting someone stopping
The network is everlasting.[53]

The Eternal Network was a conceptual site where everyone could be engaged in a practice of Permanent Creation, a term Filliou used to describe the act of "being fully present in the moment of creating, as creation."[54] The idea of Permanent Creation is summarized and expressed in a seminal action poem and performance piece titled *Le Filliou idéal / Yes – An Action Poem* (1964) (FIG. 51), in which the artist proposed that the practice of "just sitting" is an act of "dynamic stillness."[55] During the performance, Filliou "sat cross-legged upstage, motionless and silent," while fellow artist Alison Knowles "described in encyclopedic detail the physiological workings of the bodily functions of 'the poet.'"[56] *Le Filliou ideal / Yes – An Action Poem* constituted a performance work of utmost simplicity, which proposed to define the essential meaning and purpose of creative production. In Filliou's conception, as summarized by this performance work, creativity is as integral to human life as breathing. He states, "I'd like people to realise that they are already artists, and to live accordingly."[57] Filliou's desire was for people to be engaged with the work of being present in the moment of creation, as creation; and where in turn, this "attention to" or "awareness of" creation shifts the terms and values of society.

In the Eternal Network, everyone is interconnected by way of Permanent Creation, as a self-organized, self-aware, and decentred system, network, or "creative weave."[58] According to this idea, art was considered to have the potential to intervene in society in emancipatory ways: "[F]or years now I have been advocating the artistic model for society as a whole... But the artistic model implies working so much on oneself... at the same time that you change society, even more you try to change yourself..."[59]

Being a practitioner in the Dzogchen (Great Perfection) tradition of Tibetan Buddhism, Filliou's concept of the Eternal Network finds an analogy in the mind-direct transmission practices. In Dzogchen meditation practice, ***mind-direct transmission*** refers to a coordinated intelligence or awareness (*rigpa*) among and between practitioners, aimed at comprehending the

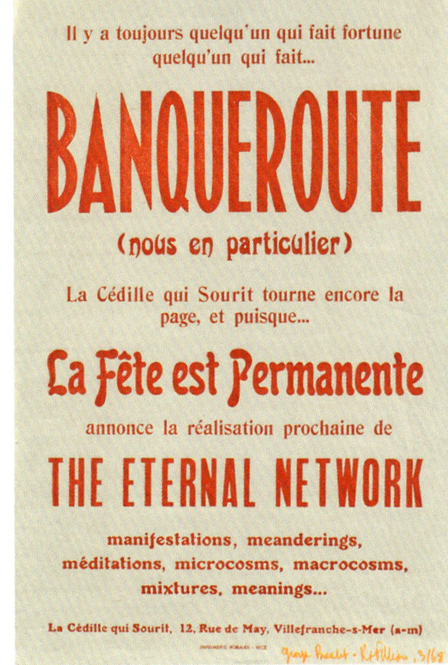

FIG. 50
George Brecht (USA, 1926–2008) and Robert Filliou (France, 1926–1987)
Poster for *Banqueroute*, La Cédille qui Sourit, Villefranche-sur-Mer, March 1968
Letterpress poster: ink on paper
49.8 × 32.4 cm
The Gilbert and Lila Silverman Fluxus Collection Gift
The Museum of Modern Art, New York, NY, USA

The Eternal Network, first announced by way of this poster, came to refer to the activation of the concept of interdependence by the means of a conceptual network of artists and creative practitioners. Central to the Eternal Network was the artistic practice of telepathy. As playful and absurd as this concept may sound, the Eternal Network could be considered a proposition for an imaginative social architecture—a mandala-like organizational structure—in which each creative practitioner, absorbed in their own creative world, was concerned with processes of self and social transformation. The Eternal Network was as real as it was illusory: a mind-object, perceptible through mind-transmission or telepathy, an analogy with the mind-direct practices of Dzogchen (Great Perfection).

10 A Filliou Sampler

Part Two—His Poem
Yes.
As my name is Filliou, the title of the poem is:
LE FILLIOU IDEAL
It is an action poem, and I am going to perform it.
Its score is:
not deciding
not choosing
not wanting
not owning
aware of self
wide awake
SITTING QUIETLY,
DOING NOTHING
Paris, 1964

Note: This work was conceived for performance, and was done at the Cafe au Go-Go in New York, on February 8th, 1965, the first part was read by Alison Knowles, while Filliou sat cross-legged upstage, motionless and silent. For the second part, Filliou stood up, spoke the words which we have printed here, then returned to his former position. Philip Corner improvised an almost silent musical accompaniment. The performance continued until all those in the audience who seemed anxious to leave had done so. It should be noted also, that the title given here names Filliou as "Le Filliou Ideal," but this title should be changed to designate any adult male poet who performs this work as "Le (name) Ideal." (*Ed.*)

Papa il est Papa 11

(La primière opinion de moi
de ma fille Marcelle)

"quand on a les cheveux sales, la poesie c'est de se laver les cheveux"
papa il est papa*

(pour mes grands amis emmett et daniel)

les enfants ont de grands yeux, de grandes dents, de grands nez, de grands pieds et de grandes mains

daniel et robert sont les parents.
emmett est l'enfant.
ils l'habillent.
le font manger.
le promènent en pousette.
le portent sur leurs epaules.
lui racontent des histoires.
jouent avec lui.
le couchent et le bercent.
l'endorment.

*Or: enfant, le poème c'est d'avoir des parents.
*Or: grand, le poème c'est de rester enfant.

1961

FIG. 51
Robert Filliou (France, 1926–1987)
Le Filliou idéal/Yes – An Action Poem, 1964
Published in *A Filliou Sampler*
(New York: Something Else Press, 1967)
Artist's book: offset printing on buff paper, staple bound, 16 pages
21.5 × 14 cm
Collection of the Morris and Helen Belkin Art Gallery
University of British Columbia, Morris/Trasov Archive
M/T 098.34

ART IS WHAT MAKES
LIFE MORE INTERESTING THAN
ART

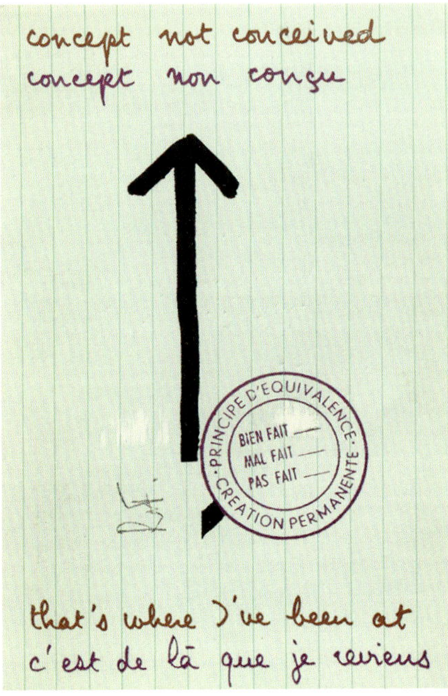

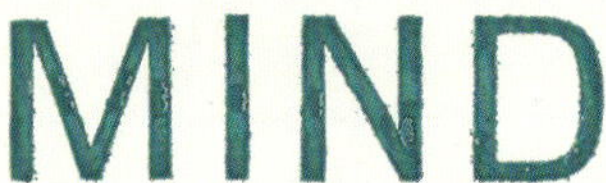

apersonalmessage, with
love from Robert Filliou

FIG. 52 (TOP LEFT)
Robert Filliou (France, 1926–1987)
Art is what makes life more interesting than art, 1995
Postcard (event invitation): ink on paper
10 × 14.5 cm
Collection of the Morris and Helen Belkin Art Gallery
University of British Columbia, Morris/Trasov Archive
M/T 126.06.35 / © Estate of Robert Filliou
Photo: Rachel Topham Photography

FIG. 53 (BOTTOM LEFT)
Robert Filliou (France, 1926–1987)
MIND: A personal message, with love from Robert Filliou, 1969/1971
Postcard: ink on paper
10.5 × 16 cm
Published by Angela Flowers
Collection of the Morris and Helen Belkin Art Gallery
University of British Columbia, Morris/Trasov Archive
M/T 126.06.44 / © Estate of Robert Filliou
Photo: Rachel Topham Photography

FIG. 54 (ABOVE)
Robert Filliou (France, 1926–1987)
Concept not conceived, 1972
Postcard: ink on paper
11 × 15 cm
Collection of the Morris and Helen Belkin Art Gallery
University of British Columbia, Morris/Trasov Archive
M/T 126.06.55 / © Estate of Robert Filliou
Photo: Rachel Topham Photography

FIG. 55 (TOP)
Robert Filliou (France, 1926–1987)
Handwritten dedication for the Eternal Network, 1973
Postcard: ink and crayon on paper
21 × 29.5 cm
Collection of the Morris and Helen Belkin Art Gallery University of British Columbia, Morris/Trasov Archive M/T 301.1-2 / © Estate of Robert Filliou
Photo: Rachel Topham Photography

FIG. 56 (BOTTOM)
Robert Filliou (France, 1926–1987)
Instructions for Telepathic Music No. 2, 1973
Postcard: ink on paper
15.5 × 22 cm
Collection of the Morris and Helen Belkin Art Gallery University of British Columbia, Morris/Trasov Archive M/T 301.1-2 / © Estate of Robert Filliou
Photo: Rachel Topham Photography

to all the members of the Eternal Network in Canadada and in the United States: greetings, sound manluck, womanluck, weatherluck. Today, after years of practicing and reflecting upon the subject, I propose to you all the composing and performing of Telepathic Music, to complement, buttress, and if need be replace all other marvelous, loving correspondences.
Day or night, day and night, send waves of greetings, sound manluck, womanluck, weatherluck, to members of the Eternal Network all over the world.
No proof of reaching and benefiting is necessary. Knowing oneself, suspecting others to be a performer of Day and/or Night Telepathic Music is sufficient. Your

R O B E R T F I L L I O U

according to a new alphabet of

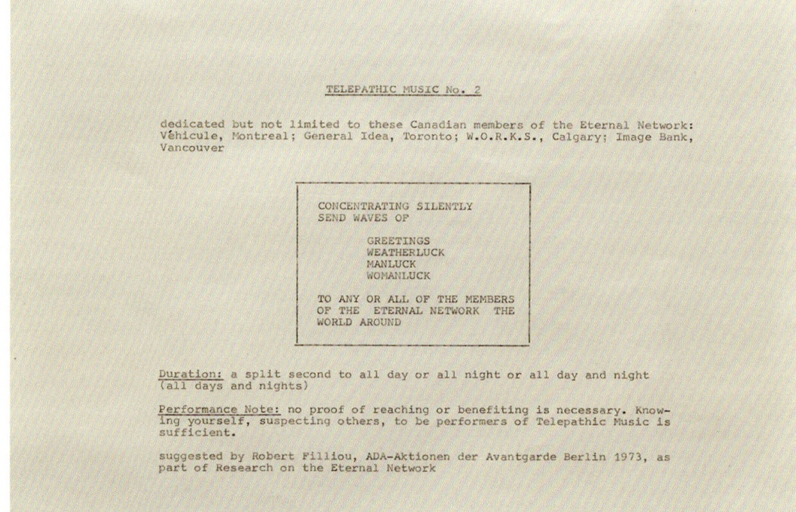

TELEPATHIC MUSIC No. 2

dedicated but not limited to these Canadian members of the Eternal Network: Véhicule, Montreal; General Idea, Toronto; W.O.R.K.S., Calgary; Image Bank, Vancouver

CONCENTRATING SILENTLY
SEND WAVES OF

GREETINGS
WEATHERLUCK
MANLUCK
WOMANLUCK

TO ANY OR ALL OF THE MEMBERS OF THE ETERNAL NETWORK THE WORLD AROUND

Duration: a split second to all day or all night or all day and night (all days and nights)

Performance Note: no proof of reaching or benefiting is necessary. Knowing yourself, suspecting others, to be performers of Telepathic Music is sufficient.

suggested by Robert Filliou, ADA-Aktionen der Avantgarde Berlin 1973, as part of Research on the Eternal Network

innermost nature of the mind. Filliou's *Research on the Eternal Network* (c. 1973) proposed to shift the terms of art by telepathically tapping into and coordinating with like-minded artists, to propose a more essential function for art, as an esoteric form of "net-work consciousness," as scholar Sharla Sava terms it.[60] In this regard, the Eternal Network exists but is simultaneously illusory as a "mind-object," perceptible through mind transmission or telepathy. Indeed, Filliou considered telepathy—for example, his extensive creative investigation titled *Telepathic Music* (FIG. 56)—as constituting part of his *Research on the Eternal Network*.[61] The Eternal Network was both an open invitation and creative metaphor for an alternate social vision that aimed at an analogy between conceptual art and tantra, where tantra is a complex, esoteric and advanced practice of Buddhism that draws on the power of the imagination and techniques of visualization to speed up the realization of Emptiness.

For Filliou, the Eternal Network was an imaginative, conceptual gateway to comprehending a non-dual relation between art and life; a means of "[closing] the gap between the artist and his public, and joining them in a common creation."[62] Filliou remarked that "young artists that we didn't know, mainly in Canada, groups like the Imagebank in Vancouver and General Idea in Toronto and WORKS in Calgary, etc., were considering their activities manifestations of the Eternal Network..."[63] He considered these Canadian artists as significant to charting an alternate course in the development of avant-garde art practices.

Whereas Fluxus proposed the relation between art and life to elicit the viewer's direct perception of the non-duality of art and life, without the mediation of the art object, for Filliou art situated in life, as life and as Permanent Creation, was an audacious though sincere artistic proposition, concerned with the creative interweaving of Buddhist teachings into life as a way of life and as art. In other words, Filliou considered life as art; but moving beyond existing definitions of art, the concepts of Permanent Creation and the Eternal Network suggest that he also regarded society as a work of art. Through his practice of Buddhism, Filliou discerned a means to imagine a new model of society liberated from the commodity conditions of postwar modernism and, emerging out of Fluxus concerns and experiments, produced a vision of society centred on his conviction of human creativity

FIG. 57
George Brecht (USA, 1926–2008)
Water Yam, 1963/1972, 6th edition (Parrot Impressions, Surrey, UK).
Artist's multiple: Black plastic box containing 91 offset lithograph printed scores
23 × 55 × 13 cm
Collection of the Morris and Helen Belkin Art Gallery University of British Columbia, Morris/Trasov Archive 31.0.0.34 / © Estate of George Brecht/SOCAN (2021)
Photo: Michael R. Barrick

Water Yam is an artist's book considered one of the most influential artworks released by Fluxus. Each edition consisted of a large number of printed cards containing open-ended event scores to spark the imagination. The event score was a critique of conventional forms of artistic representation, aiming for egalitarianism and suggesting the interpenetration of art and life. The significance of this work was in how each score suggested that everyday actions could constitute a creative "event," open and accessible to anybody.

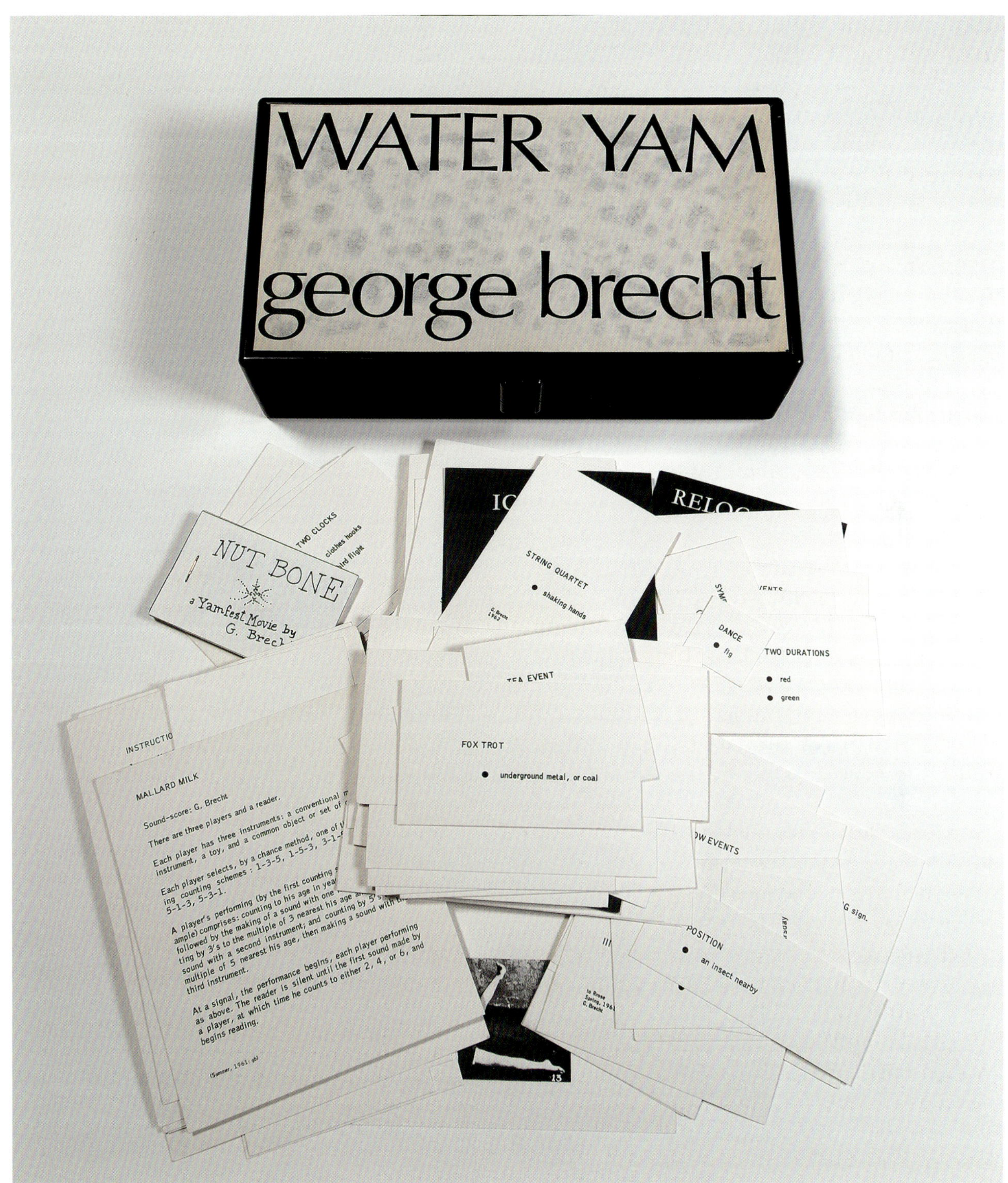

WATER YAM
george brecht
NUT BONE
TWO CLOCKS
clothes hooks
STRING QUARTET
• shaking hands
DANCE
• fig
TWO DURATIONS
• red
• green
FOX TROT
• underground metal, or coal
MALLARD MILK
Sound-score: G. Brecht
There are three players and a reader.
POSITION
• an insect nearby

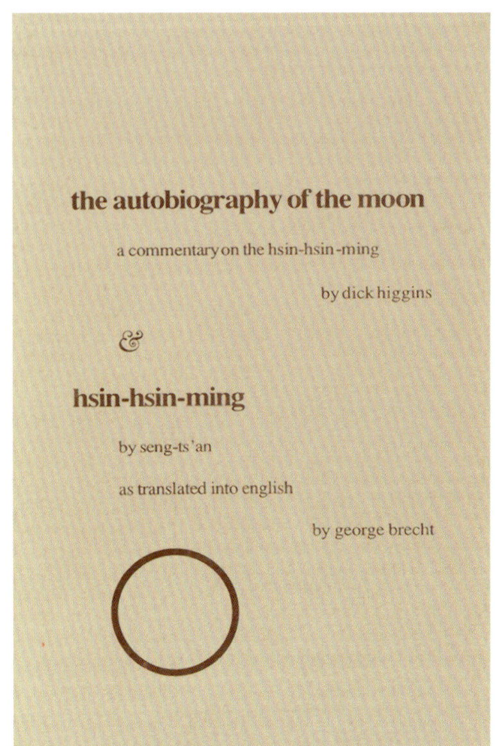

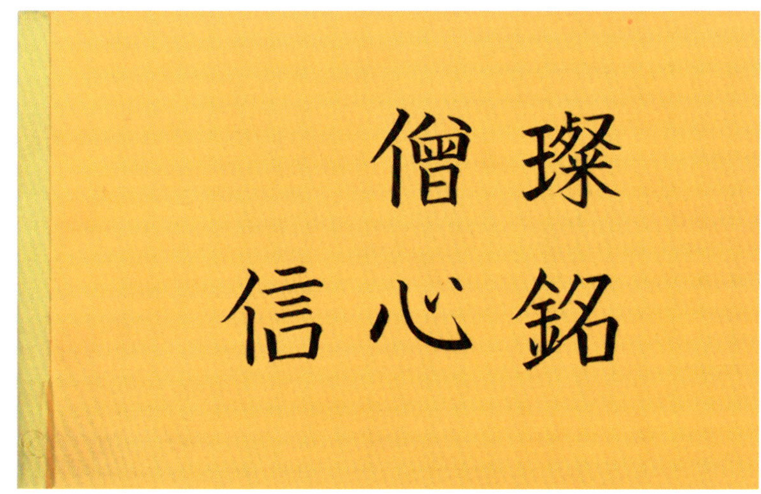

FIG. 58 (LEFT)
Dick Higgins (USA, 1938–1998), George Brecht (USA, 1926–2008)
The Autobiography of the Moon / Hsin-Hsin-Ming by Seng-Ts'an, 1991
Artists' book: 44 pages
21.5 × 14 cm
Published by Generator Press, Mentor
Photo: Stephen Topfer

FIG. 59 (RIGHT)
George Brecht (USA, 1926–2008), Robert Filliou (France, 1926–1987), Dick Higgins (USA, 1938–1998), Takako Saito (Japan/Germany, 1929–)
Hsin Hsin Ming by Seng Ts'an, 1980
Artists' book: 74 pages
11 × 16.5 cm
Facsimile re-edition. Published by Editions Lebeer Hossman, Bruxelles & Hamburg, 1984
Original edition published by Editions Lebeer Hossman, 1980 / Photo: Stephen Topfer

The *Hsin Hsin Ming*, commonly translated as "Faith in Mind," was introduced to the West as a Chan/Zen text by Suzuki in his book *Essays in Zen Buddhism* (1927). It is often studied in Western Zen circles. The authorship of the text is attributed to Seng T'san, the third Chinese patriarch. The text is concerned with the idea that Buddha and Mind are one and deals with themes of the interpenetration of time and space, non-duality, and the relationship between emptiness and form. For Fluxus artists, the *Hsin Hsin Ming* coordinated the goal of Zen practice—"no strain, no exertion, no wasting of energy"—with the goal of creative (in) activity: "not deciding, not choosing, not wanting . . . sitting quietly, doing nothing."* For Fluxus artists, the act of simply and consciously *being* (samadhi) is regarded as creative activity.

In a letter to John Cage, artist George Brecht explains the intention behind this Fluxus translation of the Chan/Zen text the *Hsin Hsin Ming*: "The minimal transcription . . . is not meant to substitute for, nor to improve upon, the translations into English . . . It is offered rather to help those already familiar with one or more of these interpretations to approach nearer to the Chinese itself, since the existing translations, in an effort to make the text more understandable, vary more or less widely from the original . . ."†

* David Doris, "Zen Vaudeville: A Medi(t)ation in the Margins of Fluxus" (1998), available at www.thing.net/~grist/ld/koppany/doris-e.htm, accessed June 29, 2020; Robert Filliou, *Le Filliou Idéal / Yes – An Action Poem*, in *A Filliou Sampler* (New York: Something Else Press, 1967).

† Letter from George Brecht to John Cage, January 7, 1981, box 40, folder 6, sleeve 13, John Cage Archive, Music Library, Northwestern University, Evanston, IL.

as a natural birthright.[64] Filliou's concept of society as a work of art, wherein each individual is engaged in a practice of creativity that promoted a deeper sense of self- and social awareness, anticipated a field of art practice now termed social practice (FIGS. 57–59).

SOCIAL PRACTICE

In 1966, the celebrated Vietnamese monk Thich Nhat Hanh visited the United States to lead a symposium on Vietnamese Buddhism at Cornell University. There he introduced the term *engaged Buddhism* to Americans, encouraging Buddhists to become more socially involved through charity, social service, education, and social activism. In the groundswell of protest against the Vietnam War, and coinciding with the concerns of the civil rights movement, feminism, environmental movements, and other progressive social causes, engaged Buddhism served to reinforce a sense of responsibility to alleviate suffering in the world. In art, engaged Buddhism contributed to a sense of collective possibility: a belief that social service and artists' actions at a civic level could contribute to greater social progress and civic change. Engaged Buddhism contributed to new modes of conceptual art practice, known variously as "new genre public art," "social practice," "engaged art," or "relational art." These practices, while rooted in the exploration of art connected with everyday life, as articulated by Fluxus artists, are best defined by their relationship to a larger agenda of community service, social justice, charity, and activist organizing.

The pioneering social practice artist Suzanne Lacy contextualizes the agenda of this radical approach to art, with relation to its connection to Buddhism:

> Since the 1970s, visual artists of varying backgrounds and perspectives have developed distinct models for an art whose public strategies of engagement are important aspects of their aesthetic language. Better defined by their relationship to a larger agenda of community or world change rather than to any specific art form, engaged artists might investigate ecological systems with scientists, create models of community development alongside planners, or work with politicians towards changes in police practice. The sources for this art are not exclusively either visual or socio-political, but derive from social necessity as perceived by these artists in collaboration

> with their audience. Such artists use the term "public" as their operative concept, connecting art in very real ways to the fabric of everyday life. They often transgress traditional artistic formats in the process of creating an art that is formally and ideologically related to the service practices of engaged Buddhism.[65]

Social practice is community oriented and collaborative; it is process driven and promotes social interaction or participation as a form of experience and aesthetics. Social practice artists variously address progressive and grassroots issues of social design. Their work is typically concerned with ideas of non-violence, social justice, citizenship, economic justice, ecological sustainability, and so on, indicating the altruistic dimension of artistic projects having a civic intent. Not all social practice artists draw from Buddhism, but for those that do, Buddhism shapes the artistic intention and methodological approach which directs them towards forms of self- and social actualization.

For example, the trailblazing composer Pauline Oliveros conceived of her pioneering work *Sonic Meditations* (1971) as a means to prioritize *listening* over *hearing* for "humanitarian purposes."[66] *Sonic Meditations* comprises a series of sound-based performance scores that represent a unique approach to sound art as egalitarian, non-hierarchical, inclusive, and non-dual (FIGS. 87–89, PAGES 111–112). Oliveros's compositions attempt to erase subject/object or performer/audience binaries, rejecting the conventional concert format binary of performer/spectator. Drawing on meditative processes based on her study of Buddhism and t'ai chi ch'uan, Oliveros's intention was to devise methods by which to deepen and develop more nuanced approaches to the cognition of sound, which she later described as "Deep Listening." Her aim was to review or restructure the performer-participant's perception of the world, in order to perceive the interconnection of all living things, as a form of healing.[67] Oliveros wrote,

> With continuous work some of the following becomes possible with Sonic Meditations: Heightened states of awareness or expanded consciousness, changes in physiology and psychology from known and unknown tensions to relaxations which gradually becomes permanent. These changes may represent a tuning of mind and body. The group may develop

> positive energy which can influence others who are less experienced. Members of the Group may achieve greater awareness and sensitivity to each other... Healing can occur in relation to the above activities when 1) individuals feel the common bond with others through a shared experience. 2) when one's inner experience is made manifest and accepted by others. 3) when one is aware of and in tune with one's surroundings. 4) when one's memories, or values, are integrated with the present and understood by others... its beauty is not through intention, but is intrinsically the effectiveness of its healing power.[68]

For Oliveros, the goal of art was to deepen forms of human interaction through the development of social awareness.[69] While Oliveros's work may not usually be considered as social practice, her approach and intentions conform to its definition—as a form of art practice concerned with defining an alternate or possible social order by processes of human interaction and participation. The aesthetic quality of a social practice work is thus internal to the creative work and emerges through participation. Social practice has less to do with how a work looks or appears or is presented or received—that is, it is less concerned (sometimes not at all concerned) with formal qualities and issues of presentation—but refers to creative processes concerned with enabling or situating an interpersonal, participatory experience that has a capacity to restructure our perception and understanding of the world. For Oliveros, this experimental and participatory approach to sound and composition conceived of listening and performance as a form of activism. In this context, activism is not simply a form of protest; it is a form of creative action and intervention designed to transform social dynamics and therefore bring about change at various scales.[70] Activism, in this sense, need not refer to practices concerned with changing the world, but can also refer to those concerned with changing the self, to see oneself in relation to and in *interconnection with* all other things. One of the features of social practice is its collectivist approach, recognizing that relief from the social conditions that produce suffering must be addressed in collective or interrelational ways, resonating with Thich Nhat Hanh's interpretation of the Buddhist concept of interdependence as "interbeing."[71]

However, as the curator and educator Mary Jane Jacob points out, Buddhism (or any religion, for that matter) can be considered

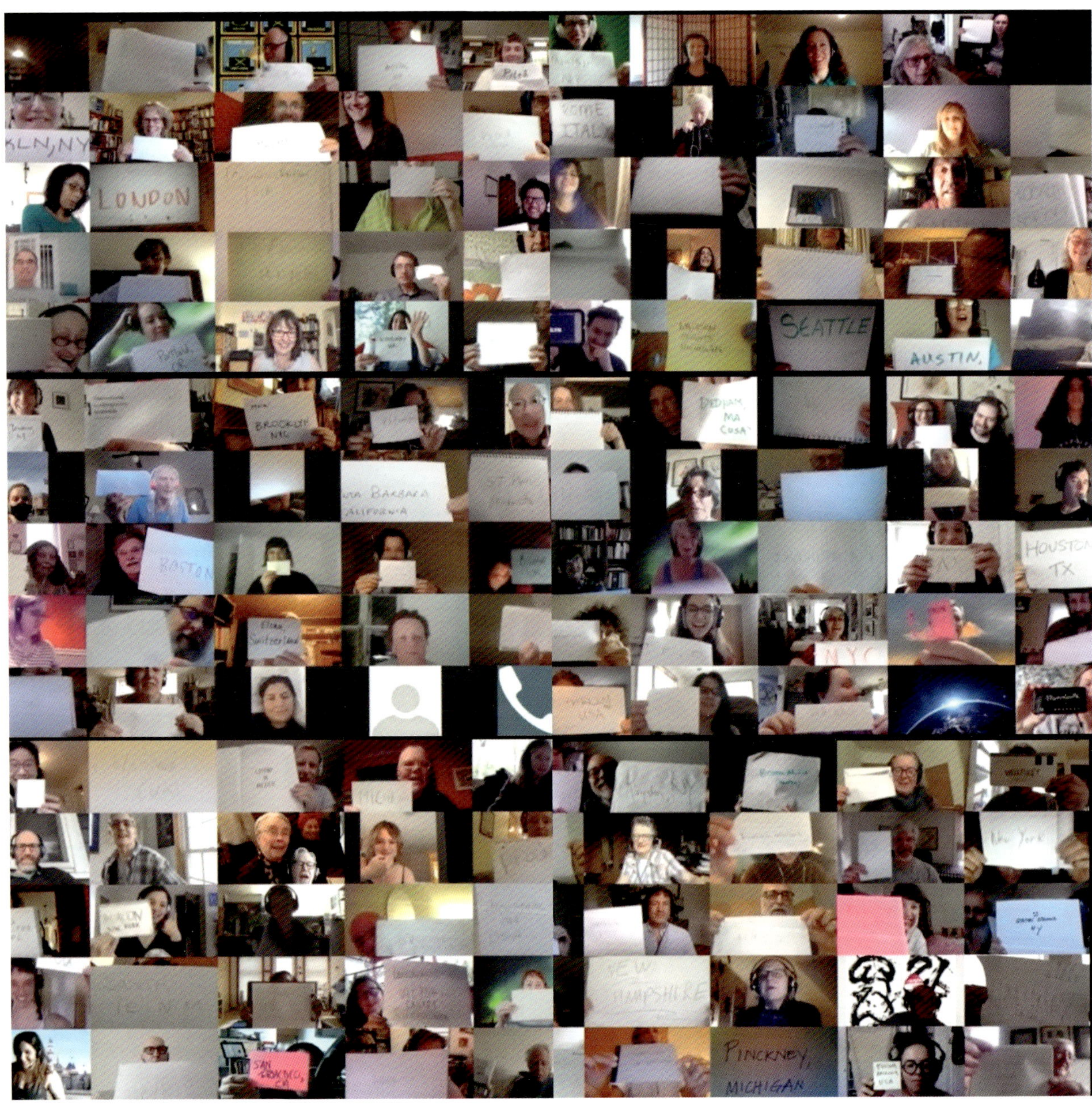
ROME ITALY
LONDON
SEATTLE
AUSTIN,
DEDHAM, MA USA
BROOKLYN NYC
BOSTON
HOUSTON TX
NYC
New York
NEW HAMPSHIRE
PINCKNEY, MICHIGAN

FIG. 60
Pauline Oliveros (USA, 1932–2016)
Worldwide Tuning Meditation, 2007
Documentation of online event hosted by the International Contemporary Ensemble, March 2–April 25, 2020. Available at www.musicrebound.com/pauline-oliveros-tuning-meditation

This iteration of Oliveros's *Worldwide Tuning Meditation* used the video-conferencing application Zoom in the midst of the 2020 COVID-19 pandemic for the presentation of a global performance of a work intended to bring communities together through meditative singing. Anyone, anywhere in the world, was invited to join from their phone or computer.

as both a "flashpoint and attraction point" in contemporary art and criticism, where the topic of religion can be considered as "frightening" or "cultish" as a consequence of the secularism of contemporary Western culture and society.[72] The value of Buddhism in the context of contemporary art, Jacob proposes, is as a "wisdom tradition" that teaches us, among other things, the meaning and potential of concepts of interconnectedness. These concepts might include, but are not limited to, the relationship between art and life, concepts of compassion and empathy, a deepening of our capacity for experience and teaching us how to sit with and experience the phenomena of creation over an extended period of time. Jacob comments,

> The point is that art can have meaning... for our lives. So that great 20th-century discourse of art and life, which we had to come to... because we had lost it through the centuries when art and life were together in many ways because of religion or other things, is something which Buddhism helps us figure out: What is the everyday gesture or practice that becomes artlike not artful but part of a way we live our lives...?[73]

Her argument is that while some contemporary Western art critics may have rejected the value of contemporary art as having a basis in religion, contemporary artists have long drawn upon—and continue to draw upon—Buddhism (and religion more broadly) as a source and foundation for art practice. Comprehending art in ways that reveal a Buddhist underpinning, however, requires so much more than simply *looking* at a work of art with a disinterested gaze. Much contemporary art requires the viewer to be curious, open-minded, and willing to immerse themselves in the *experience* of the work, where the intention of the artwork is to deepen and expand the viewer-participant's capacity for awareness or consciousness and thereby to deepen the purpose and function of art in life and society.

In another example, Vancouver-based artist Lam Wong draws richly on Buddhist concepts and references in a work titled *MA No. 1 – The Space between Objects (Wu/Mu)* (2019) (FIG. 61).[74] This work reconsiders the form and symbolism of traditional Chinese and Japanese tea ceremonies as a contemporary form of socially engaged art practice. In its traditional context, tea ceremony, closely associated with Chan and Zen ideas and cultural practices, is concerned with an aesthetic of humility, restraint, and imperfection. In Asian cultural contexts, tea

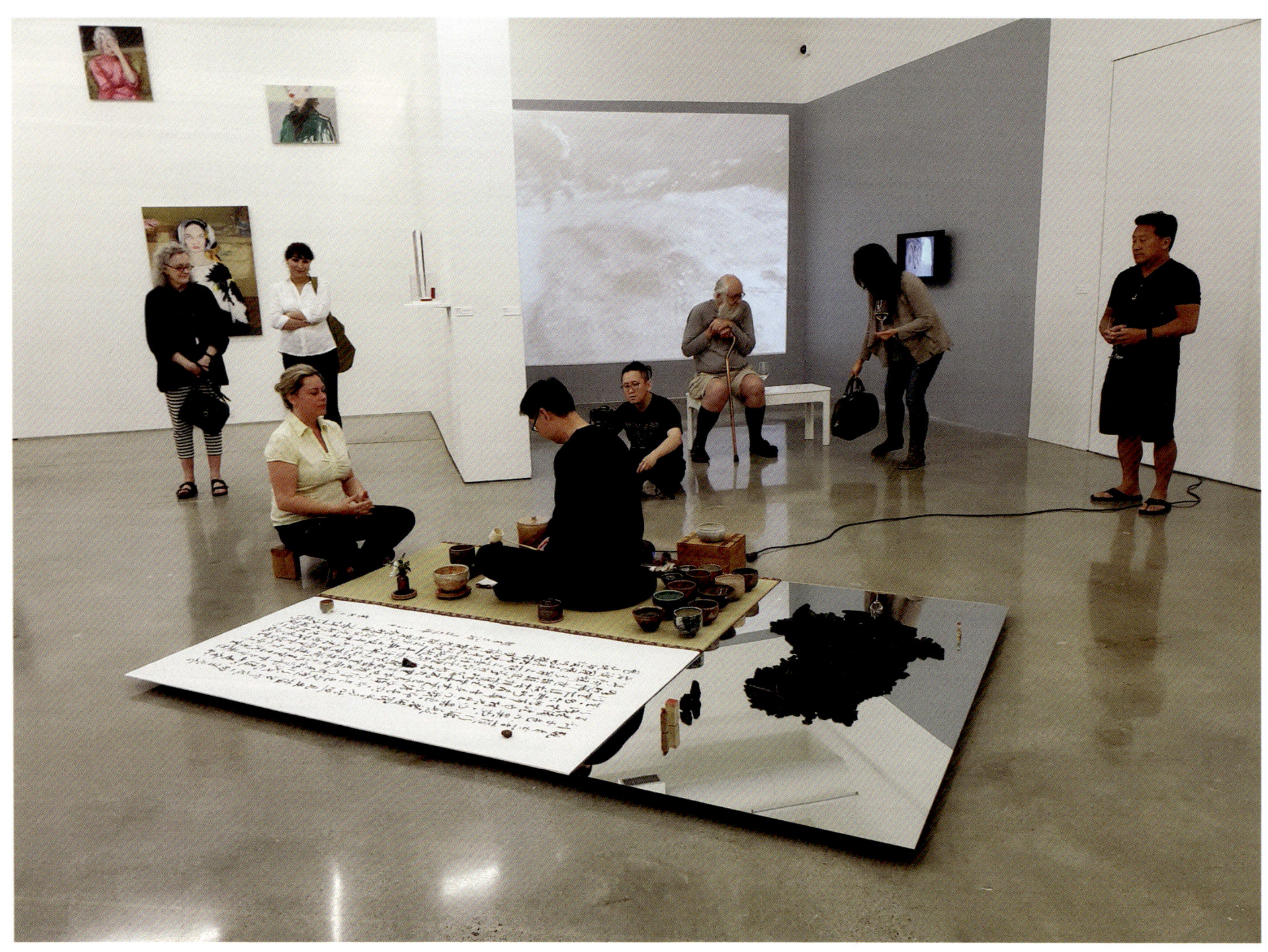

FIG. 61
Lam Wong 王藝林
(China/Canada, 1968–)
MA No. 1 – The Space between Objects (Wu/Mu), 2019–ongoing
Installation and socially engaged art practice: mirror, charcoal, seal chop, Chinese calligraphy of Heart Sutra, tea, tea seed, obsidian, teacup, wood, river rock, bamboo ladle, meditation cushion, tea accessories, ceramic tea ware, chawan
270.5 × 180.34 cm; duration, variable.
Courtesy of the artist / Photo: Mei Wong

ceremony is considered a transformative practice that situates an experience of profound peace and communion and recognizes the interdependence of things.

In this installation, Wong reframes the environment of the traditional tea ceremony as a floor sculpture comprising a large platform, having the dimension of three tatami mats. The first component of the platform comprises an actual tatami mat, where the tea ceremony is performed. The accoutrements for tea—tea bowls, teapot, ladle, and other teaware—are laid out around the tatami mat. The second component of the platform is mirrored, symbolically recalling the concept of the mirrorlike mind of empty awareness referred to by the 6th Patriarch, Huineng, in the Platform Sutra. This mirror surface supports a charcoal sculpture in the form of the Chinese character *wu/mu*, referring to the essence of the Dharma and the negations that constitute it. The charcoal sculpture also represents the hearth of the tea house, referring to ancient forms of tea ceremony relying on charcoal stoves, and representing concepts of impermanence and rebirth. The third component of Wong's tea platform is inscribed with a calligraphy of the Heart Sutra. The calligraphy serves the same function that a scroll painting would in the tokonoma of a traditional Japanese tea house, and is legible and immediately recognizable to Chinese readers and participants. The artist has placed three objects in a diagonal arrangement on the calligraphy: in the top right-hand corner, a teapot with three seeds, representing body, mind, and speech, and/or past, present, and future time; at the exact centre of the calligraphy, coinciding with the Chinese character for wisdom, is an obsidian crystal representing the *vajra*—in tantric Buddhism, a ritual implement symbolizing the properties of a diamond (indestructibility), which cleaves through ignorance to reveal the nature of reality. The *vajra* suggests endless creativity and skilful activity. A third object, an empty teacup placed on the artist's seal, symbolizes emptiness. Wong refers to a well-known Zen story of the overflowing teacup, about a scholar who visited a Zen master seeking enlightenment. According to this story, the scholar spends most of his time talking over the Zen master. The master eventually starts pouring tea for the scholar, but doesn't stop pouring. When the tea fills the cup and starts to overflow the scholar shouts at the Zen master to stop. The master responds, "You are like this cup. You ask for teaching but your cup is full. Before I can teach you, you must empty your cup."[75]

Wong's installation is richly embedded with layers of symbolism and Buddhist references, embodying what he describes as "a total knowledge" that is activated as social practice by the ritual of tea. The tea ceremony is performed by the artist with viewer-participants. Wong begins the ceremony by entering the space of the installation, circumambulating the sculpture, and bowing three times to show reverence for the ideas embodied by the artwork. This simple ritual of paying respect changes the terms of relation between the artist and the artwork, the viewer and the artwork, and the artist and the viewer-participant. His actions circumscribe a space of ritual and establish a sombre, meditative tone of engagement. The practice of tea is public, but it takes place in silence. The artist gestures for a participant, and once the participant is seated, Wong chooses a tea bowl for the guest and sets an intention for the ceremony. The tea bowl becomes a point of meditative focus throughout the ceremony. Wong describes the ceremony as a slowing of time, deliberately exaggerating the gap between movements, as gestures of bare attention, to effect a communion between the artist/tea master and the participant. The slowing of time and this practice of bare attention are intended to produce a sense of deep peace.

As a free-floating, mobile platform for tea, *MA No. 1* adapts the form and context of the traditional teahouse to create a culturally egalitarian art installation, accessible and available to anyone. Accordingly, the meaning of traditional tea ceremony is modernized and presented as a fusion of Chinese, Japanese, and Western elements, democratizing the meaning and practice of tea. As a social practice that inserts itself into non-conventional sites and cultural contexts, Wong's practice of tea acts as a counterpoint to the emotional and political charge of our current time—at the time of writing in 2021, referring to the context of COVID-19, worldwide attention on structural racism, and undeniable global climate disaster. Wong's work is transformative to the extent that it situates a generous and intimate gesture of cross-cultural, interpersonal encounter with the intention of offering respite from the stress and chaos of the world. The power of the work is in the artist's capacity to situate and host a profound exchange between and among strangers in the midst of chaos and, for a moment, to pause or suspend our preoccupation with that chaos, to effect a moment of stillness, a glimpse of empty awareness.

FIG. 62 (TOP)
Charwei Tsai (Taiwan, 1980–)
Driftwood (Heart Sutra), 2019
Performance document: India ink on driftwood
90 min.
Performed on October 27, 2019, as part of *In the Present Moment: A Research Convening*, Visual Arts Building, University of Victoria
Courtesy of the artist / Photo: Laura Gildner

The Heart Sutra has been a preoccupation in Tsai's work for over fifteen years. For Tsai, art and Buddhism coincide as practices concerned with achieving a meditative state centred on the concept of ephemerality. The Heart Sutra text is commonplace in many East Asian societies, printed on mugs, scarves, towels, decorative plaques, and other household goods. This Sutra acquired depth of meaning for Tsai by way of artistic repetition and her introspective creative and performative process. Tsai's ongoing explorations of the Heart Sutra trace the development of the artist's comprehension of the Sutra: initially as a short text learned as a child by rote, but slowly acquiring profound meaning by repeated recitation and meditation. Working with everyday, ephemeral materials, the artist gives form and expression to her meditation on the nature of Emptiness.

FIG. 63 (BOTTOM)
Charwei Tsai (Taiwan, 1980–)
Driftwood (Heart Sutra), 2019
Performance document: India ink on driftwood
90 min.
Performed on October 27, 2019, as part of *In the Present Moment: A Research Convening*, Visual Arts Building, University of Victoria
Courtesy of the artist / Photo: Laura Gildner

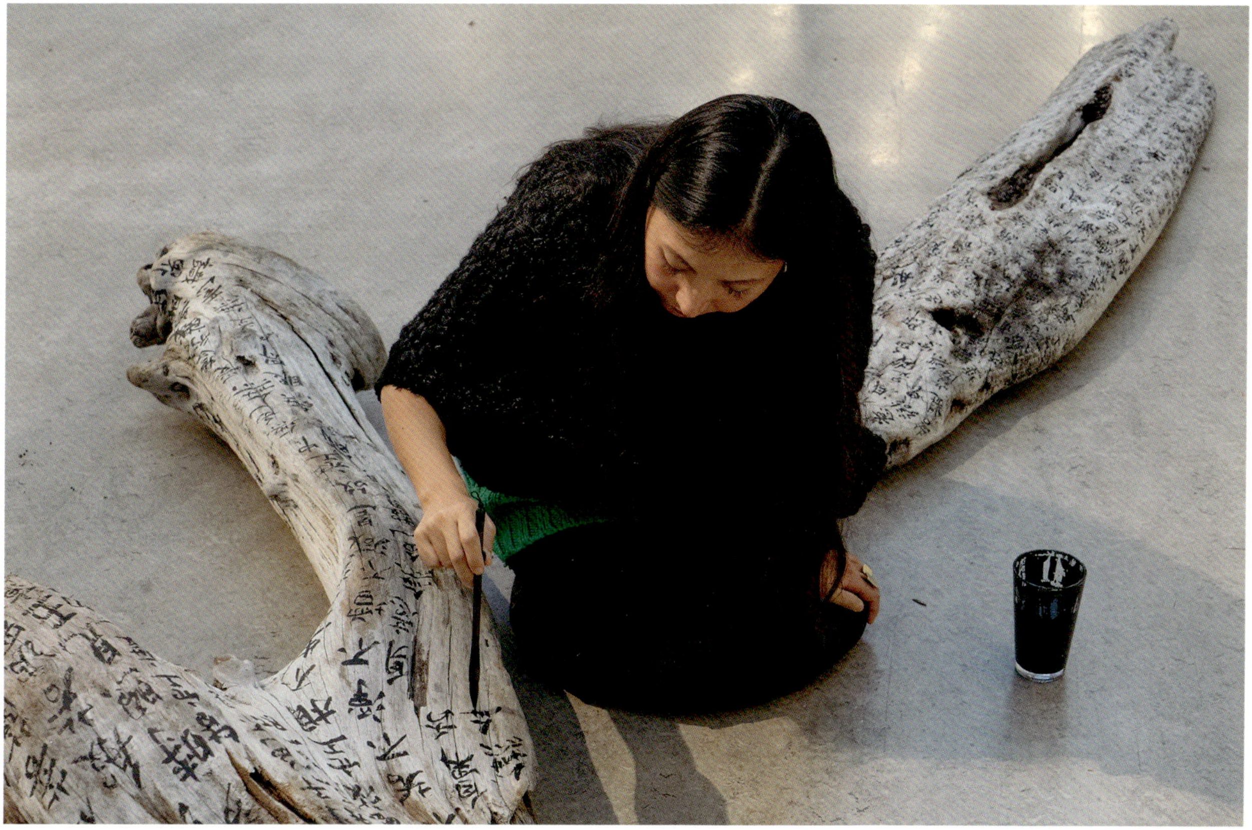

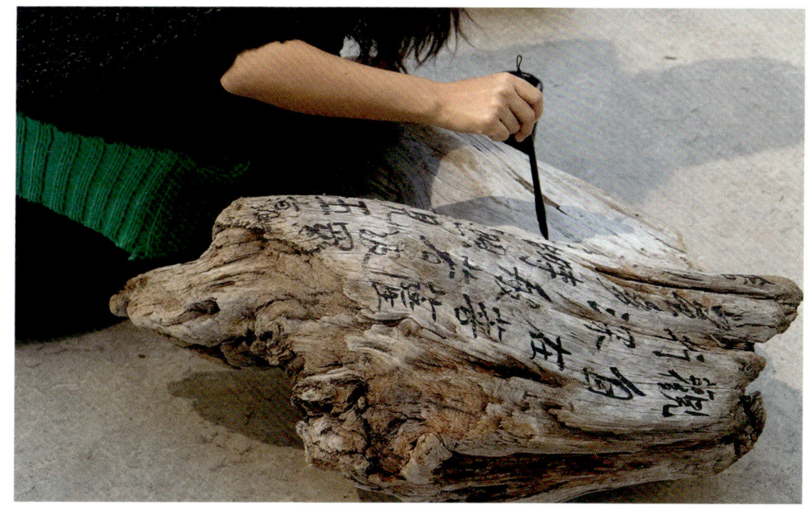

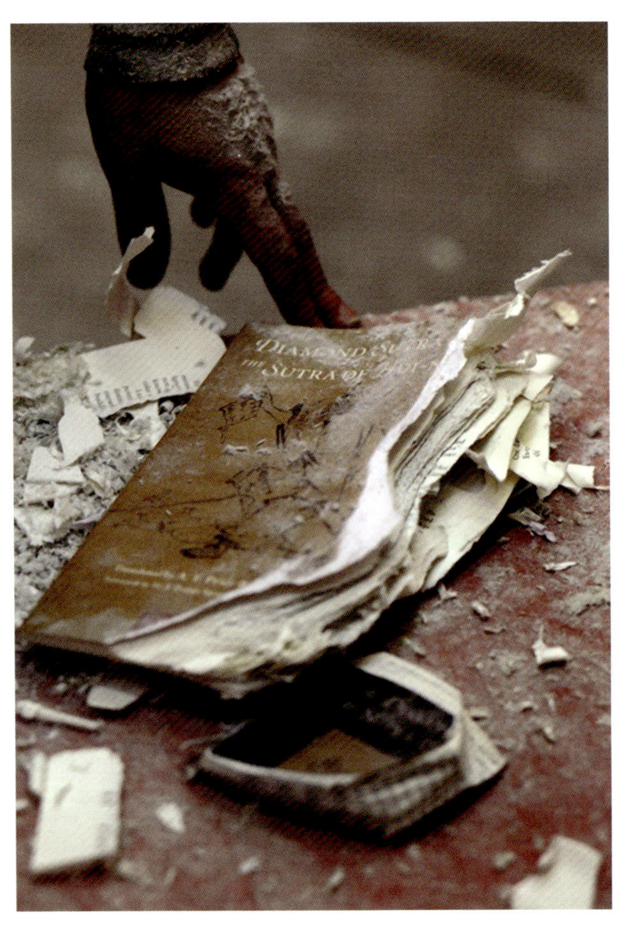

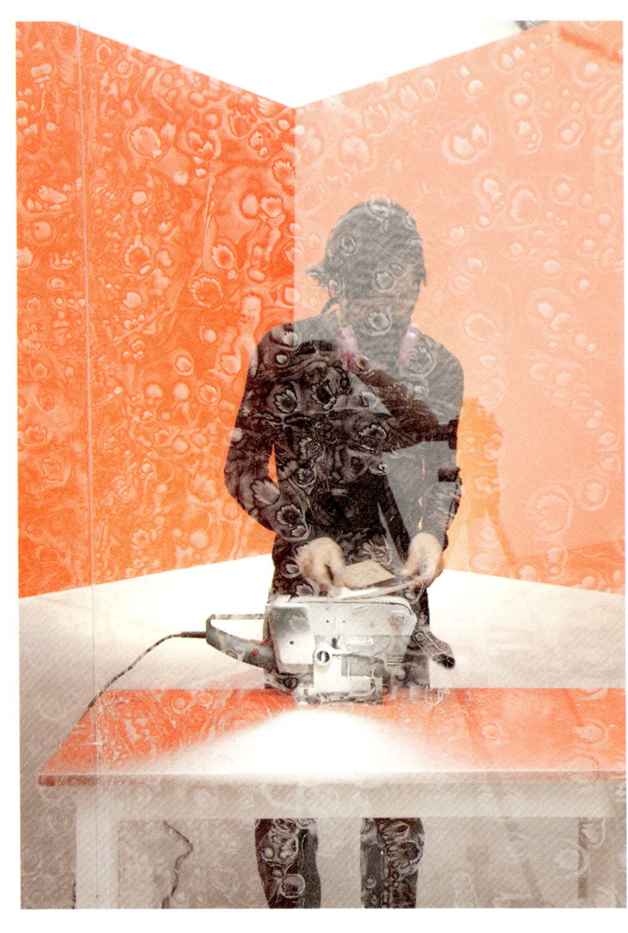

何以故阿那含名為不來而實无來是故
名阿那含
須菩提於意云何阿羅漢能作是念我得
阿羅漢道不須菩提言不也世尊何以故實
无有法名阿羅漢世尊若阿羅漢作是念
我得阿羅漢道即為著我人衆生壽者世
尊佛說我得无諍三昧人中最為第一離欲
阿羅漢我不作是念我是離欲阿羅漢世尊
我若作是念我得阿羅漢道世尊則不說須
菩提是樂阿蘭那行者以須菩提實无所
行而名須菩提是樂阿蘭那行
佛告須菩提於意云何如來昔在然燈佛所於法
有所得不世尊如來在然燈佛所於法實无
所得須菩提於意云何菩薩莊嚴佛土不不
也世尊何以故莊嚴佛土者則非莊嚴是名
莊嚴是故須菩提諸菩薩摩訶薩應如是
生清淨心不應住色生心不應住聲香味觸
法生心應无所住而生其心
須菩提譬如有人身如須彌山王於意云何是
身為大不須菩提言甚大世尊何以故佛說
非身是名大身須菩提如恒河中所有沙數
如是沙等恒河於意云何是諸恒河沙寧為
多不須菩提言甚多世尊但諸恒河尚多无數
何況其沙須菩提我今實言告汝若有善男
子善女人以七寶滿尒所恒河沙數三千大千
世界以用布施得福多不
須菩提言甚多世尊佛告須菩提若有善男
子善女人於此經中乃至受持四句偈等為他
人說而此福德勝前福德復次須菩提隨說是
乃至四句偈等當知此處一切世間天人阿脩

FIG. 64 (TOP LEFT)
Michael Zheng 郑济忠
(China/USA, 1965–)
Learning • Diamond Sutra, 2013
Performance document: Wie Kultur, Berlin, Germany, May 17, 2013
Durational performance
120 min.
Courtesy of the artist / Photo: Julia Baier

FIG. 65 (TOP RIGHT)
Michael Zheng 郑济忠
(China/USA, 1965–)
Learning • Diamond Sutra, 2013
Performance document: Wie Kultur, Berlin, Germany, May 17, 2013
Durational performance
120 min.
Courtesy of the artist / Photo: Julia Baier

Learning • Diamond Sutra is a conceptual/durational performance art piece that enacts the core teaching of the Diamond Sutra, a key text of Chan and Zen Buddhism. This enigmatic and seemingly paradoxical sutra is concerned with "cutting through" the illusion of form and materiality, challenging the "truth" of form, and thereby the perceived truth of the material world and our attachment to it.

During the performance, the artist, enclosed in a transparent chamber, uses a power sander to sand down a contemporary book copy of the Diamond Sutra in a seemingly iconoclastic gesture. The panels of the chamber are gradually covered in dust so that the audience's view of the performance is "whited out" by the performance itself. The performance comments on how the systems of knowledge that we rely on to perceive reality in fact obscure that reality; in other words, how knowledge is an illusion that limits perception.

FIG. 66 (BOTTOM)
Diamond Sutra
China, possibly Dunhuang; 7th–9th century
Handscroll: ink on paper
24.4 × 2,215.6 cm
From the Rev. Dr. James M. Menzies Collection, given by his son, Arthur R. Menzies
Art Gallery of Greater Victoria 1983.065.002
Photo: Stephen Topfer

CONCLUSION

The dissemination of Buddhism to the West describes processes of ongoing global cultural exchange that have had, and continue to have, considerable impact on 20th- and 21st-century visual art. The impact of Buddhism on art has been its ongoing contribution to the development of new approaches to art making and art experience that considers art as a site of self- and social inquiry and critique. In this context, artists regard Buddhism as a methodology of art practice that guides processes of artistic inquiry, experience, and critique, where the artistic inquiry provides insight into concepts central to Buddhism. In the West, and particularly in North America, which is the primary focus of this essay and exhibition, artists' inquiries into Buddhist concepts and practices have contributed to significant developments in the visual arts. New ideas such as the dematerialization of art, as proposed by Cage's seminal composition, *4′33″*, the practice of conceptual art, as promoted by various Fluxus artists, and the pronounced social agenda for contemporary art, as offered by artists such as Pauline Oliveros, centre a multi-sensory, interpersonal *human experience* facilitated by a work of art, rather than privileging representation or formalist aesthetics. This has, in turn, radicalized concepts regarding the meaning of a work of art and its purpose in society, where, for example, an artist such as Lam Wong considers the work of art as a conduit for the direct experience of the Buddhist concept of interdependence by way of a relational process, resulting in a full, though perhaps fleeting, experience of the present moment as "empty awareness."

In summary, what Buddhism has contributed to contemporary art is an approach to the understanding of the visual arts as relational and as emerging through practice, rather than being simply representational, performative, or iconographic. This approach to art aims for the creation of works that actualize ideas of self- and social realization on the path towards the ultimate Buddhist goal of Emptiness.

The author wishes to thank Martin Adam and Katherine Hacker for their thoughtful review and comments.

NOTES

1 Various curatorial essays and art historical texts have addressed this theme. For example, Helen Westgeeste, *Zen in the Fifties: Interaction in Art between East and West* (London: Reaktion Books, 1998); Jacquelynn Baas and Mary Jane Jacob, eds., *Buddha Mind in Contemporary Art* (Berkeley: University of California Press, 2004); Olivia Georgia, Robyn Brentano, Roger Lipsey, and Lilly Wei, *The Invisible Thread: Buddhist Spirit in Contemporary Art* (Staten Island, NY: Snug Harbor Cultural Center, 2004), exhibition catalogue; Jacquelynn Baas, *Smile of the Buddha: Eastern Philosophy and Western Art* (Berkeley: University of California Press, 2005); Martin Brauen and Mary Jane Jacob, *Grain of Emptiness: Buddhism-Inspired Contemporary Art* (New York: Rubin Museum of Art, 2010), exhibition catalogue; Vivien Greene, Harry Harootunian, Richard King, and Alexandra Munroe, eds., *The Third Mind: American Artists Contemplate Asia, 1860–1989* (New York: Guggenheim Museum, 2009), exhibition catalogue; and Ellen Pearlman, *Nothing and Everything: The Influence of Buddhism on the American Avant-Garde: 1942–1962* (Berkeley, CA: Evolver Editions, 2012).

2 "Japanese Provide for the Study of Buddhism by Foreigners," *New York Times* (December 25, 1932).

3 Tobey became a member of the Baha'i faith in 1918 and was an active member of the community. However, a central tenet of Baha'ism is the universalism of humankind. In his life and work, this belief in universalism was expressed as the interweaving of Eastern and Western influences in his art, where Zen had a special significance.

4 Mark Tobey, "Japanese Traditions and American Art," paper presented at the 6th National Conference of the U.S. Commission for UNESCO, San Francisco, 1957, and subsequently published in *College Art Journal*, vol. 18, no. 1 (1958), pp. 20–24.

5 Ibid., p. 24.

6 Barbara Johns describes Tomatsu Takizaki as "university educated in Japan, was a master in Zen and Kendo," in *Paul Horiuchi: East and West* (Seattle and London: University of Washington Press, in association with La Conner, WA: Museum of Northwest Art, 2008), p. 36.

7 Ibid., pp. 40–41.

8 In Ken Levine, *Northwest Visionaries, 1976–80*, VHS tape (Seattle, WA: Iris Films, [1979]), available online at www.youtube.com/watch?v=YDh4Zt8tK_4, accessed August 16, 2019.

9 Johns, *Paul Horiuchi*, p. 54.

10 Haema Sivanesan, "Charmion Von Wiegand's Vision of Modern Buddhism," in Maja Wismer, *Charmion Von Wiegand: Expanding Modernism* (Basel: Pretel, 2021), pp. 91–116.

11 David L. McMahan, *The Making of Buddhist Modernism* (Oxford and New York: Oxford University Press, 2008), p. 5.

12 Donald S. Lopez Jr., *A Modern Buddhist Bible* (Boston: Beacon Press, 2002), p. xxxix.

13 Ibid.

14 Ellen Pearlman, *Nothing and Everything: The Influence of Buddhism on the American Avant-Garde: 1942–1962* (Berkeley, CA: Evolver Editions, 2012), p. xi.

15 "Losing Our Religion," interview with Robert Sharf, *Tricycle* (Summer 2007), available at tricycle.org/magazine/losing-our-religion-2, accessed October 10, 2020.

16 These contentions were the subject of a conference, *Buddhism in the Global Eye: Beyond East and West*, University of British Columbia, Vancouver, August 10–12, 2016, buddhism.arts.ubc.ca/conferences/buddhism-in-the-global-eye-august-10-12-2016, accessed November 20, 2020.

17 John Cage, quoted by Kay Larson, *Where the Heart Beats: John Cage, Zen Buddhism, and the Inner Life of Artists* (New York: Penguin, 2013), p. 81.

18 Ibid., p. 82

19 Charlotte Joko Beck, "Attention Means Attention," *Tricycle* (Fall 1993), available at tricycle.org/magazine/attention-means-attention, accessed August 12, 2020.

20 Larson, *Where the Heart Beats*, p. 82.

21 The dematerialization of the art object is an idea proposed by art theorist and curator Lucy Lippard in *Six Years: The Dematerialization of the Art Object* (Berkeley, Los Angeles, and London: University of California Press, 1997).

22 David McMahan provides a useful account of the development of the Buddhist concept of "interdependence" (*pratitya-samutpada*) from its Pali origins to its contemporary conceptualization. In tracing a history of the development of this concept, he points out that "there is something *new* in the contemporary articulation of interdependence, something emerging in response to the unique circumstances of the modern world and attempting to answer questions that simply could not have arisen in the time of the Buddha, Nagarjuna or Dogen" (McMahan, *The Making of Buddhist Modernism*, p. 179).

23 Larson, *Where the Heart Beats*, p. 245.

24 John Cage, "Composition as Process," in *Silence: Lectures and Writings* (Middletown, CT: Wesleyan University Press, 1961), quoted in Larson, *Where the Heart Beats*, pp. 247–248.

25 Larson, *Where the Heart Beats*, p. 277.

26 David Doris, "Zen Vaudeville: A Medi(t)ation in the Margins of Fluxus" (1998), available at www.thing.net/~grist/ld/koppany/doris-e.htm, accessed June 29, 2020.

27 As quoted by Madeline Bocaro, "Yoko and John ... Cage," Madelinex.com (September 5, 2018), madelinex.com/2018/09/05/yoko-and-john-cage/, accessed October 15, 2020.

28 John Cage, quoted in William Duckworth, "Anything I Say Will Be Misunderstood: An Interview with John Cage," *The Bucknell Review*, vol. 32, no. 2 (1989), p. 22.

29 Toshi Ichiyanagi, quoted in Mark Swed, "A Dean of Japanese Music Talks Boundaries, John Cage and Life with Yoko Ono," *Los Angeles Times* (May 25, 2015), available at www.latimes.com/entertainment/arts/la-ca-cm-toshi-ichiyanagi-profile-20150517-column.html, accessed October 23, 2020.

30 Ibid. Midori Yoshimoto notes that around 1958, Cage invited Ono to attend D.T. Suzuki's lectures at Columbia University. She writes, "Although she had already heard Suzuki lecture at Sarah Lawrence College, she did not decline Cage's invitation" (Yoshimoto, *Into Performance: Japanese Women Artists in New York* [Rutgers, NJ: Rutgers University Press, 2005], p. 84).

31 Doris, "Zen Vaudeville."

32 Ichiyanagi, in Swed, "A Dean of Japanese Music Talks Boundaries, John Cage and Life with Yoko Ono."

33 The concept of "bare attention," also translated as "bare awareness," has a long provenance in Buddhist thought, tracing back to the Satipatthana Sutta, and is the foundation of contemporary Vipassana practice. Knowles would have encountered the concept of bare attention by way of her friendship with John Cage. See, for example, Tyler Friedman, "Interview with Alison Knowles and Hannah Higgins," *Shepherd Express* (November 15, 2013), available at shepherdexpress.com/arts-and-entertainment/visual-art/interview-alison-knowles-hannah-higgins, accessed January 27, 2021.

34 In Estera Milman, "Road Shows, Street Events, and Fluxus People: A Conversation with Alison Knowles," *Visible Language*, vol. 26, nos. 1/2 (1992), p. 103.

35 Melissa Anne-Marie Curley, "Correspondence School: Canada, Fluxus and Zen," in *Flowers on the Rock: Global and Local Buddhisms in Canada* (Montreal, QC, and Kingston, ON: McGill-Queen's University Press, 2014), p. 268.

36 Ibid.

37 Sook-Kyung Lee, "Nam June Paik: Transforming Cultures, Connecting the World," in Sook-Kyung Lee and Rudolf Frieling, *Nam June Paik* (London: Tate Museum, 2019), exhibition catalogue, pp. 10–13.

38 Nam June Paik in Otto Hahn, "Interview 1992," interview with Nam June Paik, in Klaus Bußmann and Florian Matzner, eds., *Eine DATA base*, H171, as cited by Patricia Mellencamp, "The Old and the New:

Nam June Paik," *Art Journal*, vol. 54, no. 4 (Winter 1995), p. 44.

39 Nam June Paik, in *Fluxus cc FiVe ThRee*, no. 4 (1964), available at walkerart.org/collections/artworks/fluxus-cc-five-three-fluxus-newspaper-number-4, accessed November 23, 2020.

40 Tae-seung Lim, "Moving Meditation: PAIK Nam June's *TV Buddha* and Its Zen Buddhist Aesthetic Meaning," *Dao*, vol. 18 (2019), pp. 92–94. Lim provides the example of the 6th Patriarch of Chan Buddhism, Huineng, who is depicted in a 13th-century brush painting as tearing up a sutra. While the idea of a monk tearing up a sutra is shocking, the aim of the gesture is to break through delusion and the trap of convention and formality.

41 Walter Smith, "Nam June Paik's *TV Buddha* as Buddhist Art," *Religion and the Arts*, vol. 4, no. 3 (2000), pp. 359–373.

42 Lim, "Moving Meditation," pp. 100–101.

43 Lim, following on Smith, "Nam June Paik's *TV Buddha* as Buddhist Art," p. 361, describes *TV Buddha* as an image of nirvana (Lim, "Moving Meditation," p. 106). In Sanskrit, *nirvana* literally means "extinction," referring to the "soteriological release from rebirths in samsara" that is the ultimate spiritual goal of Buddhism. Smith, however, equates nirvana with enlightenment: "This transcendent, indefinable state is to be identified with the Buddha himself." Rather than describing the state of nirvana, I suggest that *TV Buddha* more properly describes a state of samadhi, or "oneness with the object of meditation."

44 Yoshimoto, *Into Performance*, p. 96.

45 Yoko Ono, quoted in Midori Yoshimoto (transcribed and translated), "Some Young People – From Nonfiction Theater," *Review of Japanese Culture and Society*, December 2005, p. 101.

46 Ibid., p. 100.

47 Julia Bryan-Wilson, "Remembering Yoko Ono's *Cut Piece*," *Oxford Art Journal*, vol. 26, no. 1 (2003), p. 106, fn. 14.

48 Yoko Ono, quoted in Roger Perry and Tony Elliot, "Yoko Ono," *Unit* (December 1967), cited by Kevin Concannon, "Yoko Ono's 'Cut Piece': From Text to Performance and Back Again," *PAJ: A Journal of Performance and Art*, vol. 30, no. 3 (September 2008), p. 89.

49 Ibid.

50 Julia Bryan-Wilson's insightful essay considers *Cut Piece* as a response to Ono's personal experience of the Tokyo bombings during World War II and compares the aesthetics of the piece with images depicting the shredded clothing of survivors of the Hiroshima and Nagasaki bombings (Bryan-Wilson, "Remembering Yoko Ono's *Cut Piece*"). Yoshimoto similarly describes the work as a call for non-violence or pacificism, a "hope for World Peace" (Yoshimoto, *Into Performance*, p. 101).

51 Yoshimoto, *Into Performance*, p. 96.

52 For critiques of modern Buddhism, see, for example, Robert Sharf, "Buddhist Modernism and the Rhetoric of Meditative Experience," *Numen*, vol. 42, no. 3 (October 1995), pp. 228–283, or Evan Thompson, *Why I Am Not a Buddhist* (New Haven, CT: Yale University Press, 2020).

53 Robert Filliou, *Lehren und Lernen als Auffuerungskuentste / Teaching and Learning as Performing Arts* (Cologne and New York: Verlag Gebr. Konig, 1970), p. 205.

54 Refer to Laurel Fredrickson, "Life as Art, or Art as Life: Robert Filliou and the Eternal Network," *Theory, Culture and Society*, vol. 35, no. 3 (September 2018), p. 6.

55 Filliou, *Lehren und Lernen als Auffuerungskuentste / Teaching and Learning as Performing Arts*, p. 95.

56 Doris, "Zen Vaudeville."

57 In Anders Kreuger and Irmeline Lebeer, eds., *Robert Filliou: The Secret of Permanent Creation* (Antwerp: M HKA [Museum of Contemporary Art Antwerp], 2017), p. 63-E.

58 Ibid., pp. 50–51-E.

59 In Louwrien Wijers, ed., *His Holiness the Fourteenth Dalai Lama of Tibet talks to Louwrien Wijers* (Holland: Kantoor voor Cultuur Extracten, n.d.), p. 72.

60 Sharla Sava, *As If the Oceans Were Lemonade: The Performative Vision of Robert Filliou and the Western Front*, MA thesis, Department of Fine Arts, University of British Columbia, Vancouver, BC (1996), pp. 4–9.

61 Kreuger and Lebeer, eds., *Robert Filliou: The Secret of Permanent Creation*, p. 50-E.

62 Filliou, *Lehren und Lernen als Auffuerungskuentste / Teaching and Learning as Performing Arts*, p. 7.

63 In Kreuger and Lebeer, eds., *Robert Filliou: The Secret of Permanent Creation*, p. 50-E.

64 Ibid., p. 61-E.

65 Suzanne Lacy, "Having It Good: Reflections on Engaged Art and Engaged Buddhism," in Jacquelynn Baas and Mary Jane Jacob, eds., *Buddha Mind in Contemporary Art* (Berkeley, Los Angeles, London: University of California Press, 2004), p. 101.

66 Pauline Oliveros, *Sonic Meditations* (Smith Publications, 1971), musical score.

67 Refer to William Osbourne, "Sounding the Abyss of Otherness: Pauline Oliveros' Deep Listening and the Sonic Meditations," in Deborah Johnson and Wendy Oliver, eds., *Women Making Art: Women in the Visual, Literary, and Performing Arts since 1960* (New York: Lang, 2000), pp. 65–86, available at www.osborne-conant.org/oliveros.htm, accessed August 15, 2019. From 1981, Oliveros studied Zen with John Daido Loori at Zen Mountain Monastery, Mount Tremper, NY, and Tibetan Buddhism with H.E. T'ai Situ Rinpoche at Karma Triyana Dharmachakra, Woodstock, NY. Refer to Pauline Oliveros, *Deep Listening: A Composer's Sound Practice* (Deep Listening Publications, 2005).

68 Oliveros, *Sonic Meditations*.

69 As the scholar Tracey McMullen phrases it, Deep Listening "could be understood as a practice of dissolving the self by putting deep focus on the other-in-front-of-us and coming to understand the interrelatedness and co-arising of supposed 'other' and 'self'" (McMullen, "Subject, Object, Improv: John Cage, Pauline Oliveros, and Eastern (Western) Philosophy in Music," *Critical Studies in Improvisation / Études critiques en improvisation*, vol. 6, no. 2 [2010], available at wwwimprovcommunity.ca/sites/improvcommunity.ca/files/research_collection/750/John_Cage_Pauline_Oliveros_and_Eastern_Western_Philosophy_in_Music.pdf, accessed December 9, 2020).

70 Kerry O'Brien, "Listening as Activism: the 'Sonic Meditations' of Pauline Oliveros," *The New Yorker* (December 9, 2016), a vailable at www.newyorker.com/culture/culture-desk/listening-as-activism-the-sonic-meditations-of-pauline-oliveros, accessed November 24, 2020.

71 Thich Nhat Hanh's concept of "interbeing" describes the condition of the (non-)self as interdependent with all other things. Refer to Thich Nhat Hanh, *Interbeing: Fourteen Guidelines for Engaged Buddhism* (Berkeley, CA: Parallax Press, 1998).

72 Duncan Mackenzie, "Episode 209: Mary Jane Jacob," *Bad at Sports* podcast (August 30, 2009), available at badatsports.com/2009/episode-209-mary-jane-jacob/, accessed November 24, 2020.

73 In ibid.

74 This work was first installed and performed as part of the exhibition *Person/ne*, curated by Lisa Baldissera at Griffin Art Projects, North Vancouver, Canada, May 11–September 2, 2019.

75 Lam Wong, telephone conversation with the author, September 16, 2020.

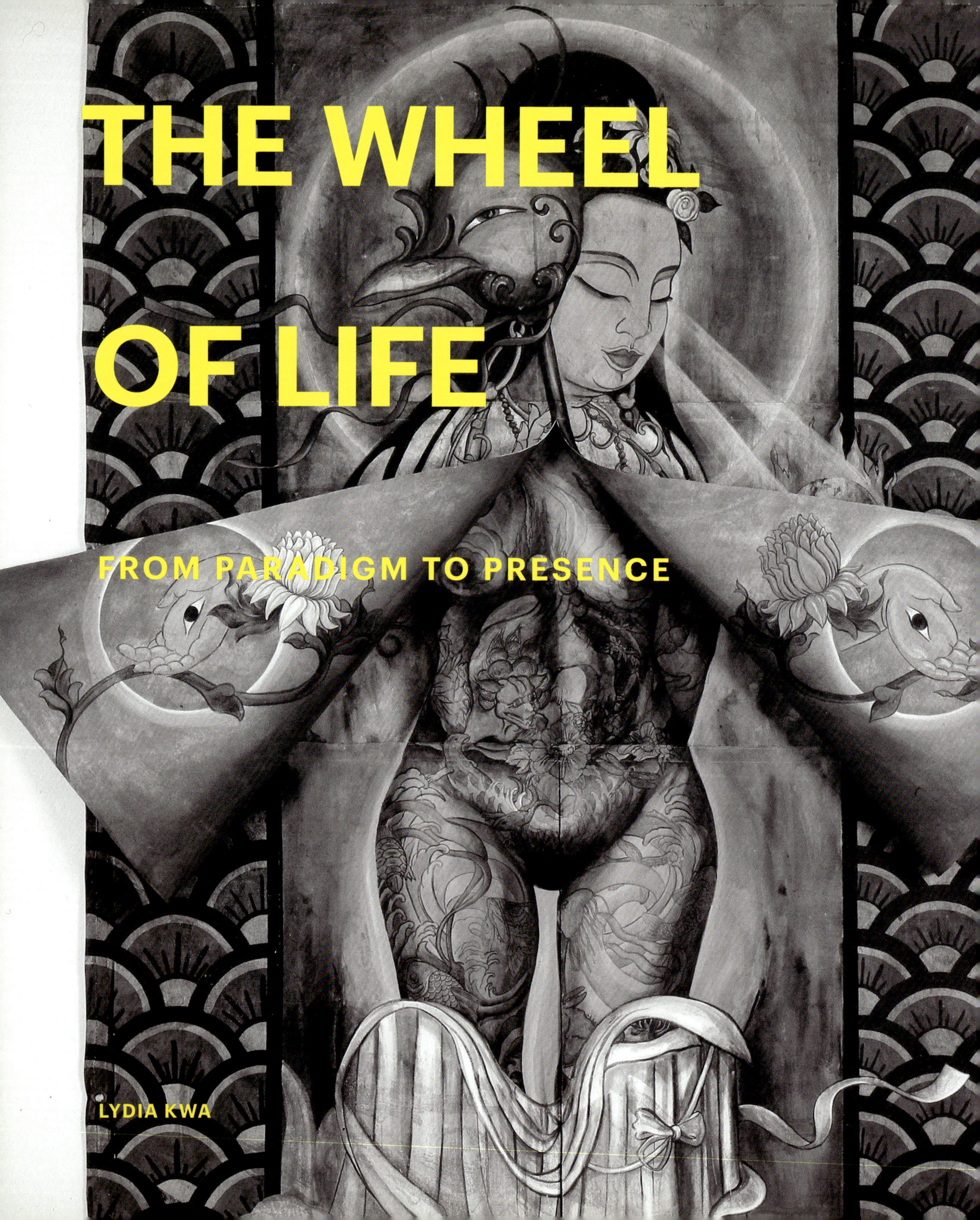
THE WHEEL
OF LIFE
FROM PARADIGM TO PRESENCE
LYDIA KWA

If you meet the Buddha on the road, kill him.

ZEN PROVERB ATTRIBUTED TO LINJI YIXUAN (RINZAI SECT, D. 866 CE)

TO DISCARD A PRECONCEIVED notion is to open up the path to discovery and to possibly apprehend multiple meanings and truths. The 9th-century Zen monk Linji Yixuan intuited that concepts of the Buddha—or the theorization of Buddhism—can become an obstacle to direct experience, and hence it would be important to not be attached to such concepts but instead release oneself in order to fully experience what is possible. The term "direct experience" has been interpreted in many ways. Although it is of course impossible to enter into an engagement devoid of past learning and personal tendencies, the notion referred to in this instance is to aspire to a state of being in the present moment as a result of practising a mind that is concentrated, free of conceptual thoughts, and free of the usual sense of subject and object as separate.[1]

To bring both attention and concentration to our experience of an artwork allows us to move beyond paradigms into the practice of present-moment experiencing.

The Wheel of Life—commonly painted on the external walls of Tibetan temples and monasteries—represents the six realms of samsara (cyclic existence of life, death, and rebirth) and the interconnectedness between these realms (FIG. 67). Where—or what—are the points of entry into this world? Three Asian diaspora artists based in Vancouver reflect on this concept of samsara and disassemble, recreate, and transform the symbolism of the Wheel of Life through the lens of lived contemporary challenges.

Howie Tsui has the imagination of a shapeshifter. The two works featured in *In the Present Moment—Mount Abundance and the TipToe People #1* and *#2* (2010)—subvert Buddhist iconographies and conventions, playfully combining the horrific with the absurd to comment on psychological and political realities. Tomoyo Ihaya pays tribute to a Wheel of Life mural at

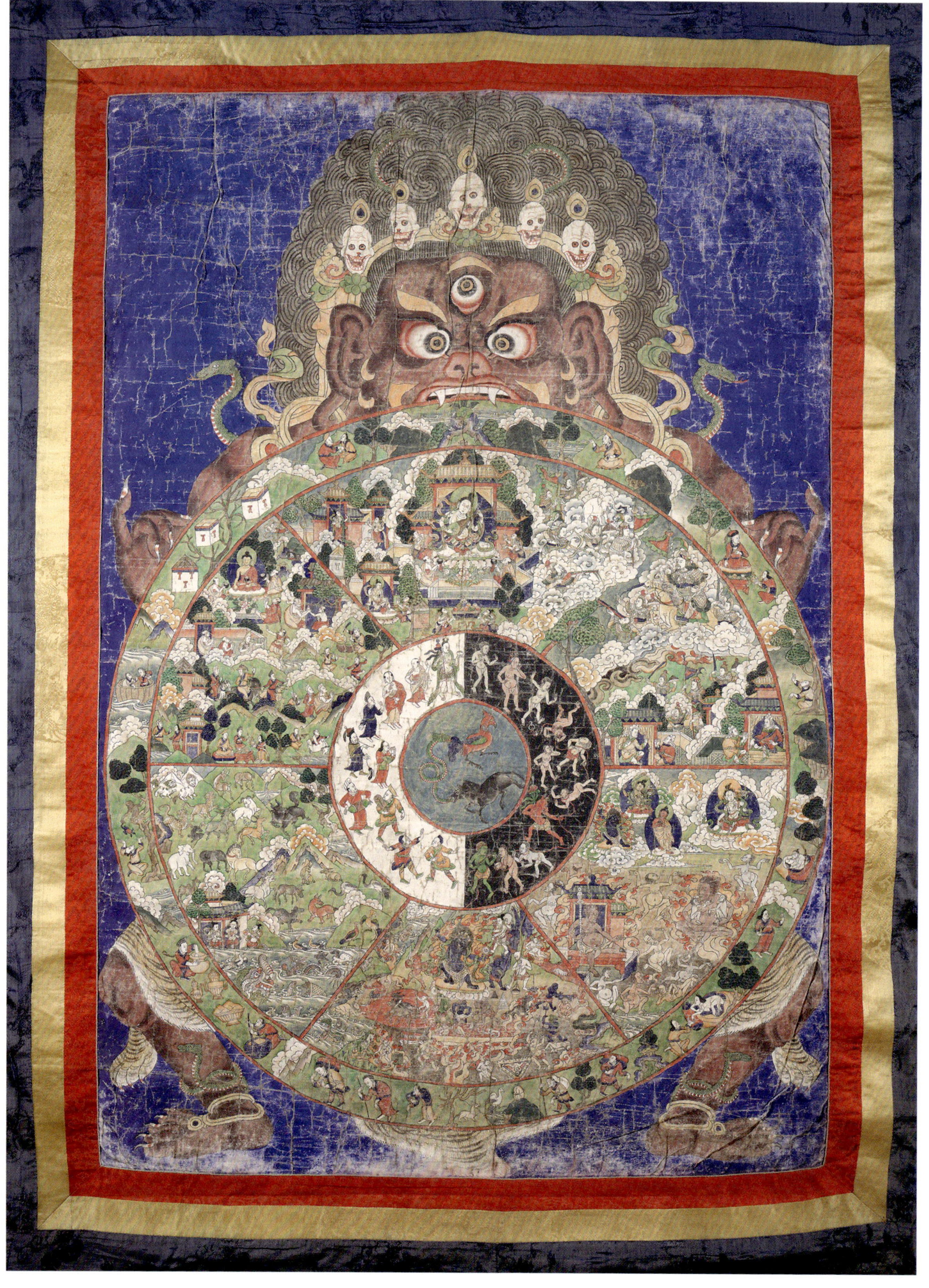

FIG. 67 (FACING)
Wheel of Life
Tibet or Mongolia, 19th century
Pigments on cloth
156.21 × 99.7 cm
Rubin Museum of Art
Gift of Shelley and Donald Rubin C2006.66.131

The Wheel of Life is mandala-like, though not an actual mandala. The image summarizes the concept of samsara, or the cycle of repeated births and deaths. The Wheel of Life is often painted at the entrance to Tibetan temples. It depicts the five (or six) divisions of beings or conditioned existence: the world of gods, the world of humans, of animals, ghosts, and hell beings (and demi-gods). It is used to help ordinary people understand Buddhist teachings.

FIG. 68 (RIGHT)
Tenzing Rigdol (Nepal/USA, 1982–)
Melong, 2013
Collage and silk brocade on canvas
167.6 × 152.4 cm
© Courtesy of Rossi & Rossi Gallery, London/Hong Kong

Drawing on the iconography of the Wheel of Life, Tenzing transforms the concept of samsara into a comment on contemporary Tibet.

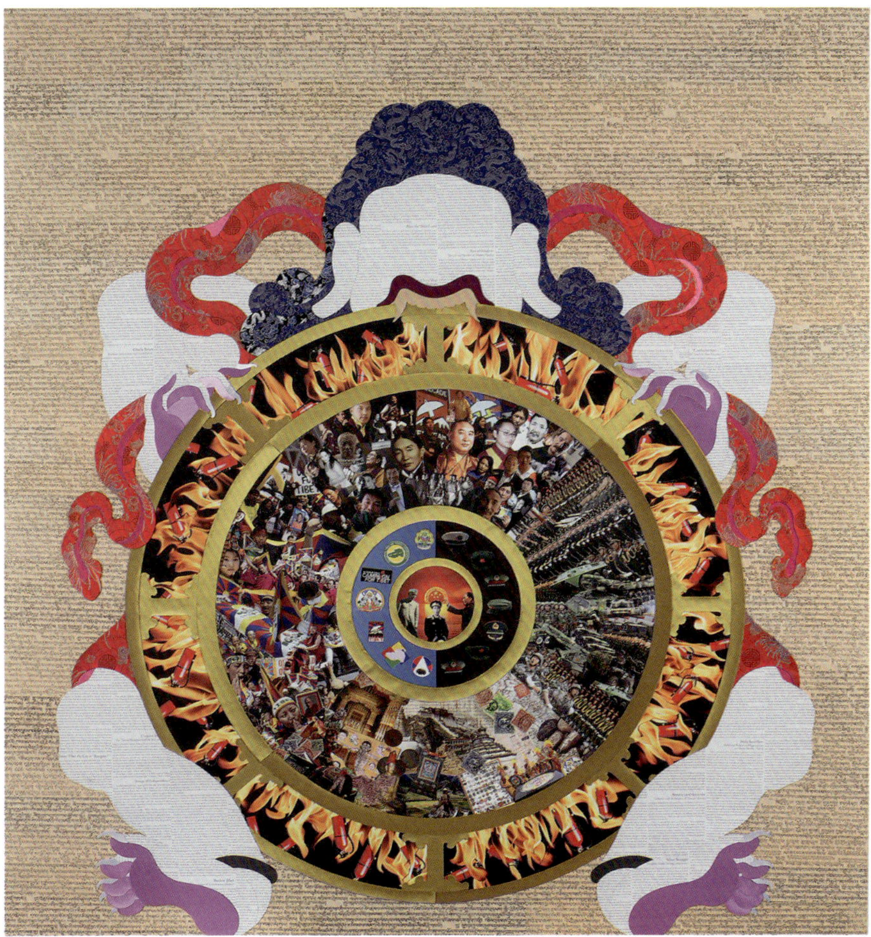

Alchi Monastery in Ladakh with two mixed-media works, *Indus Sindhu* (2011) and *Rivers Meet* (2011), interpolating her encounters as a pilgrim and traveller through India and Ladakh over the past sixteen years. Haruko Okano's viewer-activated mural *Hands of the Compassionate One* (1993) summons us to dream what could not have been otherwise imagined in waking reality, and asks us to embody compassionate response to a world in crisis.

HOWIE TSUI CITES cinema, literature, and popular culture—particularly from Hong Kong—as significant sources of inspiration. Tsui was born in Hong Kong but spent most of his childhood split between Hong Kong and Lagos, Nigeria (1979–1984). His family moved to Canada and lived in Thunder Bay, Ontario, from 1984 to 1997. While in Canada, Tsui sustained his connection to Hong Kong through VHS tapes and films; he resumed visiting Hong Kong in 2010 as an adult. Tsui was especially drawn to films and

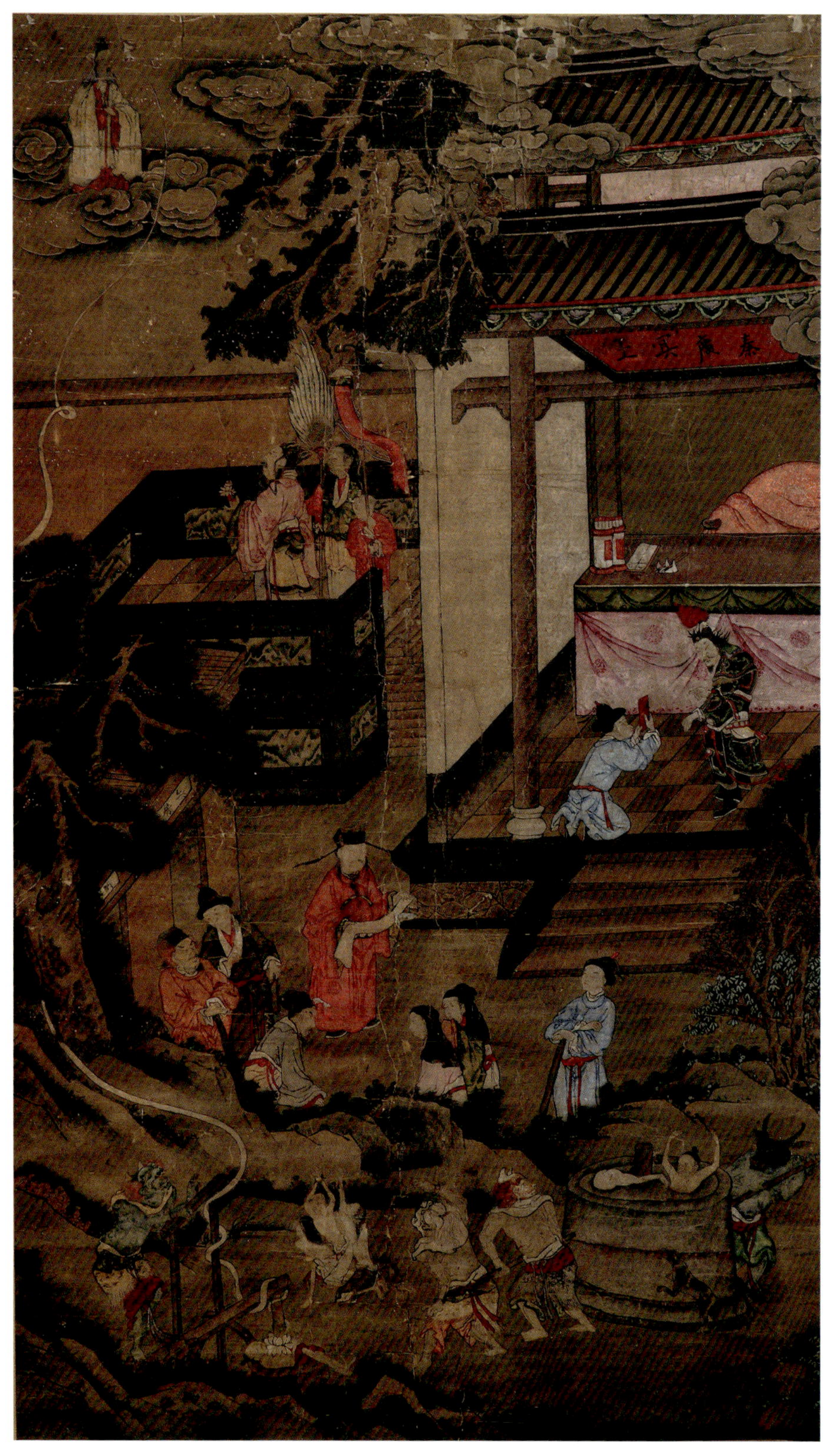

FIG. 69
Judges of Hell
From the series *Ten Buddhist Judgements of Hell*, China, c. 1700
Hanging scroll: ink and colours on cloth, mounted on silk
156 × 87.8 cm
Gift of Ernie A. Davis
Art Gallery of Greater Victoria 1989.046.001.008
Photo: Stephen Topfer

The concept of the Ten Courts of Hell combines Chinese folk beliefs with Buddhist mythologies. These hell worlds are typically depicted as a subterranean maze with various levels and chambers. The courts of hell are described as being ruled by judges, and each court deals with different kinds of gruesome punishments. This scroll painting depicts one such hell, depicting the judge and a petitioner in a chamber at the top right of the picture. In the top left corner of the picture is the figure of Guanyin, being venerated by an emperor while she bestows mercy upon a figure being tortured in the far lower reaches of this hell world at the bottom left of the picture.

TV series with *wuxia* (武俠) and *chuanqi* (傳奇) content—tales of the heroic, the spectacular, and the strange.

In this pair of *Mount Abundance* paintings (FIGS. 70–71), Tsui has combined Chinese Buddhist cosmological beliefs in hell worlds and heavenly realms with ghost stories. Subversive in tone, these works are the visual equivalent of morality tales in Chinese literary tradition.[2] *Mount Abundance* alludes to the mythical Eternally Auspicious Mountain[3] in *The Classic of Mountains and Seas* (*Shanhaijing*).[4] Tsui employs these literary references as seeds, to create what he refers to as "tense, fictive environments."[5]

By rendering invisible presences visible, Tsui challenges us to consider what we have ignored or dismissed. Non-human presences attest to wrongdoings, fears, and aggressions. Sites carry an energetic charge that may persist long after physical buildings have been demolished or even after humans have died. Life does not end at death but continues to insinuate and disrupt in the forms of spectres, chimeras, and demons.

The viewer is rattled by what is not easily or comfortably discerned. Do we laugh or are we disconcerted? Perhaps both? These paintings share much of the spirit of Tsui's earlier work *Horror Fables* (2008–2010) in which he explores fantasy landscapes of beings in struggle against powerful, oppressive structures.[6]

In *Mount Abundance #1*, a ghost bride is escorted on a tiger towards her home. Two spectres emerge from the entrance to welcome her back. Had the bride suffered a forced marriage? Was the family home ransacked? Something sinister still lingers within the dark interior of the home, now guarded by a vampire. And what are we to make of the creature in the top left corner of the painting wielding a small axe-like weapon while the crown of its head spurts blood?

In *Mount Abundance #2*, the Buddha's head functions as a sacrificial altar where a victim is being opened up by a predatory presence. Although occupying the summit, Buddha's head is not without taint—an image that implicates systems of belief and political structures that serve as platforms for abuse. How is power being exercised both personally and politically to exploit the vulnerable? The vampiric and the predatorial are driven by an insatiable lust for blood.

A monk stares into his reflection in *Mount Abundance #2*. Is the red-faced demon a part of him that he can acknowledge and tame? Or is he run by his inner demon?[7] This demon shapeshifts

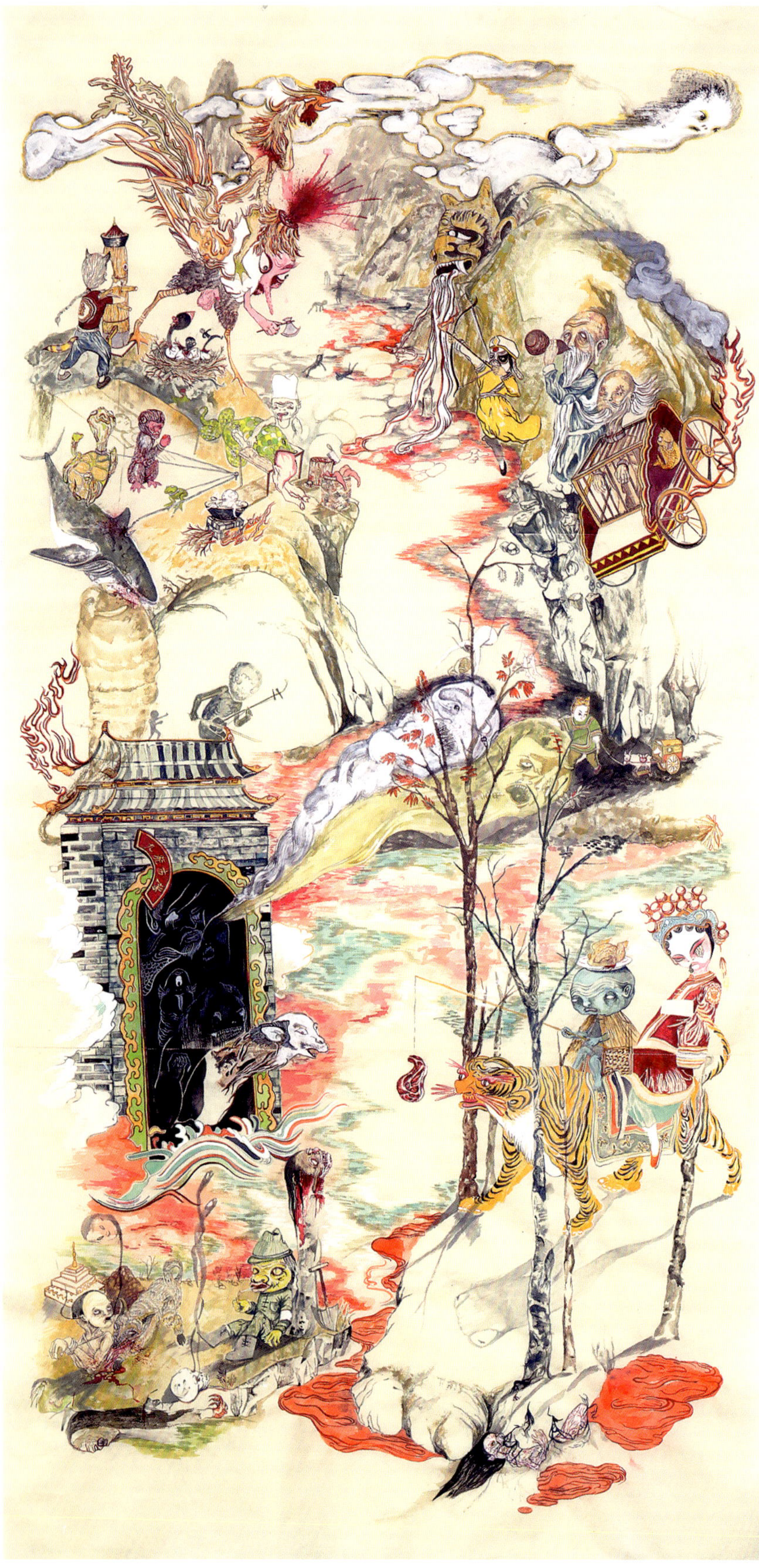

FIG. 70
Howie Tsui 徐浩恩
(Hong Kong/Canada, 1978–)
Mount Abundance and the TipToe People #1, 2010
Ink and paint pigment on mulberry paper
190.5 × 96.52 cm
Courtesy of the artist, collection of the Ottawa Art Gallery
Photo: Justin Wonnacott

FIG. 71
Howie Tsui 徐浩恩
(Hong Kong/Canada, 1978–)
Mount Abundance and the TipToe People #2, 2010
Ink and paint pigment on mulberry paper
190.5 × 96.52 cm
Courtesy of the artist, collection of Tad Freese, San Francisco
Photo: Justin Wonnacott

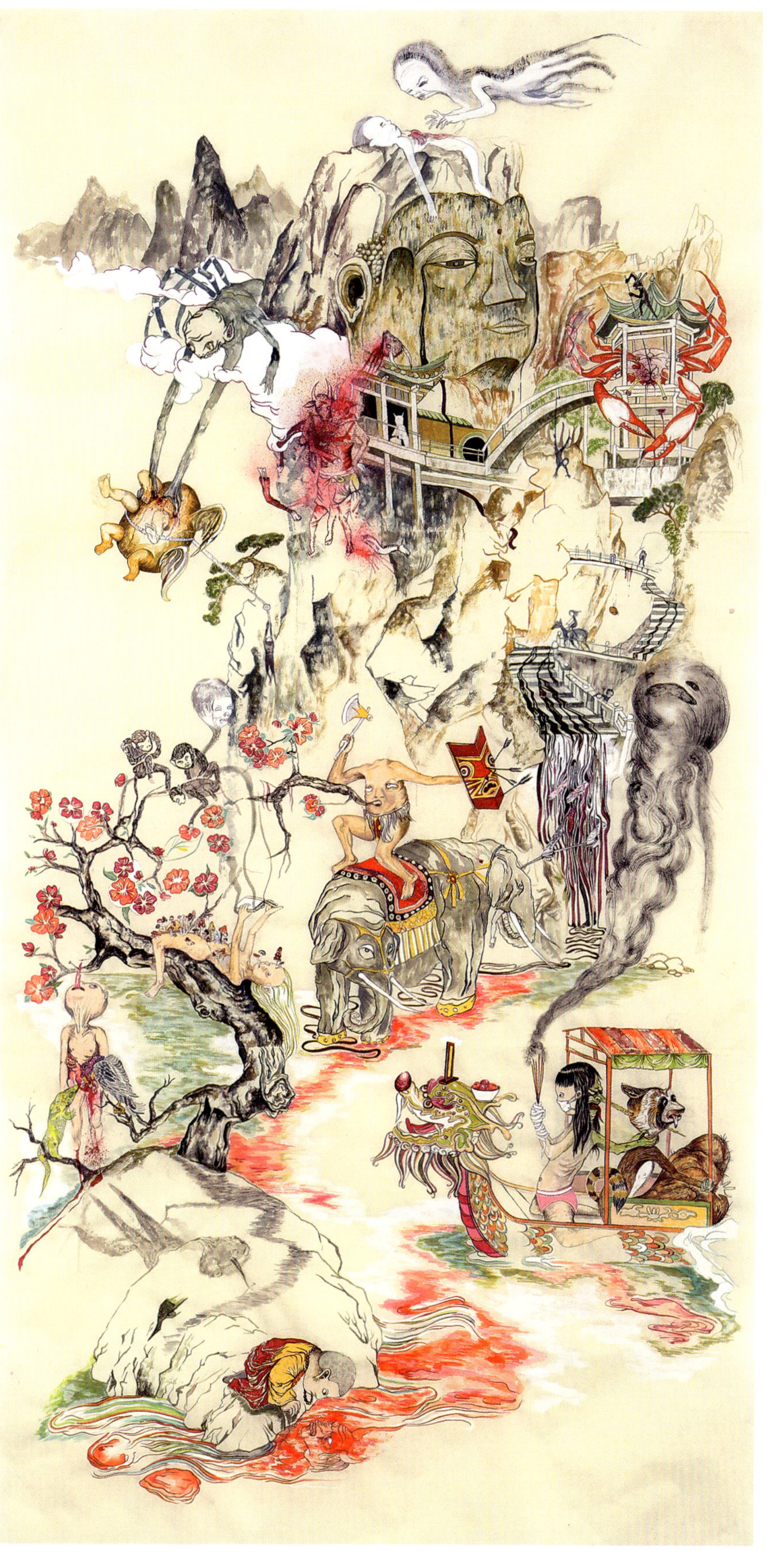

into a bloodied stream that stains parts of the allegorical landscape, reaching the legs of the elephant, on which sits the deity Xingtian (形天). Even though Xingtian was defeated and beheaded by the Supreme God, he regenerated, and formed eyes with his nipples.[8] Depending on one's values and perspective, the conclusion is either that Xingtian lost or that he has in fact emerged victorious, because of his capacity to shapeshift. The latter interpretation is favoured as Xingtian holds up his battle shield in a proclamation of victory.

A red stream traces its presence lightly through both paintings. Is this a symbol of bloodshed and violence that continues to mark our human realm? *Mount Abundance #1* and *#2* are multifarious and phantasmagorical. Although employing ancient, mythical tropes, Tsui poses questions about how fear, when not transformed through compassionate responses, takes the form of demonic manifestations of greed and materialism in our contemporary existence.

These richly saturated visual narratives suggest that life is not only fluid but often ethereal and transformative. In response to various forms of trauma, it is sometimes necessary to mutate in order to survive.

TOMOYO IHAYA GREW up in Japan familiar with the tenets of Buddhism. Even as a young person, she wondered what boundaries meant and what defined her as a person distinguishable from other humans. Ihaya went to India for the first time in 2005 with a group of Buddhist practitioners and their teacher. Since then, she has gone to India twenty-two times, and visited Ladakh seventeen of those.

Ihaya happened to be in Leh, the capital of Ladakh, when a cloudburst and heavy overnight rains led to mudslides and floods on August 6, 2010. She had arrived about a week earlier. She remembers the date of the floods because it was also the anniversary of the bombing of Hiroshima. In the midst of the devastation, Ihaya walked up a hillslope and looked down—what had existed only the night before no longer was there. Ihaya was struck by the reminder of impermanence. She remained in Leh for a month following the disaster to help. Three dogs befriended her and became her support animals during that time. She saw the corpse of a girl laid out on the pavement, still covered in mud. Ihaya was not sure who had placed the corpse there—there was no sign of anyone tending to it. Moved by the sight of the abandoned body, Ihaya felt compelled to draw it.

Both *Indus Sindhu*[9] and *Rivers Meet* (FIGS. 72–73) were created the following year, and not only bear witness to the devastation of the Ladakh floods but also celebrate communal interdependencies alongside the presences of hungry ghosts and those in the *bardo*—the intermediate state between two lives on earth. Both mixed-media works incorporate images of the Wheel of Life inspired by her favourite mural at Alchi Monastery.[10]

In *Indus Sindhu*, the figure lying on an island between the two shores is based on the drawing of the deceased girl whom Ihaya saw in Leh, while the dog figure represents Aloo, one of Ihaya's three canine companions.

Ihaya has translated the ancient Wheel of Life through her renditions in these panels, combining experiences from the 2010 Ladakh floods with details suggesting communal existence. The allusion to life, death, and the *bardo* are embedded in various sections of *Indus Sindhu*. The river, vessels, cauldron, water pump, and fire suggest vitality and the warmth of community; the corpse on the island symbolizes death; while the lone figure in the lower right of the work is in the *bardo* and the darker ground next to the figure and just below the collection of vessels alludes to the path towards the next reincarnation.

The figure lying on the farther shore is drawn from the Alchi mural. Ihaya added a water pump to this image to represent the vitality required to engage with life. The person holds an upturned vessel, unable to avail themselves of the source of life—an upturned vessel symbolizes the inability to receive teachings or learning. In contrast, a different figure bathes in the river, which stands as a testament to the ritual of purification performed by many Hindu devotees in the sacred waters of the Indus.

Figures in Ihaya's contemporary translations of the Wheel of Life therefore suggest psychological attributes, not merely physical ones. One's mind or mental orientation is enacted through different spiritual choices and behaviours.

Rivers Meet refers to the meeting of two rivers in Ladakh—one river being blue and the other a muddy brown. The tree occupies a prominent position and again is based on a sketch from the Alchi mural. Ihaya festooned her tree with apricots, recalling that apricot trees surround the Alchi monastery.

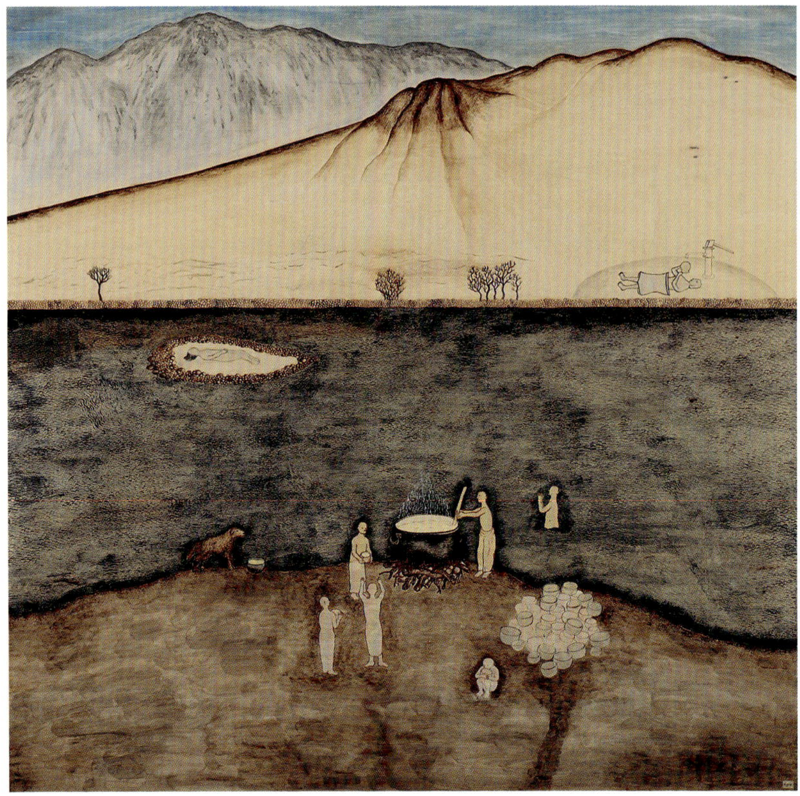

FIG. 72
Tomoyo Ihaya 井早智 代
(Japan/Canada, 1970–)
Indus Sindhu, 2011
Mixed media on wooden panel
97.5 × 97.5 cm
Courtesy of the artist, Vancouver
Photo: Image This Photographics Inc.

For Ihaya, this tree symbolizes the bridge between the god realm and the human realm. The tree is the predominant presence in *Rivers Meet*, in contrast to the smaller scale of trees in *Indus Sindhu*. While two humans wait at the foot of this tree, two others are high up in the branches, gathering fruit. Both the solitary figure floating in the sky and the being at the shore facing the blue river are hungry ghosts from the Alchi mural.

In these two artworks, the human is one of many in a larger cosmic universe. Humans, hungry ghosts, and animals are inextricably linked with the air, land, water, and mountains that form the larger landscape of our literal and metaphysical existence. The elements are present in and through us, with the river representing the source of vitality, when it is well-channelled or contained. We are reminded that water, as a source of life, can also become deadly when out of balance.

HARUKO OKANO HAD a powerful dream more than two decades ago in which the bodhisattva of compassion, Tara, appeared to her. The line between dream and embodied reality dissolved

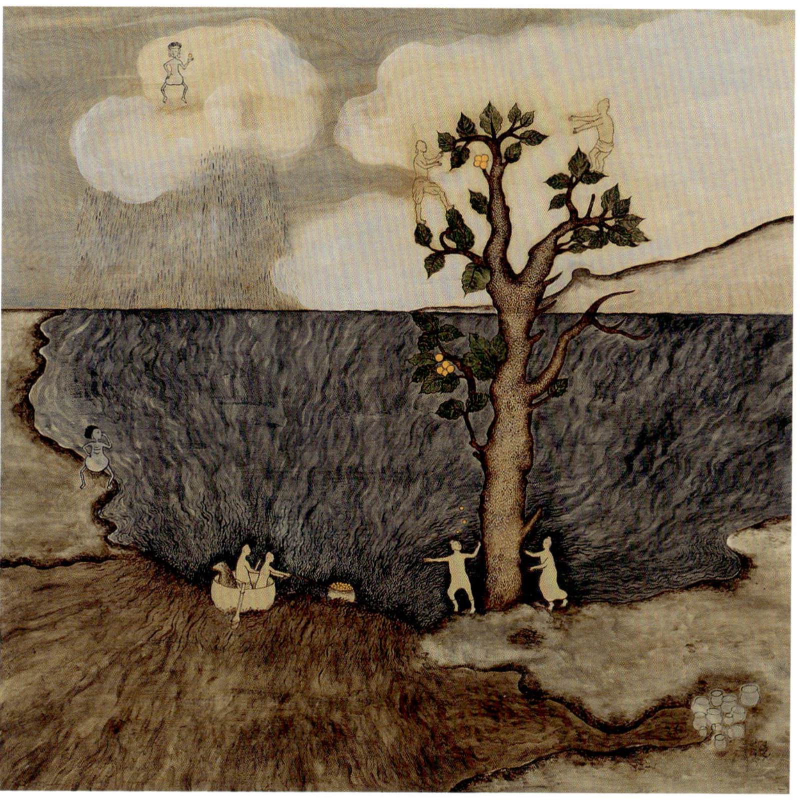

FIG. 73
Tomoyo Ihaya 井早智 代
(Japan/Canada, 1970–)
Rivers Meet, 2011
Mixed media on wooden panel
97.5 × 97.5 cm
Courtesy of the artist, Vancouver
Photo: Image This Photographics Inc.

when Okano translated Tara's compelling presence onto canvas in the viewer-activated mural *Hands of the Compassionate One* (FIG. 74). Since then, Okano has continued to discover new meanings in the work. This deity is infinitely evolving and multifarious in Okano's mural.

From an early age, Okano experienced the trauma of family tragedies and subsequently lived in a succession of foster homes. She refers to this time as growing up "white" in Toronto, disenfranchised from her Japanese Canadian roots and cultural practices. Based in Vancouver since 1976, Okano has been closely connected to her Tibetan Buddhist teacher Jetsun Kushok in Richmond, British Columbia. For Okano, Buddhist practice and art creation are inseparable, both offering healing and transformation in response to personal and collective trauma.

Held in the collection of the Surrey Art Gallery,[11] *Hands of the Compassionate One* is infused with motifs from Japanese scrolls, Tibetan *thangka* (paintings on cloth depicting Buddhist scenes) and *irezumi* (Japanese tattoo art). Although Okano previously referred to this work as being a depiction of Kuanyin, she now

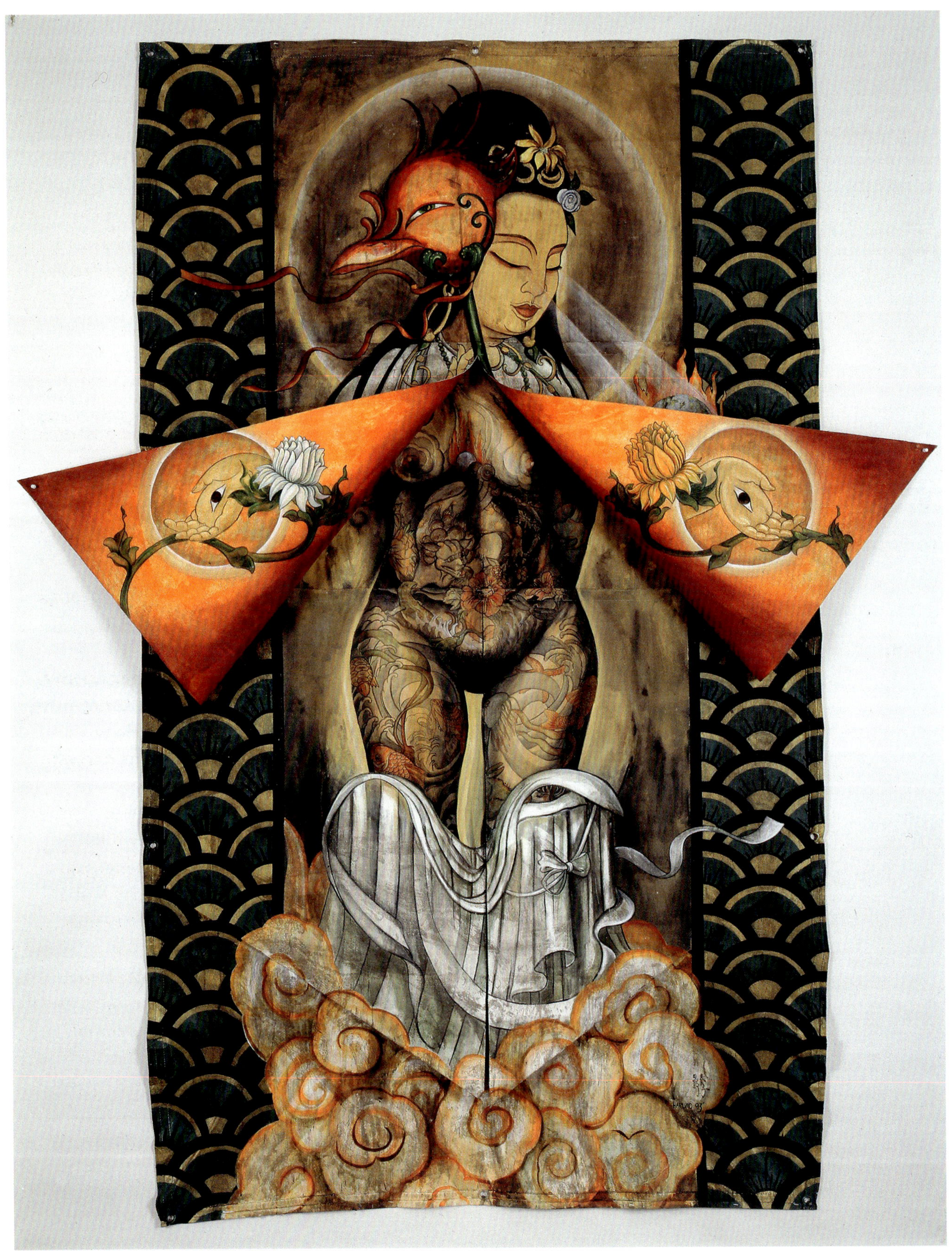

FIG. 74
Haruko Joyce Okano
(Canada, 1945–)
Hands of the Compassionate One, 1993
Viewer-activated mural transformed in three stages: acrylic on canvas with tassels
closed: 274.32 × 152.4 cm
fully opened: 274.32 × 213.36 cm
Surrey Art Gallery 1999.01.01
Photo: Al Reid Studio

chooses to refer to the work as a representation of Tara, as this deity is central to her Vajrayana practice.[12]

The mural has several incisions through it: a vertical one that starts from where Tara's right middle finger meets the staff bearing the phoenix's head, down to the clouds below her body; and four angled incisions in the shape of two Vs that meet the vertical incision. At the base of each of the four sections hangs a red-threaded ornament that allows for the sections to be lifted to expose the bodhisattva's body. Movement, engagement, and embodiment are some themes invoked as viewers reveal deeper layers beneath outer appearance.

At the first layer, Tara cups a world in flames in her left hand, her gaze soft yet beneficently focused on that world. Her right hand clasps a staff with the head of a phoenix. The hand postures on this top layer of the mural recall the use of ritual objects in the practice of Vajrayana: the *vajra* (an indestructible or diamond weapon) in the right hand and a *ghanta* (bell) in the left. The symbolism of these two ritual objects is rich and vivid—variously referring to concepts of form (*vajra*) and emptiness (*ghanta*); skilful means/compassionate action (*vajra*) and wisdom (*ghanta*). Taken together, *vajra* and *ghanta* symbolize the principle of non-duality.

Does the act of transformation, as represented by the phoenix, lead to a greater capacity to act compassionately? By prompting viewers to uncover layers of the bodhisattva, does Okano wish to inspire us to enter into an engagement with others, as part of a matrix of interdependent existences, instead of holding ourselves as separate beings unrelated to others?

Okano depicts Tara as pregnant. In Vajrayana, the Womb Realm is a metaphysical space inhabited by the Five Compassion Buddhas.[13] Another possible association is with the deity Mahamata Prajnaparamita, the Mother of all Buddhas, whose womb holds the birth of enlightenment.

When the top two layers of the mural are peeled back, we see that Tara is carrying in her womb a creature known variously as a foo dog or a guardian lion. In Buddhism, the creature symbolizes the protection of the Dharma and guards the entrances of temples and sacred sites.

As Robin Laurence observed in her 2007 essay "Haruko Okano: *Hands of The Compassionate One*," the layers of canvas are somewhat reminiscent of flayed skin.[14] In an earlier work,

Transvisceral Borders (1997), at grunt gallery, Vancouver, Okano created skins through the cultivation of kombucha fungus.[15] Okano painted them to resemble body skins covered in tattoos. Skin, as she described in her artist statement, functions as both barrier and link.

With the four flaps of *Hands of the Compassionate One* lifted, the viewer perceives Tara's body as covered with tattoos reminiscent of *irezumi* tattoo art.[16] By alluding to tattooing predominant among the yakuza in Japan,[17] Okano invokes a specific outsider culture and incorporates and transmutes that language into her rendition of the bodhisattva. Okano has called her use of *irezumi* tattooing a symbol of the Japanese Canadian experience of forced displacement and internment that occurred towards the end of World War II.[18]

A few lines excerpted from a poem inscribed on the back of the mural read,

> For I am the first and the last,
> I am the honoured and the scorned one,
> I am the whore and the holy one,
> I am the wife and the virgin,
> I am the barren one . . .
>   and many are her sons.
> I am the silence that is incomprehensible.
> I am the utterance of my name.[19]

The excerpt further reinforces the notion that reviled or wounded parts of the psyche can undergo healing and transformation by invoking the presence of Tara.

Okano's bodhisattva of compassion relates to the world in unconventional ways, marked with the signs of the outcast or outsider, while also containing the transformative capacity of the phoenix—a cycle of birthing and dying in the act of personal and collective transformation. Drawing on traditional iconography, Tara is depicted with eyes in the palms of her hands. All four hands clasp *utpala* (blue lotus) flowers of slightly varying shades—the *utpala* being associated with Tara. Perhaps the various colours suggest a range of blessings that may accrue from Tara's deeds?

Okano invites us to see beyond the visible in order to penetrate to the ineffable spirit of the compassionate one. As we contemplate the multiple layers of *Hands of the Compassionate*

One, we are initiated into the possibility of Tara's being and invited to embody her compassion.

THE WORKS OF these artists suggest that in art practice, as in meditation, the intent is to embody the ever-evolving present moment. Assumptions or preconceived notions interfere with the fullness of our understanding. On the other hand, when direct experience informs art practice, what results from the work is a power that affects both the artist and viewer. Howie Tsui, Tomoyo Ihaya, and Haruko Okano have drawn on imagination as well as their personal experiences to create visual worlds that allude to the Wheel of Life; yet each artist has gone beyond the traditional paradigm to meaningfully translate the symbolism for contemporary times. As viewers, we are offered the opportunity to engage with their works through a mind of concentration, moving beyond paradigm into the practice of present-moment engagement.

LYDIA KWA is a poet, novelist, and clinical psychologist living in Vancouver. Her books include *Oracle Bone* (Arsenal Pulp Press, 2017) and *The Walking Boy* (Arsenal Pulp Press, 2005/2019), which draw on Buddhist imagery while subverting classical Chinese literary tropes and forms. Kwa has been a Tibetan Buddhist practitioner for two decades.

NOTES

1 Anne Klein, *Meeting the Great Bliss Queen: Buddhists, Feminists, and the Art of the Self* (Boulder, CO: Snow Lion, 1995).

2 For example, in Chinese literature, *Pu Songling: Strange Tales from a Classical Chinese Studio*, translated by John Minford (Penguin Classics, 2006).

3 Richard Strassberg, *A Chinese Bestiary: Strange Creatures from the Guideways through Mountains and Seas* (Berkeley: University of California Press, 2002).

4 Anonymous, *The Classic of Mountains and Seas*, translated by Anne Birrel (Penguin Classics, 1999).

5 Howie Tsui, website, www.howietsui.com.

6 Howie Tsui, *Horror Fables*, exhibition curated by Natalia Lebedinskaia, Art Gallery of Southwestern Manitoba (January 17–March 16, 2013), agsm.ca/horror-fables, accessed July 19, 2021.

7 Tsui cites a story in Masaki Kobayashi's film *Kwaidan* as an inspiration: In "In a Cup of Tea" (*Chawan no naka*, 茶碗の中), various persons' energies take turns becoming trapped in a bowl of water.

8 "Xingtian and the Supreme God Di came to this place and struggled against each other for ultimate power. The Supreme God cut off Xingtian's head and buried him at Eternally Auspicious Mountain. Xiangtian's nipples then transformed into eyes, and his navel became a mouth. He performs a dance with an axe and shield" (Strassberg, *A Chinese Bestiary*, p. 171).

9 *Sindhu* is the Hindi word for the Indus.

10 Ihaya's favourite mural at Alchi Monastery is much smaller than others there. She said that the mural is crumbling, which was why she was also motivated to copy some images, as photography was not allowed. The Wheel of Life depicted on this mural is about 75 cm in diameter.

11 Robin Laurence, "Haruko Okano, *Hands of the Compassionate One*" (2007) and Haruko Okano, "Artist's Statement" (1993), Surrey Art Gallery, www.surrey.ca/sites/default/files/media/documents/Okano1.pdf, accessed July 19, 2021.

12 Kuanyin is the Chinese name for the bodhisattva known as Avalokiteshvara in Sanskrit, and Tara is an emanation of Avalokiteshvara. Since Okano has been practising Vajrayana Buddhism for many years, with Tara as one of her primary foci, she now finds it more meaningful to talk about this work as a representation of Tara.

13 "Womb Realm," *Wikipedia*, en.wikipedia.org/wiki/Womb_Realm

14 Laurence, "Haruko Okano, *Hands of the Compassionate One*."

15 *Transvisceral Borders*, grunt gallery (1997). From her artist's statement: "Over the months of working in this repetitive manner, much of what I intellectualize about Buddhism I began to understand from experience. Animate and inanimate, animal and vegetable become one . . . The more basic my activities became, the more I understood the true nature of my own mind, and *Transvisceral Borders* was only the beginning."

16 For more on this form of tattoo art, see "Man Creates the Largest Collection of Tattooed Human Skin in the World," artFido (March 28, 2019), www.artfido.com/man-creates-the-largest-collection-of-tattooed-human-skin-in-the-world/

17 See "Yakuza Tattoos: Japanese Gang Members Wear the Culture of Crime," RattaTattoo (n.d.), rattatattoo.com/yakuza-tattoos-japanese-gang-members-wear-the-culture-of-crime/, accessed July 29, 2021.

18 Zoom conversation with the author, April 25, 2021.

19 These lines are part of a much longer poem found at Nag Hammadi.

THE SOUND OF THE MANDALA

 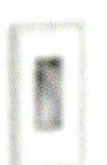        

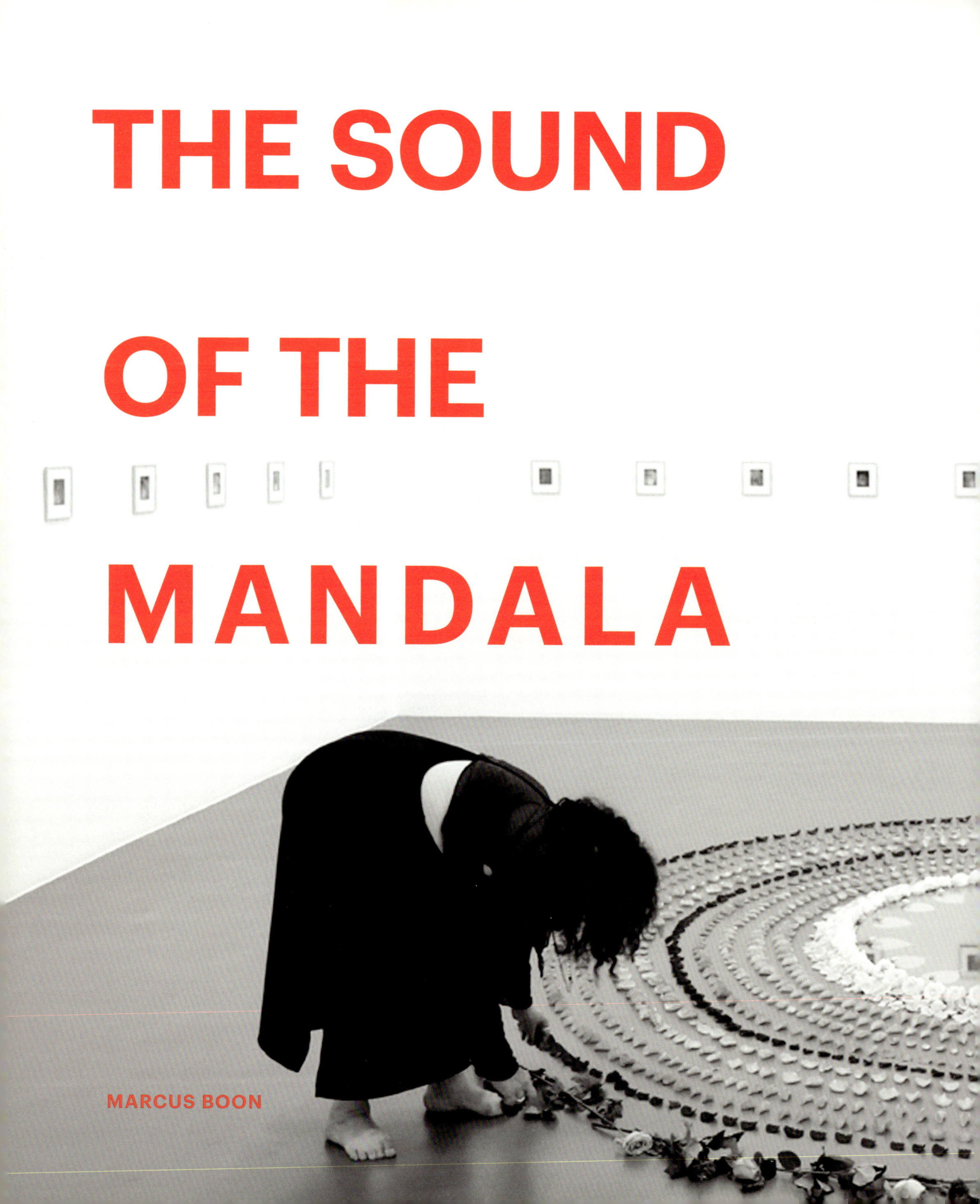

MARCUS BOON

FIG. 75 (BELOW)
Werner Herzog (Germany, 1942–)
Wheel of Time, 2003
Documentary film still

A mandala is a ritual diagram, a matrix or model of a perfected universe, which the practitioner enters into, as an environment, to accelerate the process of transformation into Buddhahood. A mandala is not just an image or object, but a practice. One of the most famous mandalas in the Tibetan tradition is the Kalachakra, which refers not only to concepts of space but also to cycles of time: from the cycles of the planets to the cycles of the breath, everything is under the influence of time. The Kalachakra practice coordinates concepts of cosmological space and time with the psycho-physical space and time of the practitioner.

FIG. 76 (OVERLEAF)
Buddha Shakyamuni and Two Disciples, Sixteen Arhats, Two Monks and Four Lokapalas
Central Tibet, 17th century
Thangka: opaque watercolour on cotton
68.5 × 45.7 cm
Gift of Max Tanenbaum, Toronto, 1980
National Gallery of Canada 26835

This *thangka* (consecrated scroll painting) depicts the historical Buddha, Shakyamuni, accompanied by acolytes and the guardians of the four directions (*lokapala*). When a practitioner encounters and meditates upon an image of the Buddha, they enter into a "perfected field" of expanded awareness and exalted possibility. In other words, they enter into a mandala, a ritual threshold or gateway to the realization of one's own Buddha-nature.

To appreciate Tibetan art we must appreciate ourselves, the fact of our being, our quality of awareness and all that is manifested therein. Tibetan art is a part of this miraculous process of manifestation, not a comment on it or an attempt at an entertaining alternative to it. If we fully understand this art, then we are aware of being Buddhas in a Buddhafield. If we fully understand ourselves, then we are aware of being Buddhas in a Buddhafield.[1]

TARTHANG TULKU, 1972

IN TANTRIC OR "ESOTERIC" Buddhism, the word *mandala* denotes a spatial field of enlightened activity, a cosmology describing the interrelation of universes populated by various deities. Usually, the term *mandala* refers to the visual representation of such a field, either in the form of a painting or sculpture, although it can also refer to the field itself as it is visualized and invoked in ritual and meditation practice. The sadhana (rituals) associated with the generation of this field, and the techniques involved, are described in a text called *tantra*, which includes the mandala (or spatial image), the mantra (or sonic activator of the field), the mudras (or gestures associated with the generation of the field), and the yogas (or instructions for meditation associated with the generated field). Taken together, the geometric space of the mandala can be considered a deification and spatialization of

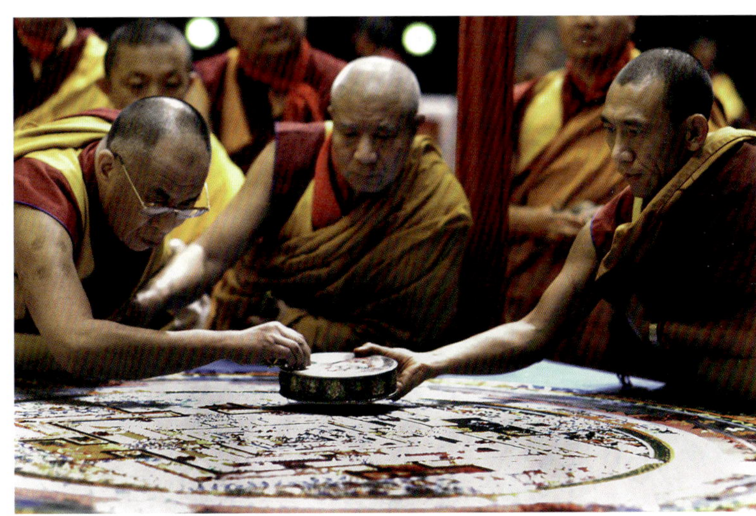

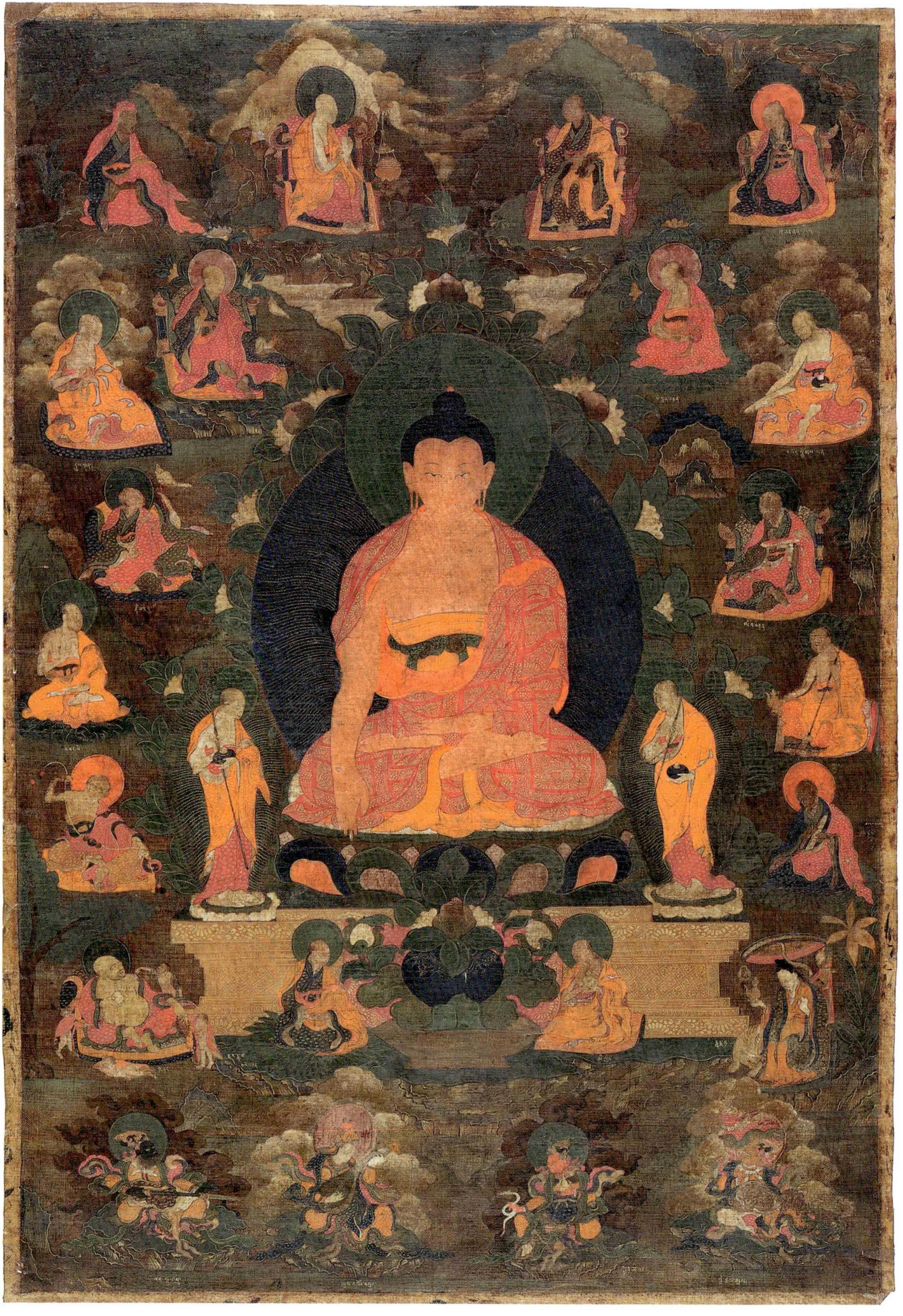

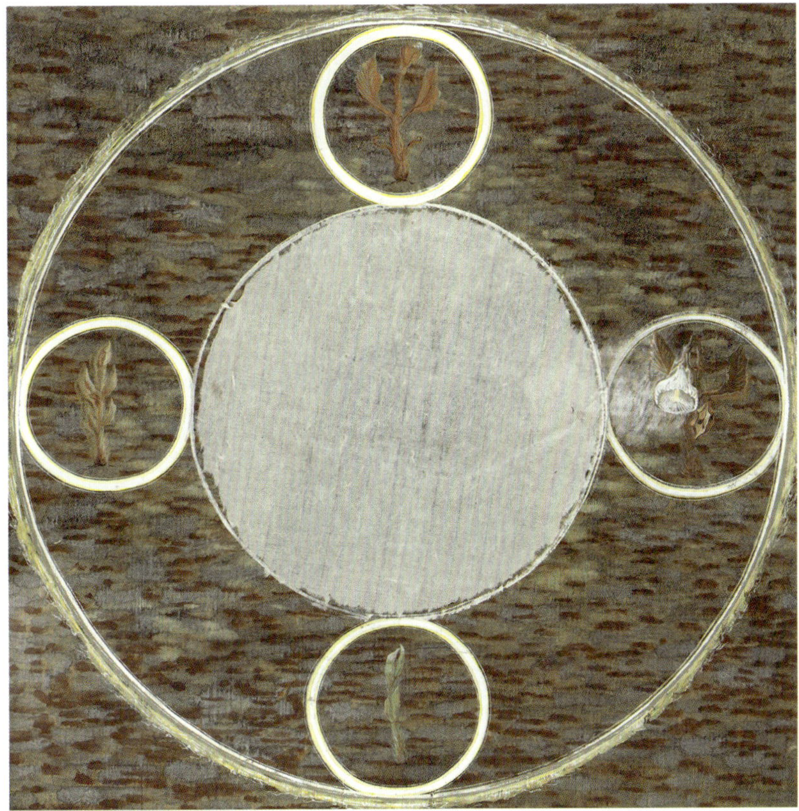

FIG. 77
Morris Graves (USA, 1910–2001)
Black Buddha Mandala, 1944
Tempera with collage on paper, mounted on canvas
69.5 × 67.9 cm
Gift of the Marshall and Helen Hatch Collection, in honor of the 75th anniversary of the Seattle Art Museum
Seattle Art Museum 2009.52.99
© Morris Graves Foundation; Courtesy of Michael Rosenfeld Gallery LLC, New York, NY
Photo: Elizabeth Mann

The mandala form has been a persistent theme in modern art in North America. One of the first known paintings depicting a mandala in modern art is *Black Buddha Mandala* by Morris Graves. Graves claimed that the *Black Buddha Mandala* appeared to him in a dream. He recorded that he saw two concentric circles of light against a sepia-dappled slatelike ground. Within this luminous mandala appeared four smaller circles, one after another, which contained different stages of a plant bud as it progressed towards flowering. Finally, a voice addressed the artist with the words "You see the eternal laws are working." Then another mandala appeared at the centre, and it contained the image of a seated black Buddha. Graves recorded the vision in this painting but later felt the Buddha image too personal to display, so covered it with a circle of rice paper.

doctrinal principles. As such, these deities might embody the five aggregates of consciousness, the senses or bodily organs—but also the physical and cosmological principles of the phenomenal world. A mandala is a very dense, compacted tool of memorization—but it is more than that too since its goal is transfiguration of the being of the practitioner in the direction of enlightenment.

According to Buddhist studies scholar Kimiaki Tanaka, the first mandala to appear in the West was a Japanese three-dimensional mandala, which the French Orientalist Emile Guimet displayed at the 1878 World Expo in Paris. The ritual object, stripped of its ritual context by imperialism and colonialism, set the stage for its appearance as an art object.[2] Mandalas are mentioned in passing in Walter Evans-Wentz's popular translations of Tibetan texts,[3] but they first become an object of focus in Carl Jung's *Psychology and Alchemy* (German, 1944; English, 1953), in which Jung describes a 1938 encounter in Darjeeling, India, with a Tibetan lama who explains to him the nature of Tibetan mandalas, emphasizing that the externally generated mandala is not

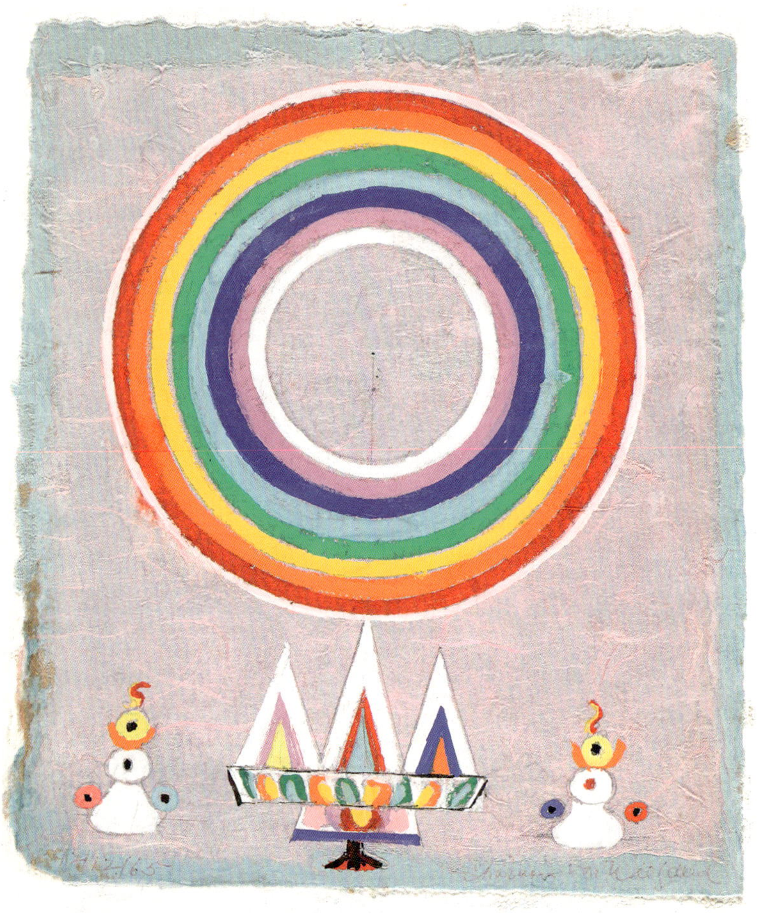

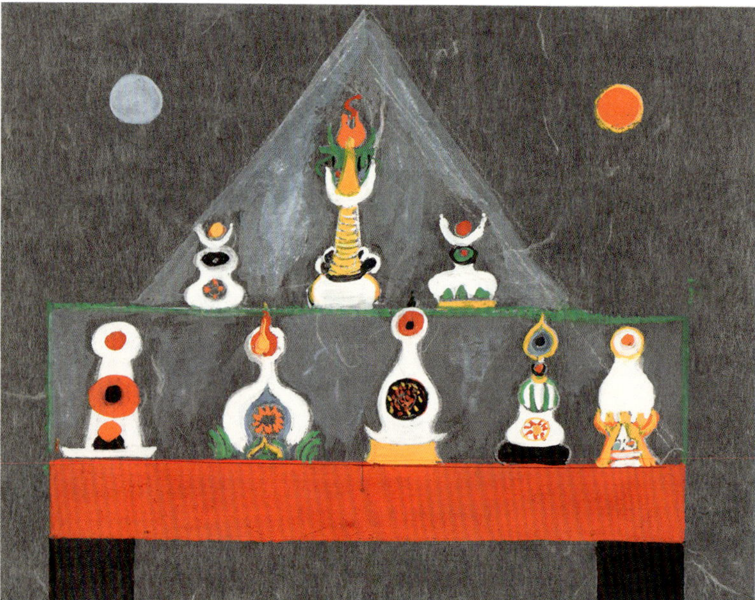

FIG. 78 (TOP LEFT)
Charmion Von Wiegand
(USA, 1896–1983)
Offering to the Universe (#226),
1965
Gouache on paper
17.8 × 15.6 cm
Gift of the Estate of Mark Tobey
Seattle Art Museum 87.39

Photo: Elizabeth Mann

FIG. 79 (BOTTOM LEFT)
Charmion Von Wiegand
(USA, 1896–1983)
Untitled (#199), 1963
Gouache on paper
19.7 × 24.8 cm
Gift of the Estate of Mark Tobey
Seattle Art Museum 87.38

Photo: Elizabeth Mann

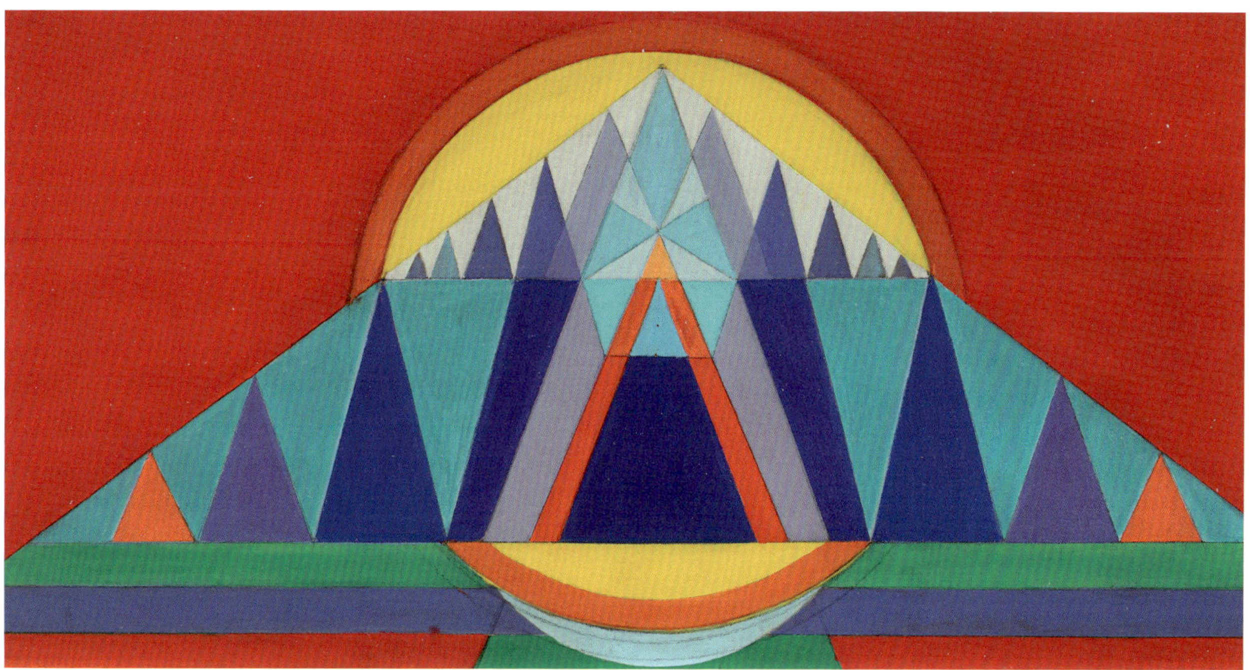

FIG. 80
Charmion Von Wiegand
(USA, 1896–1983)
Untitled, 1964
Oil on masonite
35.6 × 71.1 cm
Michael Rosenfeld Gallery LLC, New York, NY

Photo: Ryan Sobotka

as important as the internally generated one. Jung swiftly draws a psychological conclusion from this, and then observes the presence of mandala-like imagery in a variety of historical cultures, including medieval Christianity.[4] In 1949, Italian Tibetologist Giuseppe Tucci published the first book on mandalas in a European language, *Theory and Practice of the Mandala* (translated to English in 1961), but other scholars in his milieu, such as Mircea Eliade, also discussed mandalas.[5]

The earliest mandala-like images in the *In the Present Moment* exhibition reflect the complex and entangled histories of Buddhist mandalas, and the processes by which they were rendered available as part of visual and sonic art practices in the West. Morris Graves's *Black Buddha Mandala* (1944) (FIG. 77), has a mysteriously early creation date and may reflect his visits to Japan and the important legacy of Japanese mandalas associated with Shingon and Pure Land Buddhism.[6] Charmion Von Wiegand's geometric paintings from the 1950s and 1960s (FIGS. 78–81), Jordan Belson's mandala-like films such as *Samadhi* (1967) (FIG. 83), and the mandala images composed by Harry Smith and Bruce Conner around the same time all reflect a complex iconographic genealogy. This would include the impact of theosophical texts such as Annie Besant and Charles Leadbeater's remarkable

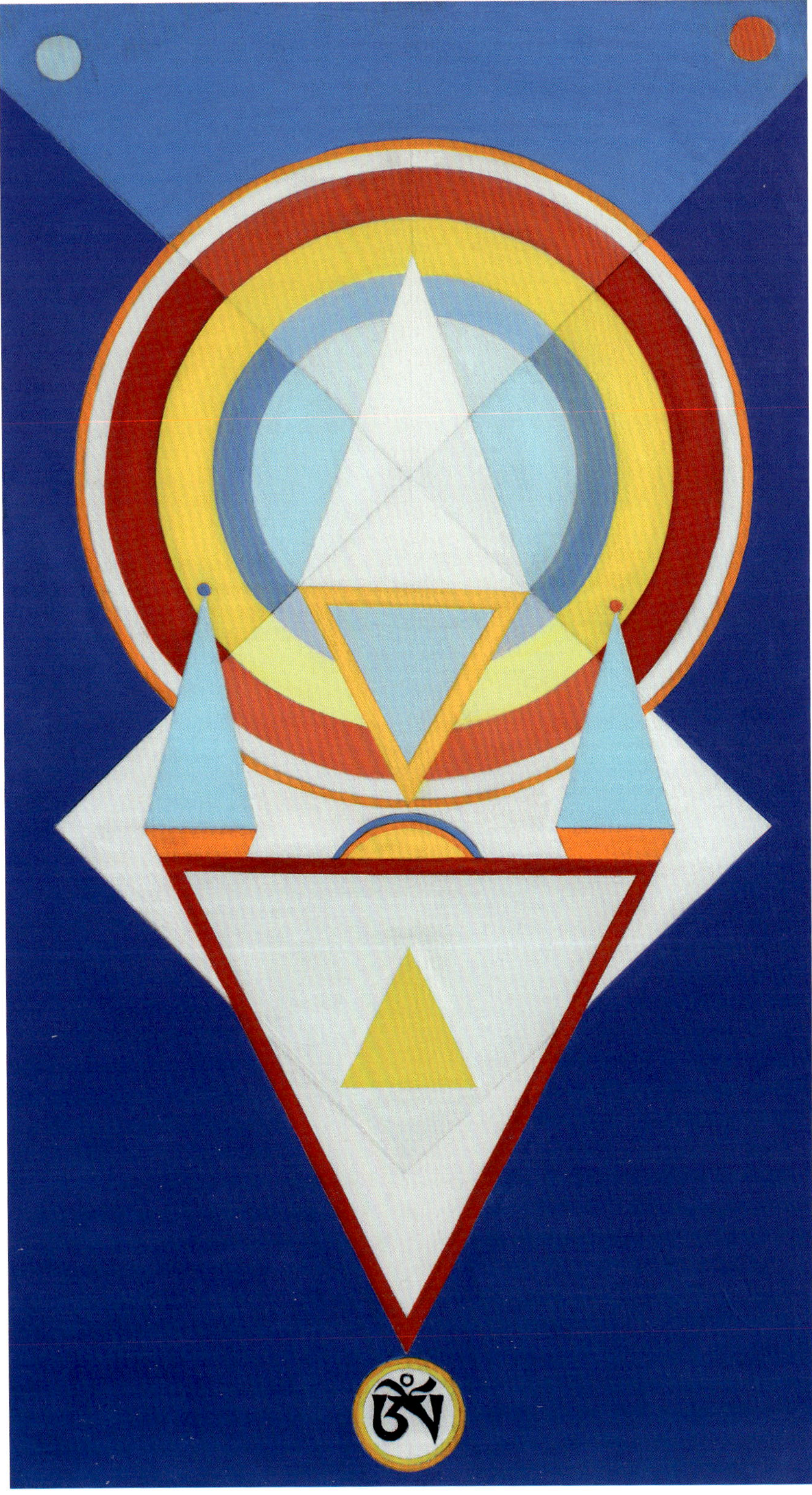

FIG. 81 (LEFT)
Charmion Von Wiegand
(USA, 1896–1983)
Invocation to the Adi-Buddha,
1968–1970
Oil on canvas
127 × 68.6 cm
Michael Rosenfeld Gallery LLC, New York, NY
© Estate of Charmion Von Wiegand; Courtesy of Michael Rosenfeld Gallery LLC, New York, NY
Photo: Ryan Sobotka

Charmion Von Wiegand was one of the first American artists to embrace Tibetan Buddhism in the mid-1960s, having met and befriended members of both the Kalmyk and Tibetan refugee communities. Her paintings visualize the experience of Tibetan Buddhist shrine meditation, incorporating concepts of sound (mantra), form (yantra), and ritual colour. The symbolism of the Tibetan altar was important in her paintings.

A mandala can be any image or device that functions to facilitate the realization of the non-duality of individual and cosmos. A mandala can take the form of a sand drawing, a thangka, an altar, a stupa, even a city or country. The human body can also be understood as a mandala. In mandala practice, a sacred cosmology is invoked into the body to promote expanded awareness that offers new possibilities of being.

FIG. 82 (FACING TOP)
Jack Wise (USA/Canada, 1928–1996)
Mandala, 1978
Gouache on paper
57 × 57 cm
Anonymous gift
Art Gallery of Greater Victoria 1992.045.019
Photo: Stephen Topfer

For many artists, the mandala form represents a deeply personal spiritual vision. In 1966 Jack Wise travelled to India, where he studied Buddhism with Tibetan refugees. The mandala, alongside other symbols of Tibetan Buddhism, became a recurrent theme in Wise's work.

FIG. 83 (FACING BOTTOM)
Jordan Belson (USA, 1926–2011)
Samadhi, 1967
Film still
© Center for Visual Music, Los Angeles

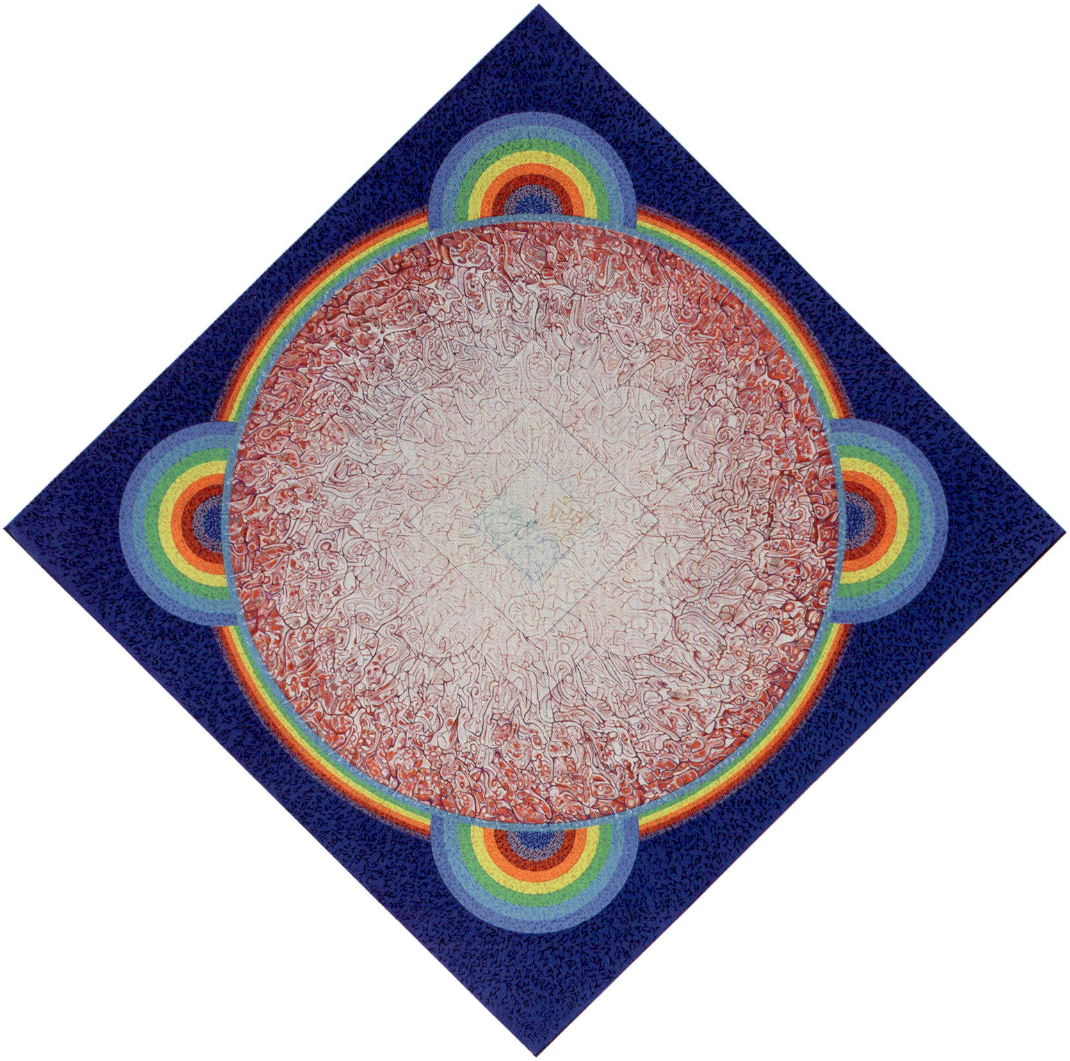

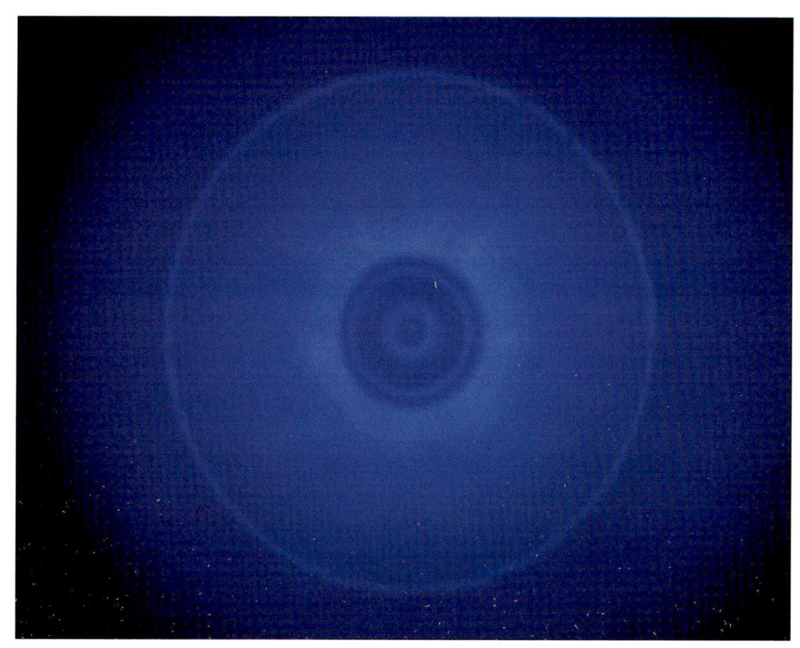

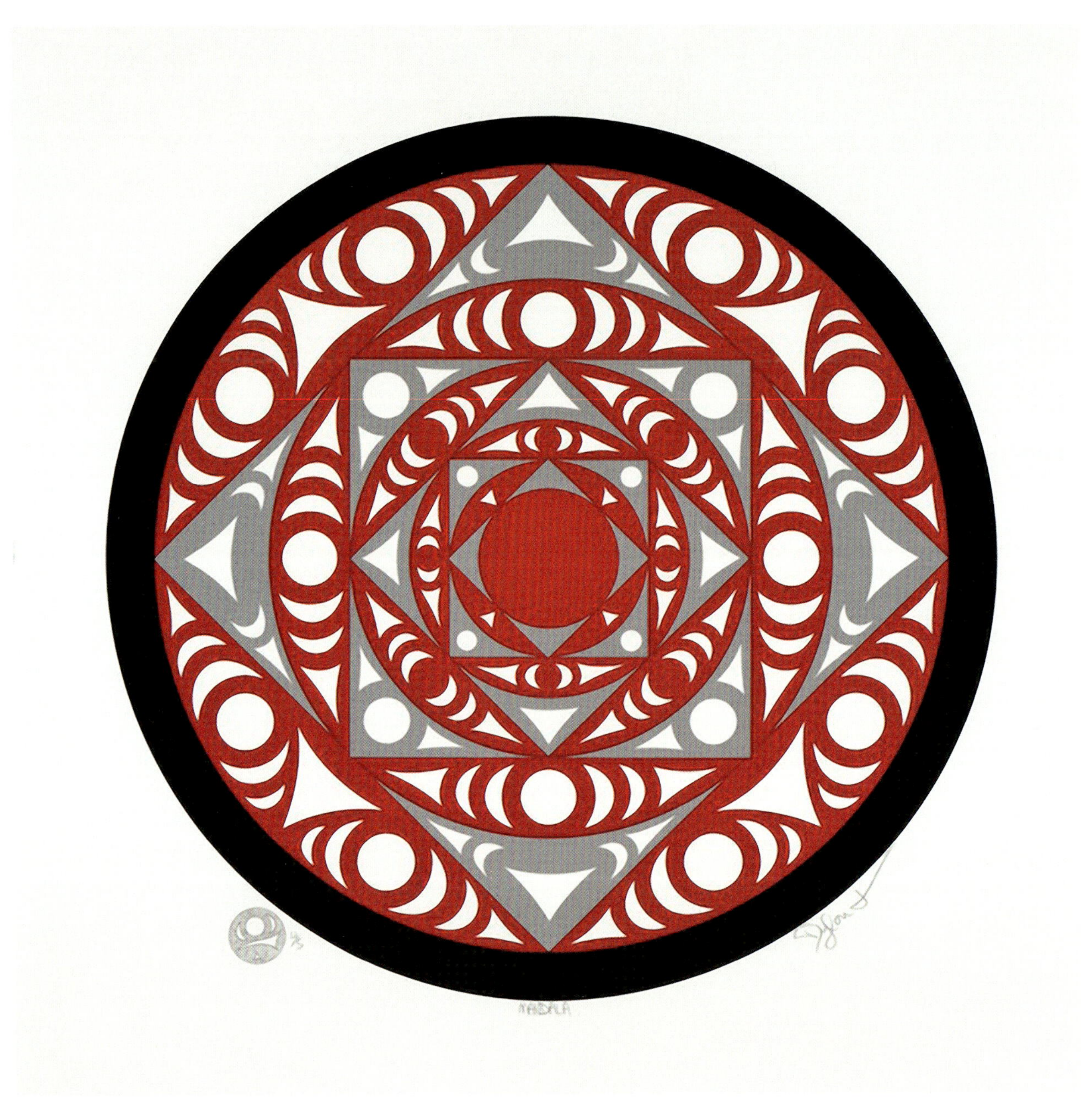

FIG. 84 (FACING)
Qwul'thilum (Dylan Thomas) (Coast Salish, Lyackson First Nation/Canada, 1986–)
Mandala, 2010
Silkscreen: ink on paper
55.9 × 55.9 cm
Courtesy of the artist

Qwul'thilum (Dylan Thomas) is a West Coast First Nations artist and practising Buddhist who finds analogies between Buddhist sacred geometries and Coast Salish designs. These cross-cultural connections and relationships are important to Qwul'thilum because so much of Coast Salish culture has been lost. He states, "I enjoy doing cross-cultural art because... art is one of the things that makes us human [and] helps me to feel the unity of humankind."*

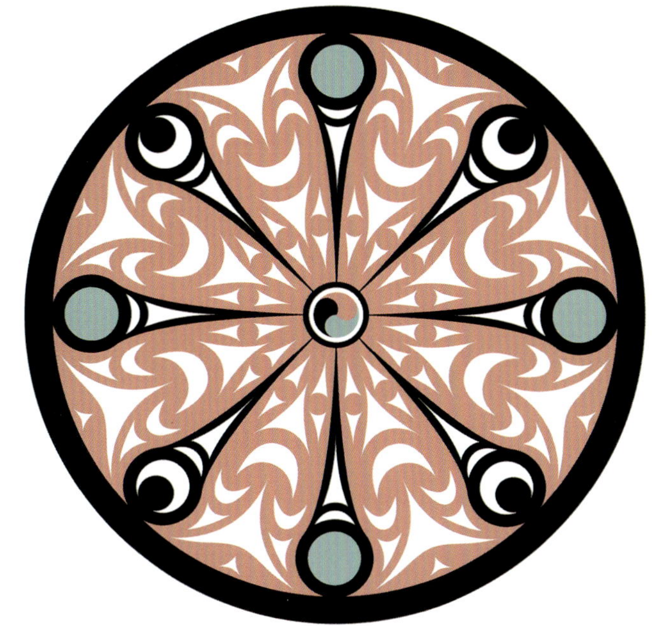

FIG. 85 (TOP)
Qwul'thilum (Dylan Thomas) (Coast Salish, Lyackson First Nation/Canada, 1986–)
Dharma Wheel, 2016
Serigraph: ink on paper
55.9 × 55.9 cm
Courtesy of the artist

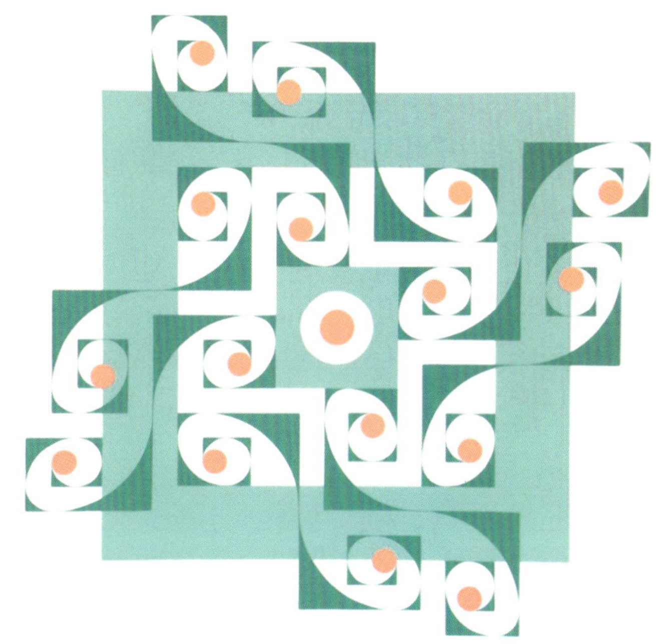

FIG. 86 (BOTTOM)
Qwul'thilum (Dylan Thomas) (Coast Salish, Lyackson First Nation/Canada, 1986–)
Bodhi Tree, 2016
Acrylic on canvas
91.4 × 91.4 cm
Courtesy of the artist

* Qwul'thilum (Dylan Thomas), interviewed by Marina DiMaio in "Art as a Spiritual Practice: Q&A with Dylan Thomas," *AGGV Magazine* (June–August 2021), available at emagazine.aggv.ca/art-as-a-spiritual-practice-qa-withdylan-thomas.

book *Thought Forms* from 1905 (an influence on the general move towards abstraction reflected in the early-20th-century work of Hilma af Klint, Wassily Kandinsky, and others) and art-historical presentations of Hindu tantra images such as Ajit Mookerjee's *Tantra Art* (1967). Jung's various writings on the subject and their integration into art therapy were also significant, as were museums and galleries with collections of Tibetan and other Asian ritual objects and images, temples of Asian Buddhist immigrant communities in the United States, and finally, a more general interest in "sacred geometry"—although the term itself dates to the 1970s.

In terms of the history of the Buddhist mandala in the West, the arrival of Tibetan Buddhist teachers in Europe and the United States in the late 1960s and early 1970s marks an important transition. The first art book devoted to mandalas, José and Miriam Arguelles's *Mandala*, was published in 1972 by Shambhala Publications, with a forward by Chogyam Trungpa, who arrived in the United States in 1970. Trungpa gave an important and brilliant seminar on "the mandala principle" at The Tail of the Tiger in 1972 (but it was only published in 1991, as *Orderly Chaos*). Tarthang Tulku, a young Nyingma lama, moved to the Bay Area and curated at least two exhibitions of Tibetan art in the early 1970s. His *Sacred Art of Tibet* (1972) contains important attempts (not dissimilar to Trungpa's) to draw attention and understanding away from the formal and decorative qualities of the mandala as "sacred geometry" towards a broader but also more precise sense of mandala as "mind palace," to be generated by a practitioner with a view to achieving enlightenment or Buddhahood.

WHEN CONSIDERING THE relationship between mandala and sound art, there are at least two significant categories: first, works of sound art that explicitly reference an idea of mandala, whether accurate or not; second, the importance in the history of sound art of works that involve the generation of a sonic field given a spiritual value, whether presented as a field of awareness, one of vibration, or otherwise.[7] Given the importance of the mantra (a sacred sound formula to be verbally or mentally recited) in generating and empowering the mandala in a tantric ritual, sound can, and clearly has, played a role in the practice of generating the enlightened field that is called a mandala. Furthermore, there is a more than synesthetic quality to the "mandala principle" as found in Asian religions, in which corporeal, mental, semiotic, sensual, material, and gestural elements can evoke or substitute for each other in tantra's non-dual weave or continuum.

In terms of the first category, the work of Pauline Oliveros is exemplary. Indeed, Oliveros is the only major composer/sound artist outside of Japan to emphasize mandalas as part of her practice. In her text "On Sonic Meditation" (1973), Oliveros introduces the image of a circle with a point at the centre as the basis for the meditation exercises which would go by the name of Deep Listening (FIGS. 88–89). Oliveros observes:

> The proper relationship of attention and awareness can be symbolized by a circle with a dot in the center… The dot represents attention, and the circle, awareness. In these respective positions, each is centered in relation to the other. Awareness can expand, without losing center or its balanced relationship with attention, and simultaneously become more inclusive. Attention can be focused as fine as possible in any direction, and can probe all aspects of awareness without losing its balanced relationship to awareness.[8]

In a 1980 lecture entitled "MMM: Meditation/Mandala/Music," Oliveros elaborated on the ways in which she has used mandala principles in her work.[9] She began with an awareness-focusing meditation, then showed images of mandalas from various cultures and traditions, after which she led listeners through a series of "mandala meditations." Then came a discussion of mandalas in her own work, from a four-pointed star drawn in her childhood, followed by observations on the ways in which mandalas allowed Oliveros to gradually move away from a more traditional form of compositional notation based on staves and notes to a spatial/diagrammatic form based on a mandala. According to Oliveros, it was the process of working with audio tape and electronics, as well as solo and group improvisation, that led to the shift from traditional notation to mandalas in *Pieces of Eight* (1964). The mandala, in this case a circle whose perimeter marks the temporal division of the piece into two-minute segments of the circle, provides a way of visualizing the piece as a whole and the different kinds of activity within it, some of which, such as the use of taped sounds, could not be notated traditionally.

It is instructive that Oliveros's work during the period of *Pieces of Eight* was conducted at the San Francisco Tape Music Center—during a period where West Coast–based visual artists like Bruce Conner and Jordan Belson were also exploring mandalas in their

FIG. 87 (LEFT)
Pauline Oliveros (USA, 1932–2016)
Lullaby for Daisy Pauline, 1979
Published in *Software for People: Collective Writings 1963–80* (1984)

FIG. 88 (BELOW)
Pauline Oliveros (USA, 1932–2016)
The Wheel of Life, 1979
Published in *Software for People: Collective Writings 1963–80* (1984)

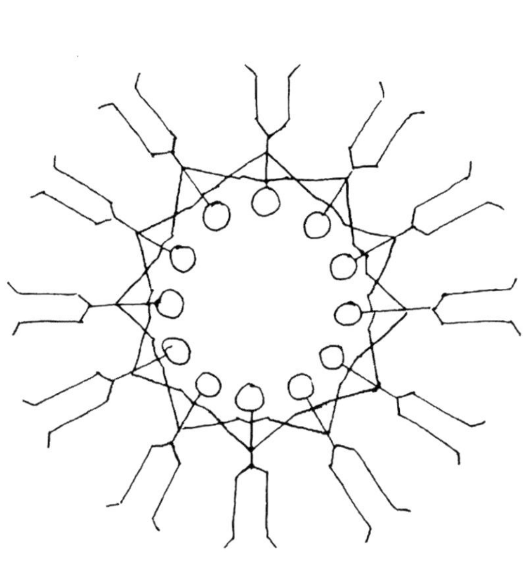

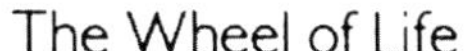

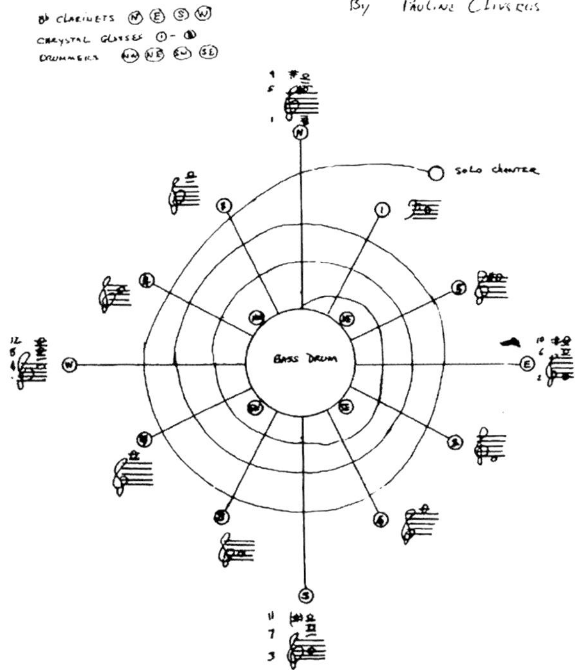

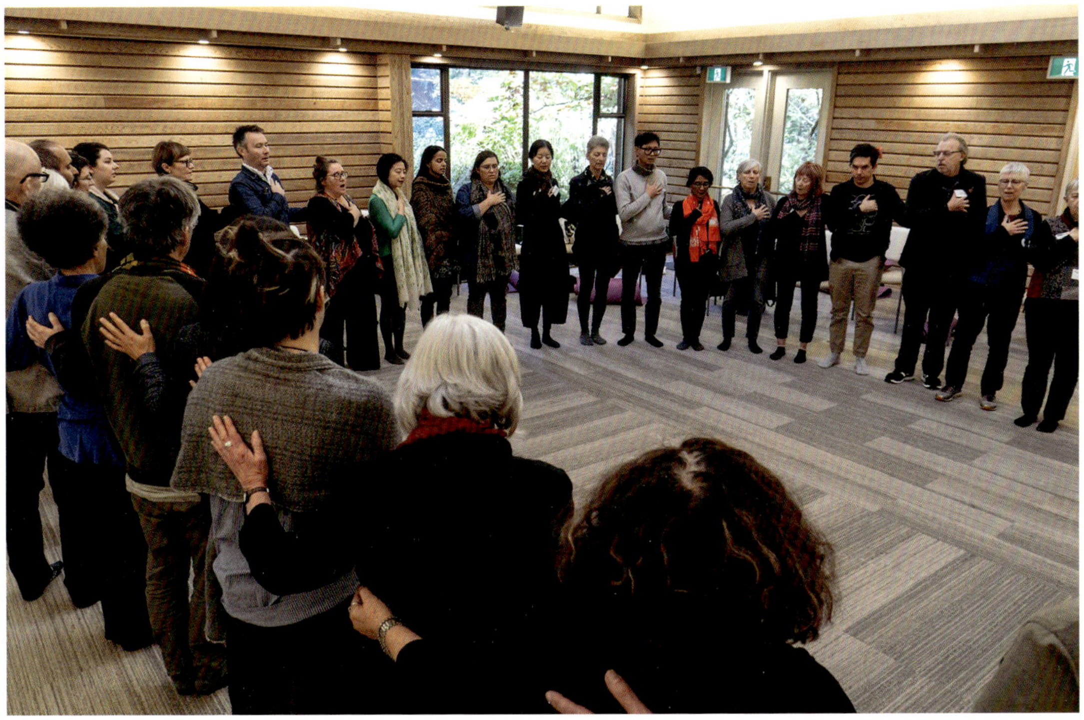

FIG. 89
Tina Pearson (Canada, 1956–)
Deep Listening® into Sounding: An Introduction to the Practice of Pauline Oliveros, featuring Heart Chant, 2001
Workshop presented on October 27, 2019, at *In the Present Moment: A Research Convening*, University of Victoria
Photo: Kirk Schwartz

Oliveros's *Heart Chant* was presented at a workshop during *In the Present Moment: A Research Convening*, led by Victoria-based artist and musician Tina Pearson. *Heart Chant* is a "Deep Listening" meditation intended to develop the potential of listening as a means of fostering community and healing through sound. It was written in response to the September 11, 2001, terrorist attacks in the United States.

visual works and where multimedia happenings, such as the Trips Festival and Ken Kesey's Acid Tests, with their use of light projections, as well as the broader iconography of psychedelia as found in underground comix and event posters, clearly reference mandala imagery.[10] Minimalist composer Terry Riley, also associated with the Tape Music Center, published his *Keyboard Study #2* in 1967 in *Aspen* magazine; here the mandala's concentric circles consist of staves and notes radiating out from a central stave. In the interlocking patterns of his celebrated composition *In C* (1964), one also finds a similar though more complex cyclical principle. And in fact there is a rich history of mandala-like circles as notational devices, from John Coltrane's well-known 1961 diagram of the circle of fifths (which he sent to Yusef Lateef) to Iannis Xenakis's geometrizations of composition in works such as the *Polytopes* (1966). But see how quickly and easily it is to drift from "mandala" to "mandala-like"?

In her lecture, Oliveros goes on to describe other uses for mandalas in designing sonic works. In *AOK* (1968), the mandala provides a floorplan for positions of performers. In *Wheel of Fortune* (1969) and *Meditation on the Points of the Compass* (1970), it provides a visualization of a stage; then, for the latter, an arrangement of the performers and audience. In short, in the transition from "music" to "sound art," the mandala offered a capacious and flexible mode of diagramming the many elements whose conscious organization, or attunement, would be considered not just incidental or auxiliary aspects of the work, but integral elements that could be specified in the democratization of the relationship of musicians, composer, and audience, as well as the ways in which sounds would be made and experienced.

This concept of mandala as arrangement of sonic space has been taken up in various ways. Bernhard Leitner's arrangement of speakers in space in his *Soundcube* (1969) and *Le cylindre sonore* (The Sound Cylinder, 1987) treat the architectural and technical organization of sonic space as a mandala-like frame. Karlheinz Stockhausen, in his opera *Samstag aus Licht* (Saturday from Light, 1982), uses two mandalas inscribed or projected onto the stage, in which melodic fragments are spatialized within the mandalas in a sequence that the musician follows, moving from location to location.[11]

FIG. 90
Avadana Stories: The Law of Cause and Effect
Tibet, 18th century
Thangka: gouache on cotton with silk mount
image: 61.2 × 43.5 cm
Gift of Mr. A.S. Wyllie
Art Gallery of Greater Victoria 1963.176.001
Photo: Stephen Topfer

Mandalas coordinate concepts of cosmological space and time with human mental and physiological functions, and with the law of karma. In Buddhism the law of karma, or cause and effect, governs "the nature of things." It is considered a fundamental natural law. The Avadana stories relay the noble deeds of the past lives of the Buddha, and thereby teach the law of karma. Here the Buddha as a mandala extends through past and future time.

TO TAKE A step back from the use of mandalas as visual diagrams, either for the notation of the sequence of sounds in a piece of music or sound art or to represent the design of the space in which music happens (including the placement of performers, audience, speakers, and composer), one might add here a separate category of pieces of music that are explicitly thematically engaged with ideas of mandala. In this category we might include Japanese composers Toshiro Mayuzumi's *Mandala Symphony* (1960) and Somei Satoh's *Mandala* (1982). Mayuzumi, one of the most important postwar Japanese composers, sounds very clearly in the tradition of post-Messiaen serialist orchestral composition—the symphony seems to describe a passage around a field that consists in a sequence of locations with particular melodic and harmonic structures, each separated from each other via silence (or in Japanese, *ma*, or negative space). Mayuzumi apparently built some of the motifs of the symphony from the harmonics of Japanese temple bells. Satoh's *Mandala* consists of a drone whose pitch structure is modulated over the course of the piece, with Satoh's *shomyo* vocal chanting enmeshed in sustained tone electronics to create a powerful vibratory field.

This raises a broader issue of drone-based works—usually presented as music, as composition, but having many of the elements of sound art. Drones are a key aspect of developments in

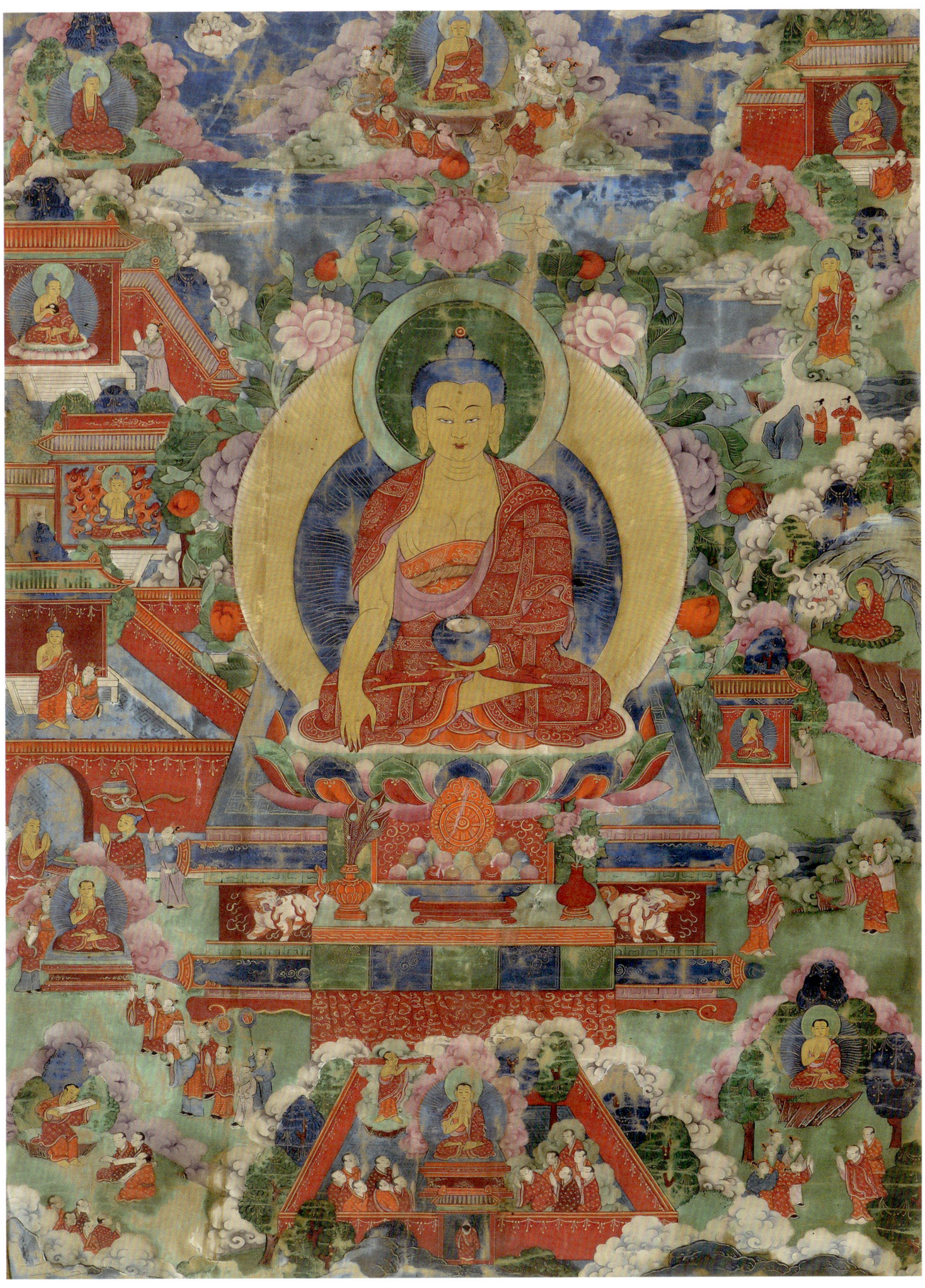

postwar composition, and most of the more important drone composers explicitly associated their work with particular Asian religious or aesthetic traditions—whether Stockhausen, Cage, La Monte Young, or another. Young, for example, was interested in the tambura drone that accompanies Indian classical music, and gagaku, the Japanese court music, as far back as the 1950s.[12] Young's collaborations with visual artist Marian Zazeela in the creation of the *Dream House* (1970–present), a sound and light environment featuring Young's drones and Zazeela's calligraphic/light sculptures (which Young has described as a "mandala"),[13] saturates and entangles the visual and aural fields. Thus, when we look for works explicitly connecting drones or sonic space to ideas of an enlightened Buddhist sonic field, it is a younger generation of composers that we look to. For example, Catherine Christer Hennix's performance of Stockhausen's *Unbegrenzt* (Unlimited) from *Aus den Sieben Tagen* (From the Seven Days) in 1974 involves a reading from the *Guyasamajatantra* as part of its expansive sonic space. French composer Eliane Radigue, who was associated with the San Francisco Tape Music Center but started studying Tibetan Buddhism with Tibetan lama Pawo Rinpoche in 1975, has produced a number of works in which shimmering synthesizer-generated electronic fields are connected to Tibetan Buddhist texts and practices, notably the works *Trilogie de la mort* (Trilogy on Death, 1985–1993) and two Milarepa-related recordings.

When looking at the history of modern art, and perhaps of sound art in particular, evidence of the mandala principle can be found, even when the particular kind of Buddhism to which the artist has been exposed (which in North America from 1945 to 1970 means Zen) actually has little or no explicit reference to mandalas. Even so, it is the shift from thinking about art as object or linear composition to thinking about art in terms of process and field that is significant here. John Cage's fundamental insights and innovations can be thought of in these terms: *4′33″* "notates" the phenomenological field in which the event of the composition's performance occurs in much the same way that a Buddhist meditation might draw awareness to this field, which includes both subject and object. Consider also Cage's much-told story of entering an anechoic chamber in 1951 and hearing two sounds, which the room's engineer explains as follows: "The high one was your nervous system in operation. The low one was your blood in circulation."[14]

The most important Japanese philosopher of the Kyoto School, Nishida Kitaro, in his attempt to generate a modern philosophy that integrated insights of Asian religious traditions and practice, emphasized the importance of space, place, or topos as a kind of field of "pure experience" out of which phenomenal reality emerged.[15] In the post–World War II period, the figure of the field can be found everywhere—in computation and systems theory, in quantum field theory, in Alexander Grothendieck's mathematics of the topos, in gestalt psychotherapy, even in the geopolitics of the Cold War. In the arts, it is there in abstract expressionism painting fields, in Fluxus's and the Gutai group's expansions beyond the canvas to the general field of action of the artist, whether in the studio or in social space; in the rewiring of artistic practice via electronic media and technologies, as in the work of someone like Nam June Paik. It is there in concept art's framing of art in terms of a mental or cognitive field of action. In all of this there is a Buddhist trace, often difficult to disentangle from the traces of other Asian religious traditions—because Asian aesthetics, even if a gross simplification, arguably have been sympathetic to field models and ontologies for a very long time. And it was from this sympathy that the mandala principle was developed.

Thus, when looking at many of the sound art scores in this exhibition (which are by no means exhaustive, just as the category of sound art itself is open to dispute and reframing), there is much evidence of concern with this field principle. For example, the "gathas" of Jackson Mac Low (FIGS. 91–92) are complex acrostic patterns of mantras which are simultaneously conceived of as text and as visual images which function as the basis of oral performance (and which in fact have a corollary in the Kunzang Khorlo form of traditional Tibetan poetry, which consists of a mandala-like acrostic grid that may be read in several directions, and which are painted onto the sides of temples). John Giorno developed a complex multimedia poetry and poetics that intersected ideas of the field derived from Charles Olson and his "projective verse" with Andy Warhol's and Robert Rauschenberg's interest in found materials as generators of patterns in a field (FIG. 93). While Giorno's early poetry used found texts and subjected them to processes of repetition, whether the famous double columns used in his printed poems or the echo and other electronic effects used in performance, Giorno shifted, around the time that he met his guru, the great Nyingma lama Dudjom Rinpoche in 1971, to treating all thoughts that appear in his

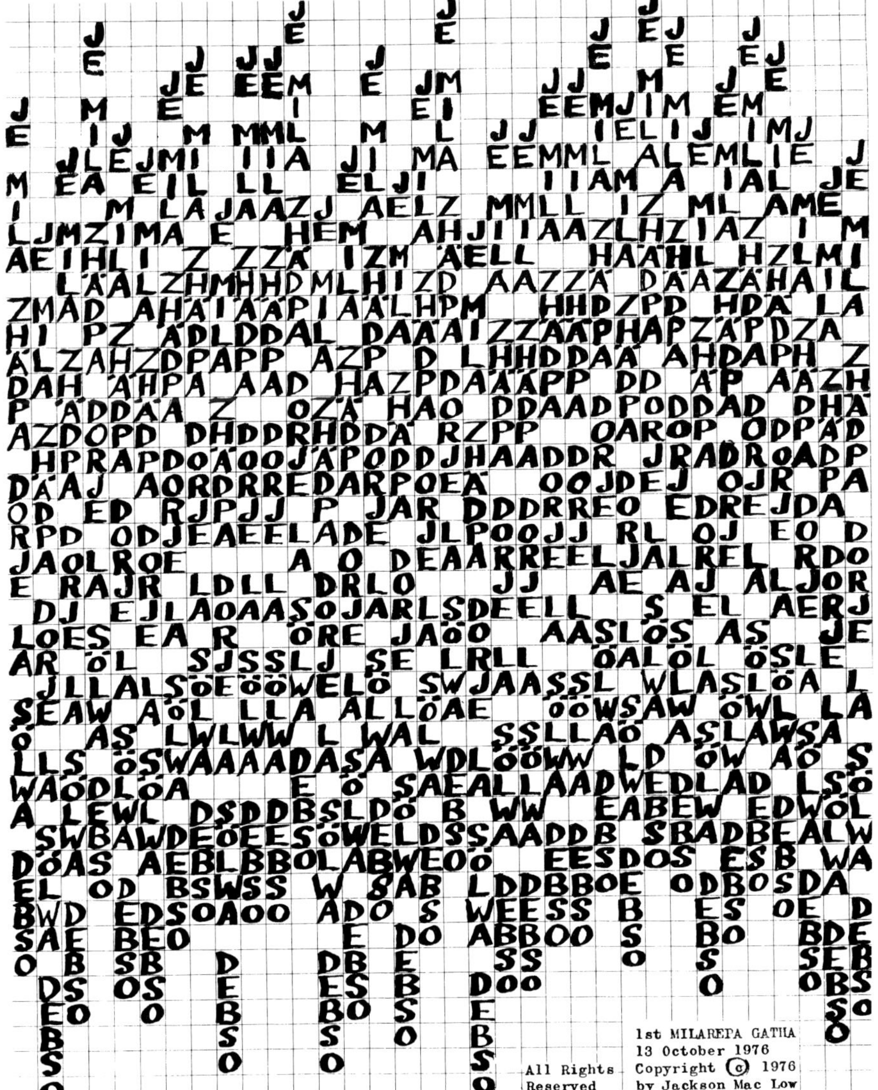

FIG. 91
Jackson Mac Low
(USA, 1922–2004)
Milarepa Gatha, 1976
Ink on paper
27.5 × 21.25 cm
John Cage Archive, Northwestern University, Evanston, Illinois (Cage 022/06/03/001)
Reproduced with kind permission of the Estate of Jackson Mac Low

A gatha is a verse or poetic metre recited in rhythm with the breath. Jackson Mac Low's gathas could be described as "mandala-form" drawings, merging language with visual thinking. This gatha consists of the individual letters of a mantra, drawn omni-directionally on graph paper. The poet described them as Buddhist performance scores that "encouraged performers and hearers to give 'bare attention' to the letter-sounds,"* where a mantra can be understood as the sound-body of a buddha or deity.

* In Brett Littman, "Jackson Mac Low: Lines–Letters–Words," *In Their Own Words*, Poetry Society of America (January 20–March 19, 2017), available at poetrysociety.org/features/in-their-own-words/jackson-mac-low-lines-letters-words.

FIG. 92
Jackson Mac Low
(USA, 1922–2004)
Tara Gatha, n.d.
Ink on paper
27.5 × 21.25 cm
Reproduced with kind permission of the Estate of Jackson Mac Low

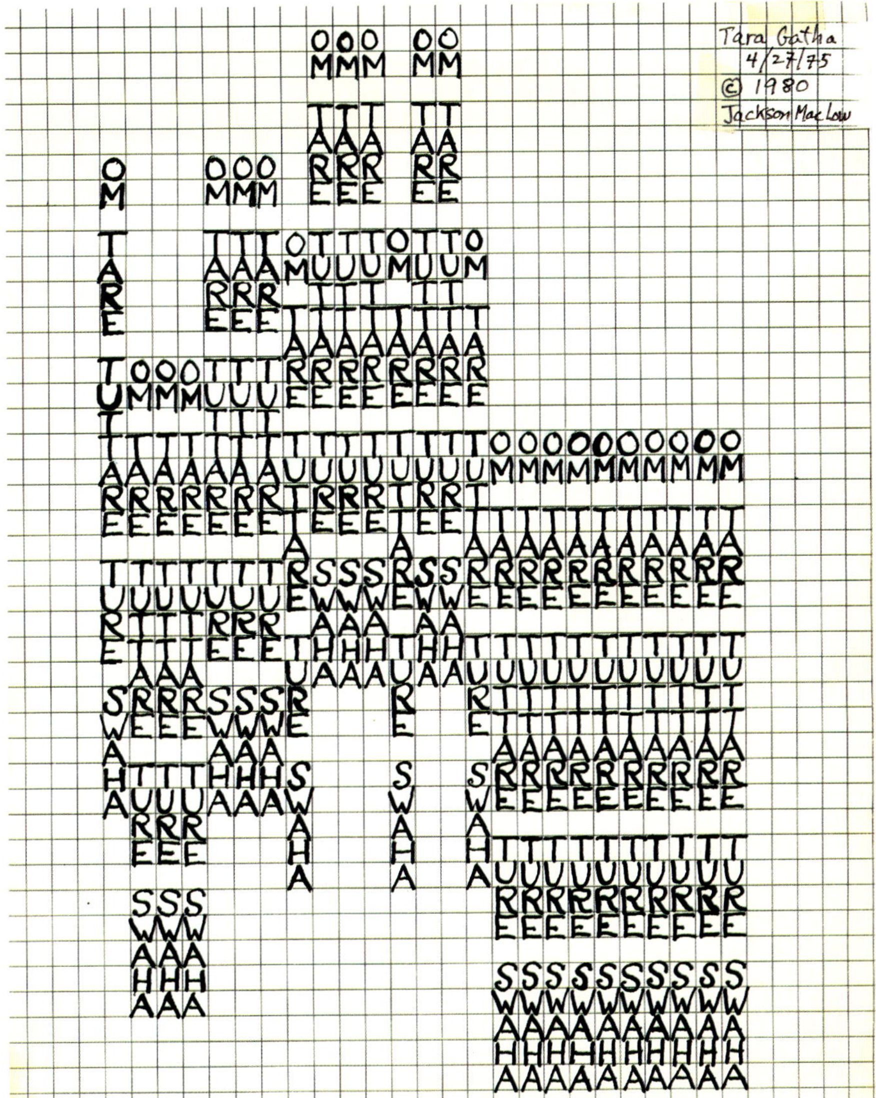

SNOW
DAHLIAS
SHARP AS CAT PISS

VOLUMINOUS
VOLUPTUOUS
BORGAINVILLEA
ARE FLAMES LICKING
WHAT CANNOT BURN

CHERRY
BLOSSOMS
ARE RAZOR BLADES

DAFFODILS
BAPTIZED
IN BUTTER

FIELDS OF
DAISIES
ARE THE PEOPLE
WHO BETRAYED ME

ARMFULS OF
HONEYSUCKLE
AND COLUMBINE

HYACINTHS
ARE THE SONGS
OF SUICIDES

LILACS
LUXURIOUSLY
LICKING THE AIR

LILLIES OF THE VALLEY
LILLIES OF FUR
LILLIES OF FEATHER
LILLIES OF FIN
LILLIES OF SKIN

LUPINE
WERE SELF-SERVING
AND UNKIND

ALMOST
MISS AMERICA
ROSE

ORCHIDS
ARE THE TONGUES
THAT LIED

MAY ALL THE TINY BLACK INSECTS
CRAWLING ON THE
PEONIES
BE MY SONS AND DAUGHTERS
IN FUTURE LIVES

POPPIES
HAVE POCKETS
PACKED WITH
NARCOTIC TREATS

BIG BUNCH OF
ONE THOUSAND
RED ROSES
ARE ALL THE PEOPLE
I MADE LOVE TO

SUNFLOWERS
SNUGGLE
THEIR HEADS ON MY LAP
AND GAZE UP AT THE SKY

NECKLACES OF
WISTERIA
BOWING TO
MAGNOLIA MAMAS

CHRYSANTHEMUMS
ARE A GARLAND OF
SKULLS

FIG. 93
John Giorno (USA, 1936–2019)
Welcoming the Flowers, 2007
Portfolio of 18 screen-printed poems on two-ply museum board
Each print: 41.91 × 41.91 cm
Printed and published by Durham Press
Image courtesy of Durham Press, Inc.

The New York poet John Giorno met his teacher, Dudjom Rinpoche, in 1971, and was a practising Buddhist for almost fifty years, until his death in 2019. His poetry has been noted for incorporating Buddhist imagery with the profane and pornographic. He describes words as a mirror and poetry as holding a mirror to the minds of his readers. His approach to poetry is deeply informed by Buddhist concepts of the mind and Dzogchen concepts of direct awareness.

mind, whether internally generated or phenomenologically perceived, as "found materials" which could be subjected to a field arrangement. While in his late works, such as the *Welcoming the Flowers* (2007) poem/paintings, he abandoned this method, the text paintings still retain a mandala/field-like practice in which a thought or a phrase condenses onto the surface of a painting, suggesting the complex transits of image, idea, sound, written syllable, geometric structure, and colour field that are characteristic of Tibetan mandalas.

THE MANDALA, as it was developed in India, Tibet, and East Asia, is a vast and profound system of interlocking elements and practices whose coherency was and is dependent on a community of practitioners and scholars actively engaged with all of the elements of the system such that their meaning was/is alive. Modern artworks derived from mandalas, sound based or otherwise, rarely if ever reflect any such systematic knowledge—indeed, it is likely that someone immersed deeply in the system would be highly unlikely to make art—although there are interesting exceptions, such as the Tibetan Buddhist lama and filmmaker Dzongsar Khyentse Rinpoche. Thus, most art that is indexed to an explicit principle of mandala involves only a tiny glimpse or flash of a system whose complexity the artist is likely unaware of. Yet such flashes are also signs of life, insofar as they reactivate the basic questions about ourselves and the universe that the formulation of the mandala in Asia over the last 2,500 years also sought to address. Buddhism itself is an unfinished project so long as some of us remain unenlightened.

Thanks to Alan Cummings, Aki Onda, Michele Laporte, Chrysanne Stathacos, Raymond Foye, Vincent de Roguin, Haema Sivanesan, and Christie Pearson for advice and information.

MARCUS BOON is a writer and Professor of English at York University in Toronto. He is the author of *The Road of Excess: A History of Writers on Drugs* (Harvard UP, 2002), *In Praise of Copying* (Harvard UP, 2010), and *The Politics of Vibration: Music as a Cosmopolitical Practice* (Duke UP, forthcoming) as well as co-author with Timothy Morton and Eric Cazdyn of *Nothing: Three Inquiries in Buddhism* (U. Chicago, 2015). He co-edited *Practice*, a collection of writings on practice in the visual arts, with Gabriel Levine (MIT/Whitechapel Documents of Contemporary Arts series, 2018), and edited Buddhist poet John Giorno's *Selected Poems* (Counterpoint, 2008).

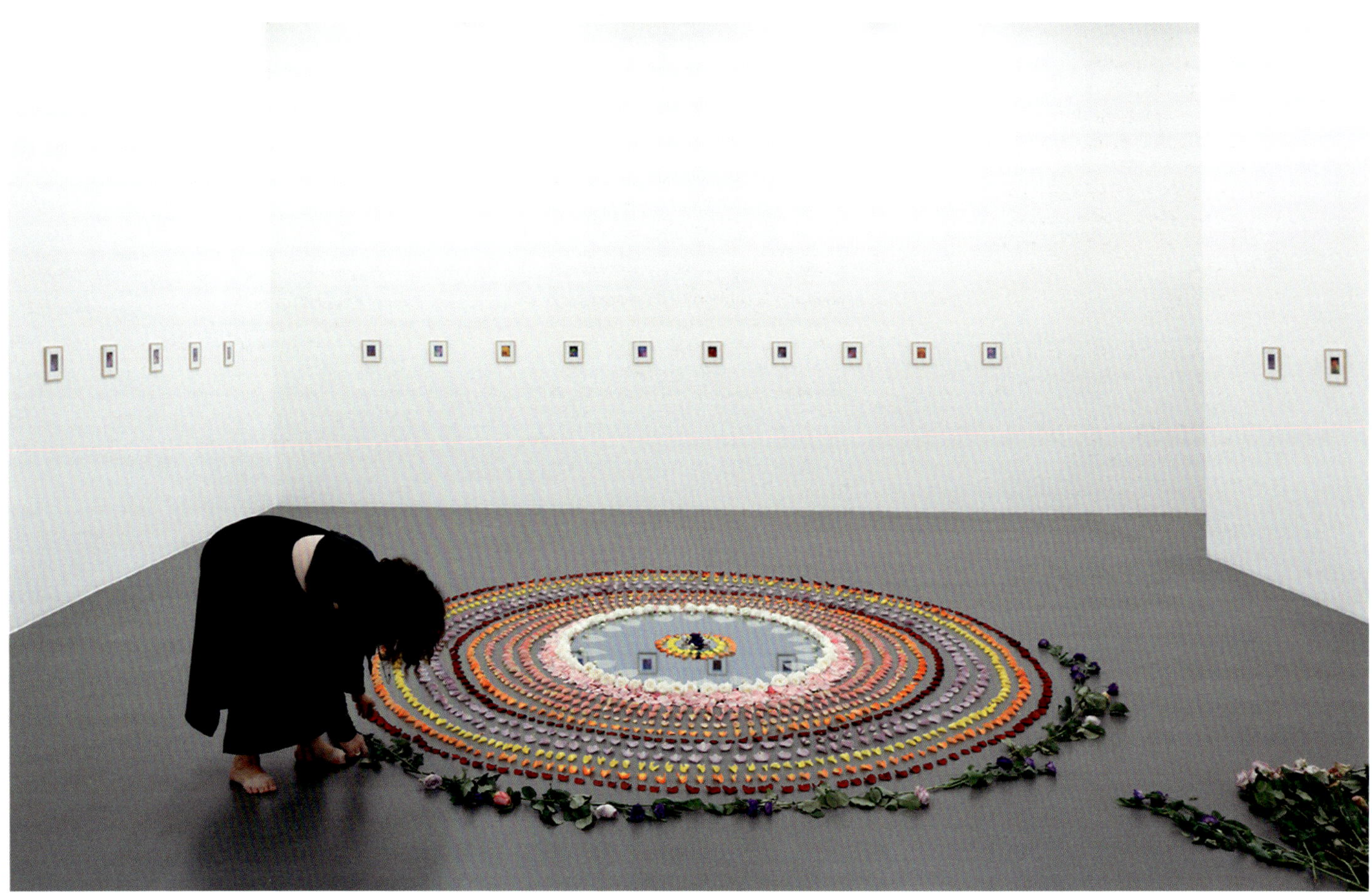

FIG. 94
Chrysanne Stathacos
(Canada, 1951–)
Rose Mirror Mandala, 2013
Installation: roses, bodhi leaves, blue mirror and glass; dimensions variable
The Temptation of AA Bronson, Witte de With Center for Contemporary Art (now Kunstinstituut Melly), Rotterdam, Netherlands
Courtesy of the artist
Photo: Matthias Herrman

Chrysanne Stathacos's introduction to Buddhism coincided with the death of friends to AIDS in the 1990s. The Buddhist concept of impermanence gave her an important perspective on death. Stathacos's practice is concerned with understanding the feminine in and through Buddhism, as a student of Jetsunma Tenzin Palmo. Her mirror mandalas deal with the idea of impermanence, fleeting beauty, and the role of the feminine in Buddhism and nature. Stathacos describes her installations as being concerned with the creation of sites of spiritual intent in secular contexts.

NOTES

1 Tarthang Tulku, *Sacred Art of Tibet* (Berkeley, CA: Dharma, 1972), p. 6.

2 Kimiaki Tanaka, *An Illustrated History of the Mandala* (Somerville, MA: Wisdom, 2018), p. 7.

3 See, for example, W.Y. Evans-Wentz (ed.), *Tibetan Yoga and Secret Doctrines* (London: Oxford University Press, 1935), pp. 72, 324.

4 C.G. Jung, *Psychology and Alchemy* (London: Routledge, 1953), pp. 95–223.

5 Giuseppe Tucci, *The Theory and Practice of the Mandala* (London: Rider and Co., 1961), first published as *Teoria e pratica del Mandala* (Rome: Astrolabio, 1949). See also Mircea Eliade, *Yoga: Immortality and Freedom*, translated by Willard R. Trask (Princeton: Bollingen, 1958; first published by Payot in France, 1954), pp. 219–227.

6 Elizabeth ten Grotenhuis, *Japanese Mandalas: Representations of Sacred Geography* (Honolulu: University of Hawaii Press, 1998).

7 There is very little scholarship on Buddhism and sound art, but see the catalogue for the Rubin Museum's groundbreaking 2017 exhibition *The World Is Sound*, in *Spiral: The Sound Issue* (2017), a journal published by the Rubin. See also the relevant sections of Jacqueline Baas, *Smile of the Buddha: Eastern Philosophy and Western Art from Monet to Today* (Berkeley: University of California Press, 2005) and *The Third Mind: American Artists Contemplate Asia*, edited by Alexandra Monroe (New York: Guggenheim Museum, 2009).

8 Pauline Oliveros, "On Sonic Meditation," in *Software for People: Collected Writings 1963–80* (Baltimore, MD: Smith, 1980), pp. 140–141.

9 Pauline Oliveros, "MMM: Meditation/Mandala/Music," in Oliveros, *Software for People*, pp. 214–268.

10 See David Bernstein, ed., *The San Francisco Tape Music Center: 1960s Counterculture and the Avant-Garde* (Berkeley: University of California Press, 2008). On psychedelics and mandalas, see Alex Grey, "Vajravision," in *Zig Zag Zen: Buddhism and Psychedelics*, edited by Allan Hunt Badiner and Alex Grey (San Francisco: Chronicle, 2002).

11 For a discussion of Stockhausen, see Wayla Joy Ewart Chambo, *The Devil and the Details: Negotiating Virtuosity, Agency, and Authenticity in Karlheinz Stockhausen's* Kathinka's Gesang als Luzifers Requiem *for Solo Flute*, doctoral thesis, University of North Texas, 2015.

12 See Peter Lavezzoli, *The Dawn of Indian Music in the West* (London: Continuum, 2007).

13 "La Monte Young and Marian Zazeela at the Dream House: A Conversation with Frank J. Oteri," videotaped by Randy Nordschow, transcribed by Frank J. Oteri, Randy Nordschow, Amanda MacBlane, and Rob Wilkerson (NewBoxMusic, 2003), p. 28, available at https://2104310a1da50059d9c5-d1823d6f516b5299e7df5375e9cf45d2.ssl.cf2.rackcdn.com/nmbx/assets/54/interview_young.pdf.

14 In John Cage, "How to Pass, Kick, Fall, Run," in *A Year from Monday: New Lectures and Writings* (Middletown, CT: Wesleyan University Press, 1969), p. 134.

15 Nishida Kitaro, "The Logic of 'Topos' and the Religious Worldview," *The Eastern Buddhist*, new series, vol. 19, no. 2 (Autumn 1986), pp. 1–29.

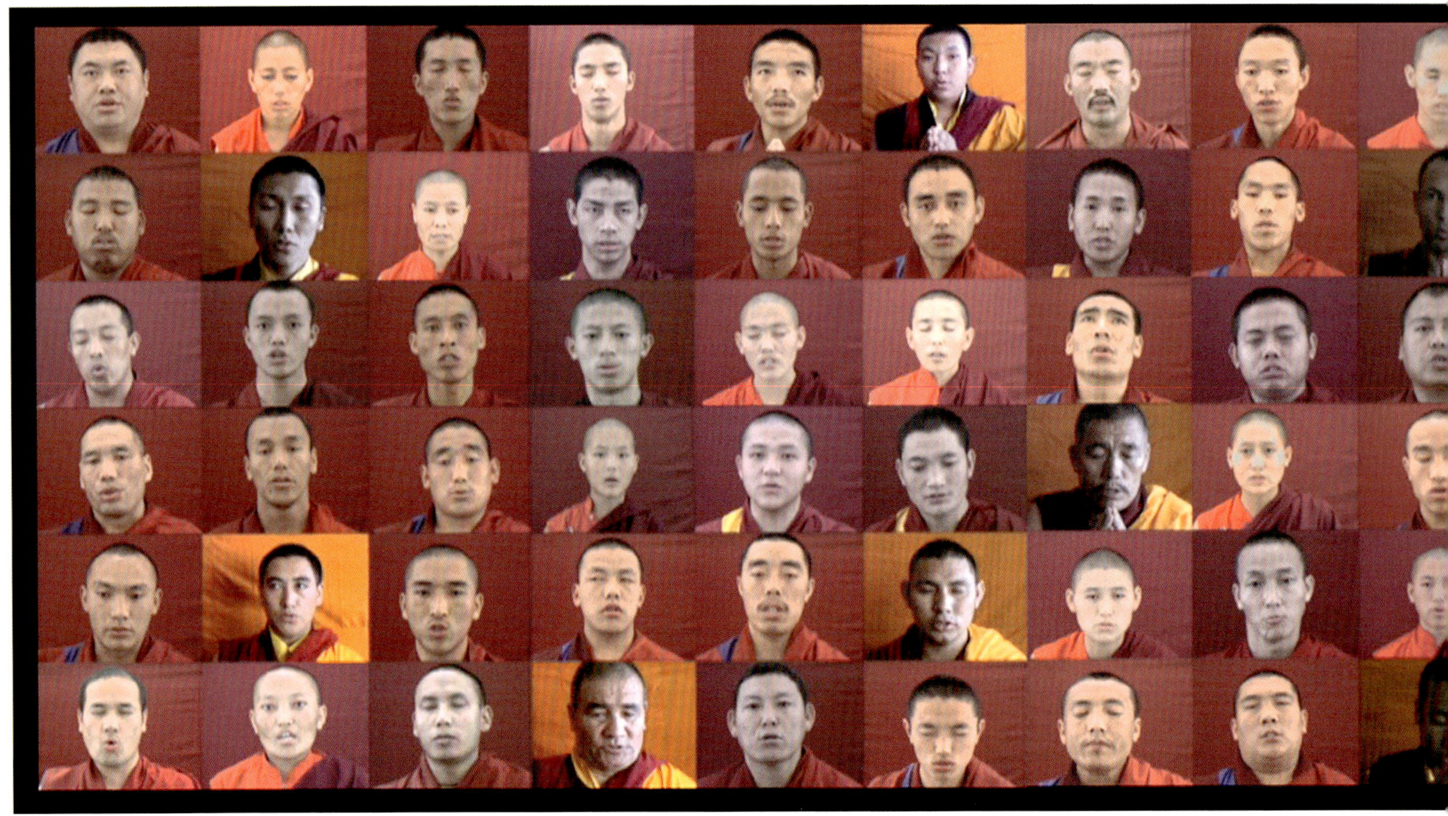

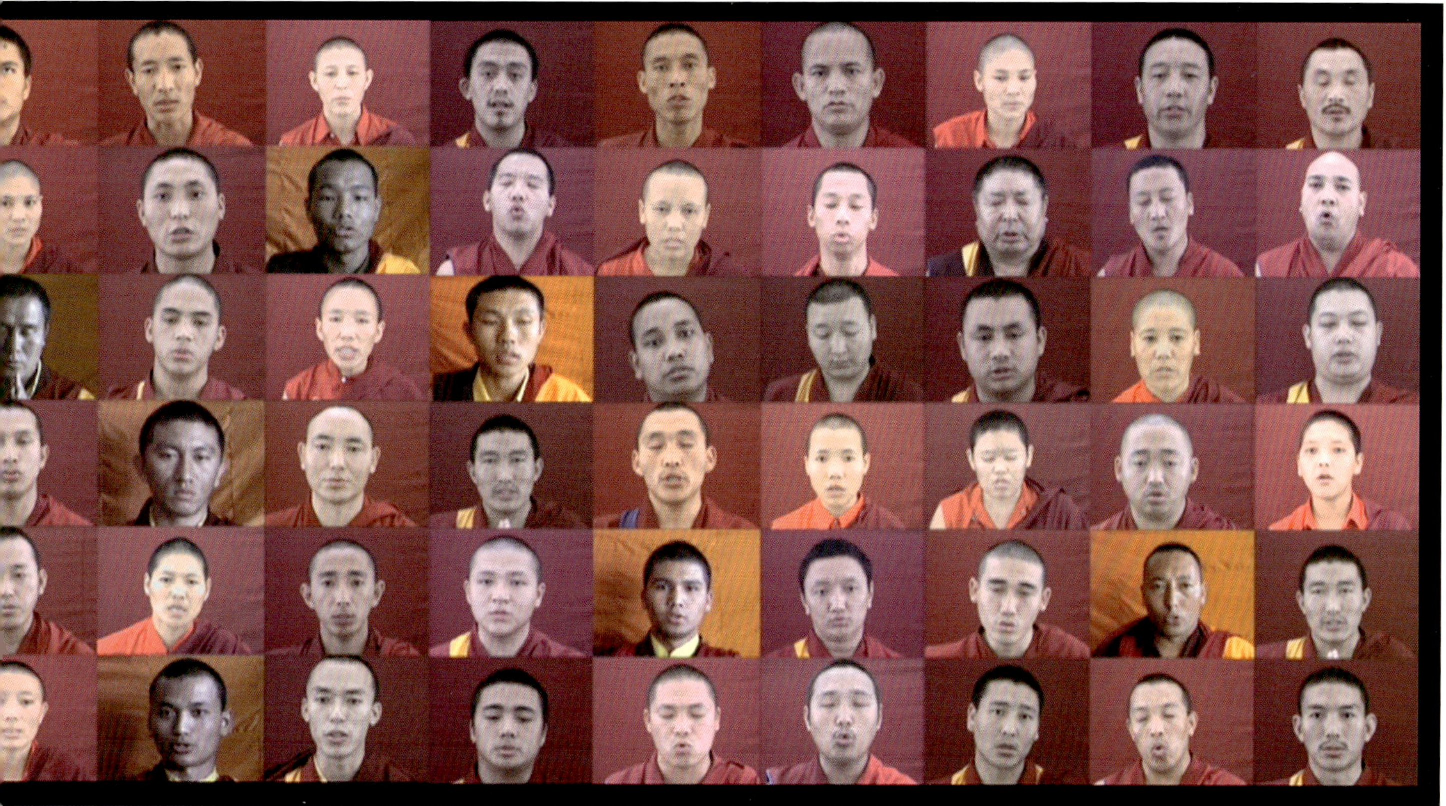

FIG. 95
Marina Abramovic
(Serbia/USA, 1946–)
Waterfall, 2000–2003
Three-channel video installation
dimensions variable

Waterfall is a video projection commissioned by representatives of His Holiness the 14th Dalai Lama. It consists of images of 108 Tibetan monks and nuns chanting, creating a "waterfall" of sound. In an interview with musician Laurie Anderson, Abramovic provided some background to this work. She explained,

"The Dalai Lama wanted to have a concert, with sacred music from the five different Buddhist traditions around the world, all on one stage . . . It was to take place in the music center in Bangalore, in southern India . . . I was invited to choreograph them. There were 106 [*sic*] monks . . . I was thinking that the form could be a human pyramid. It took five weeks to build these steps of wood on wheels—it had to roll on and off the stage, and they had one minute and 10 seconds to get all 106 [*sic*] monks standing in position onstage. We had to rehearse a lot; they weren't used to this kind of stage presence. And when it was finished—I had been in the monastery for more than a month—the chief monk came and said, 'It's so nice, but we can't use this pyramid.' And I said, 'What do you mean?' And he said, 'Because in the Buddhist tradition there is no hierarchy.' You know, I couldn't understand how they could let me work all this time, every single day, for five weeks and not tell me it wouldn't do. They told me that they hadn't wanted to offend me. I was crying. And they said this simple thing: 'Let it go.' Then at the concert they sat anywhere they wanted to and sang and it was perfect."*

* "Marina Abramovic by Laurie Anderson," *BOMB Magazine*, #84 (July 1, 2003), available at bombmagazine.org/articles/marina-abramovi%C4%87.

A SOCIAL VISION FOR ART

MANIFESTING THE BUDDHA-NATURE

LOUWRIEN WIJERS

IN AN INTERVIEW at my home in Amsterdam on October 11, 1981, the French Fluxus artist Robert Filliou said to me:

> Buddhism has been important in art for a very long time. But the connection has been for the preceding generations, like John Cage, through Zen Buddhism. Already at the time of Dadaism, the work of Duchamp in particular was very Zen. Since the events that befell Tibet from 1949 on, Tibetan Buddhism has come to the West. This is one of the most important things going on at the end of this century. The coming of Tibetan Buddhism to the West will shape the future of humanity. And what is so interesting is, that Padmasambhava had made a prediction of it. Now in the Dordogne [France] we have two Tibetan centres side by side, representing two of the four schools of Tibetan Buddhism. We have a Kagyupa Centre, with the perfectly accomplished master Lama Gendun, and we have a Nyingmapa Centre, where the head is His Holiness Dudjom Rinpoche—one of the four spiritual leaders of Tibet. These monasteries exist ten kilometers from the Lascaux caves and ten kilometers from Les Eyzies, where Cro-Magnon was found. When this was explained to both Dudjom Rinpoche and Karmapa, they thought that was fantastic and said: "Where it all started, it starts again." All this auspicious prehistorical life that went on along the Vezere river... Dudjom Rinpoche calls the Vezere river "the jewel that fulfills all wishes".. So now that our Tibetan masters are with us, we know that the Vajrayana, "the way of the diamond," the "lightning way to instant enlightenment" is where I find the connection with art. The lightning way is the artist's way, cutting through directly... because art is not worth doing unless it is total commitment to art.[1]

Contemporary art came up quickly in my first interview with His Holiness the 14th Dalai Lama of Tibet, on April 15, 1981, at his residence in exile in Dharamsala, India.

I SAID: Personally, I come from the background of Western visual arts. For more than twenty years the contemporary visual arts have been less concerned with painting and sculpting and, instead, artists have been seeking truth and wisdom. They have expressed their findings through physical performance or they have spread their ideas through mass media, like television, video, film, books, and magazines. In Germany the number one artist Joseph Beuys even founded a political party and entered the elections for the presidency of West Germany promising that he would "change politics into art."

DALAI LAMA: Good! [*laughs*] Very good... [*laughs*]

I ASKED: Could Your Holiness make a statement on art in general, and on the most beneficial task that artists can perform in society?

DALAI LAMA: Hmm... Art. Hmm... All your questions are complicated [*laughs*]... In modern art there is, I think... One of the very important ways is to express your own feelings, as well as it is a way to teach or influence other people. So, no doubt, a very, very important role in human society. I think, you see, we are talking and generally we are not lacking the technology, or science. We are lacking the real human feeling. In other words, kindness—or human understanding, or a human sense of brothers and sisters. I think, you see, an artist can express about the human feelings. That is, I think, one of the important, effective roles of artists. An artist can contribute many things... Anyway, now we, our human mind, is too much involved in external ways. In outer aims. We are trying to go into space. Millions and millions of dollars are spent on these things. Nothing wrong. But still, we have much inner space, I think, that has not yet been exploited... And sometimes, you see, I feel this human skull is very small, yet it is very complicated and very sophisticated. So, there are many, many inner spaces which are not yet exploited, or used. So, in this present time I think we should investigate or think

FIG. 96
Mark Ginsburg, "An Audience with His Holiness the Dalai Lama"
In *Interview* magazine, Christmas 1979, vol. 9, no. 12
Photo: Courtesy of the Warhol Museum, Pittsburgh, USA

This interview, for Andy Warhol's *Interview* magazine, was the first ever interview that the Dalai Lama gave in the United States during his first tour of North America in 1979, twenty years after leaving Tibet to live in exile in Dharamsala, India. The full interview is available at markginsburgmedia.com/the-dalai-lama.

An audience with His Holiness

THE DALAI LAMA

by Mark Ginsburg

For 6 million Tibetan Buddhists, the story of Tenzin Gyatso, Fourteenth Dalai Lama, the supreme temporal and spiritual leader of Tibet, is as important as the rising sun. The journey began with a vision which led a search party to a two-year old peasant boy; on his body were the eight marks that distinguished his thirteen predecessors. At the age of four he assumed leadership of Tibet. Now, forty years later, he lives in exile in Dharamsala, India with seventy thousand of his refugee followers. From his upbringing in the Potala, a palace which contained the tombs of past Dalai Lamas within it's thousands of chambers, to his treacherous undercover flight from the invading Chinese across the world's highest mountains, the Dalai Lama remains a revered and essential figure in the changing Buddhist world.

In reference to the ravaging of virgin forests by woodcutters, Chekhov wrote: "All Russia echoes with the sound of the ax." So in the Tibetan regions, the Chinese ax daily severs the Buddhist way of life, squashes it's monastic tradition, and obliterates the inner lives of it's people. Little more than their dependence on the yak remains unaffected. To know that the Dalai Lama is not bitter is to taste the strength of a man whose Mongolian title means "Ocean of Wisdom." As we talked in a guest house at Harvard on the last stop of an arduous forty-nine day visit and speaking tour, His Holiness was alert and lively. As he hitched up his bi-colored robes of rough cotton and swung a bit of maroon fabric over his shoulder, his small face produced expressive and open. During the conversation his deep voice pitches. much resonant giggling and laughter at astonishing intervals and

MARK GINSBURG: Do you ever wish you occupied a more humble position?

HIS HOLINESS: You mean an ordinary role? Yes, as a simple Buddhist monk. That's the best way to lead one's life. But at the same time you see, in order to help, in order to be of service to certain communities, or human beings in general, my present position is something helpful. So from that viewpoint, it's okay. Or even better.

MG: Has technology affected our vision of the way we want society to operate?

HH: Definitely, no doubt. Strong effects, strong influence. It circles around the greater concern or involvement with money, and therefore this constant need to rush about and do things.

MG: What is your earliest memory?

HH: A certain moment which occurred when I was two or three years. At some point, some location. I was playing, mainly.

MG: I know you enjoy gadgets and tinkering with electronic devices. Have you ever invented anything?

HH: *(laughing)* I never invented anything but I've always had the urge to try and make something.

MG: What impact do you think you could make on the people of the United States? Are you playing a role here?

HH: I do not really have a particular role that I want to play or feel I am playing. As a Buddhist monk it is my duty to explain to those who take interest in Buddhism, a certain Buddhist technique. Beside that I have no particular aim or objective. Generally my purpose is to try to promote a sense of love, kindness, and moral principle. Those people whom I met in the last few weeks generally have a favorable attitude towards my remark. This is all I wish to contribute.

MG: Would this be the same in any country you visit?

HH: *Yes!* Wherever I go. My real message is one word—kindness, and love. During the last few weeks, wherever I go, I always talk about love and compassion. Some people may be tired of it. *(laughing)* I'm always teaching compassion, love and love and love. It is refreshing, and not complicated but simple, though difficult to practice. We want happiness, not suffering.

MG: But surely the problems in America are different from those in India or other countries where you have spoken.

HH: Certainly there are different problems, but basically I always think of the deeper level. On that level, it's more or less the same.

MG: What level would that be?

HH: The human level. Beyond different cultures and races. Beyond that, we all are, you see, the same human being. I'm talking on that level. Now we need respect; sincere relations to each other. Helping each otehr and sharing suffering on the basis of love and compassion. It is all the same humanity.

MG: What brings you to the U.S. now, rather than before?

HH: This was not my choice, it's from the U.S. Government's attitude. In the past, they were showing a red light; I did not come.

MG: When you were very young, who did you turn to for help with key decisions that changed your life?

HH: I think—collective. I sought advice from several people, as much as possible. Then I'd feel more convinced, irrespective of what name or position that person had.

MG: Now, is it the same?

HH: Yes. But now, of course, I myself have gained more experience. So much easier to make decisions.

MG: Did you find the freedom and democracy here that you had heard so much about abroad?

HH: Very open society, very open. There is a certain amount of freedom, and it seems very good.

MG: How can you get Buddhism to reach a typical American who is wedded to the car and television set without having him think it's just another cult or religion?

HH: In my mind, without involving any philosophical things or certain beliefs, just act as an honest human being. And lead an honest and good life. That is the real religion, the real Buddhist practice. All religions are on that line. That is the real necessary involvement. Besides that, as a Buddhist, whether we believe in God or rebirth is a different matter. The important thing is daily life, this very life. We must remain honest. Some little contentment is better, but men are always greedy. No time to fulfill all your desire. We must have the facilities but at the same time it is better to have contentment, and more tolerance and patience. You see, we want happiness, it comes from these thoughts. Through greed, competition, anger, hatred, you cannot get real peace, real happiness.

MG: In your Buddhist practice you have meditation. Here we have no systematic means of keeping people honest. Many attitudes, particularly in older people, are fixed. People say, "I'm too old to change," or "That's the way I am." How would you respond to this?

HH: *(laughing)* All right then. Nothing can be done.

MG: Has the role of the Dalai Lama changed very much through time?

HH: The basic attitude may not change, but there may be differences. For instance, the first four Dalai Lamas remained only religious figures, saintly scholars. The Fifth Dalai Lama also became the head of temporaral power. So it changed. In the future it may change again. But the basic purpose as the important Buddhist head, as the Buddhist son, is helping others and serving as father. That will remain the same.

MG: Regardless of whether it's called the Dalai Lama or some other name?

HH: You mean my own soul, or self?

MG: Yes.

HH: Hmm. Then you see in the past, I don't know. As a Buddhist practitioner you believe from low level, from ordinary level, through life practice trying to become better and better and better. So it's changing. But as I myself practice Bodhisattvayana, sincerely devoted to serving for others, so in future life I will probably remain in that line, and maybe become more . . . better.

MG: Are you mostly interested in speaking to younger generations?

HH: After all, in the future, the younger generation is the most important. Anyway, younger people will face the problems. Due to good communications, through television and newspaper, different countries have become closer and closer. More open, more liberal attitude towards different cultures, which is positive. The younger generation is more open to this. And they have the main responsibility for the future.

MG: How do you know what is going on in the rest of the world in your exile in Dharamsala?

HH: Through newspaper and the radio broadcast. The BBC, Voice of America, Radio Australia, Radio Moscow, Radio Peking, and so on.

MG: Do you listen to broadcasts often?

HH: Every morning I listen. And I read the magazines, *TIME* and *Newsweek*.

MG: Do you compare your role to that of the Pope's, in any way?

HH: There is not much you can compare! But of course the basic message is the same: peace and love. But then we have different reasons. I, as a Buddhist, just emphasize the human need. In the Christian theory, the reason is God, the wishes of God.

MG: Do you think there is cause for other societies to see the effects of technology on our society as backward in any way? I am suggesting that improvements in technology and high living standard have not led to greater maturity in our people.

HH: It definitely is an advanced society, and historically quite a young nation, from that respect there may be some effects. And also, it is so multi-cultured. Good effects and bad effects, with multi-culture and short history. It seems that here is a society, though I'm not criticizing, with decent facilities and life goes very easy. Sometimes the human standard, and human courage becomes spoiled, the mind becomes soft, and sometimes too superficial. It is worthwhile to think more, and deeper. Everything goes very quickly here, and that affects your mind. You think of some point to investigate, and roughly think, "Yes, this is it," without sufficiently going deeper.

MG: How do you think the biological and scientific knowledge we have about reproduction and conception has changed our attitudes towards human life? Science seems to give us so many answers to age-old mysteries and wonders.

HH: If you further investigate and talk with doctors, still there is a certain point which could not find an answer. How to perform the physical, that is more or less clear. But besides this physical self, we are experiencing the consciousness of mind. What is the nature of that consciousness, how does it exist? How much relation is there between matter and consciousness? Can consciousness produce by matter, or matter produce by consciousness? These things are yet to solve in science field. So, you see, still there are mysteries.

MG: Are you in contact with Buddhist followers inside Tibet?

HH: Yes, but my contact with Tibetans inside is mainly as a Tibetan, and not on religious matters. I try to carry the movement outside according to the wishes of the Tibetan people. For that I must know what is going on inside,

50

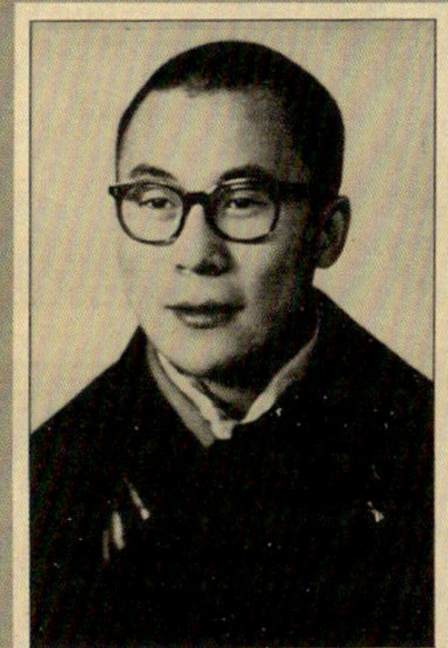

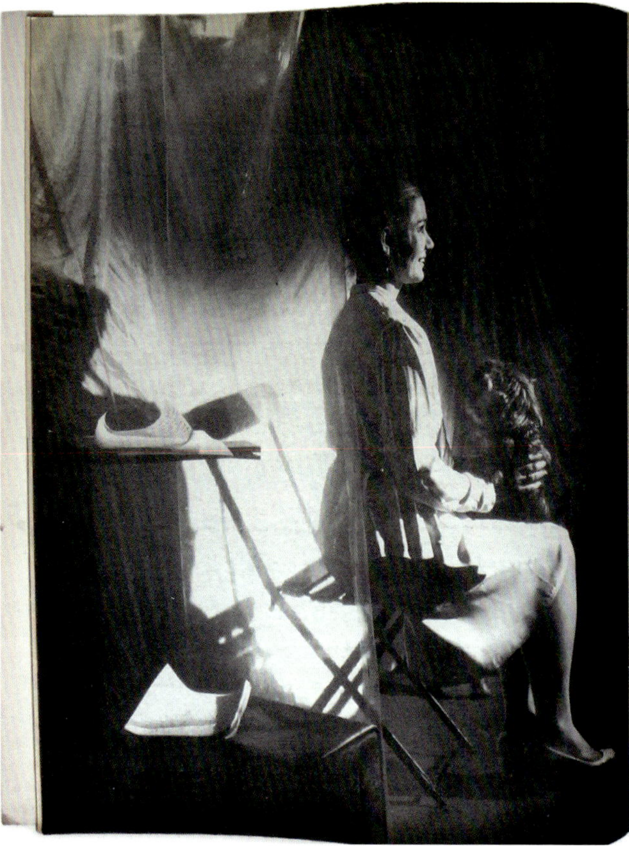

ANDY WARHOL TALKS TO LOUWRIEN WIJERS

(The conversation takes place at the Centre d'Art Contemporain in Geneva on Sunday June 8, 1980, between three and four o'clock in the afternoon. When I enter the room Andy Warhol and Bob Colacello, the editor of Interview magazine, are already seated. Andy Warhol asks me immediately if I've brought a camera and says that I should have a small automatic camera and do my own photos of all the people that I meet. He suggests the tiny Minox camera. It sounds attractive to me and I want to follow his advice, so in a more or less apologizing way I say:)

LOUWRIEN WIJERS: This time Egon (von Furstenberg) is doing the photographs...

ANDY WARHOL: On really. Oh...

L.W.: In Holland the Boymans-van Beuningen Museum of Rotterdam does a whole Beuys-year, with lots of events. For that occasion I did the book with Joseph Beuys that you had in your pocket all day, yesterday.

A.W.: Oh yes, yes. Very nice...

L.W.: At a certain point while talking to Joseph Beuys in his studio in Dusseldorf my publisher made the remark that I should now do a book with you. Joseph Beuys immediately said: 'Why don't you come to Geneva and I will introduce you to Andy.' Since we were that day discussing an article that I am going to do on Joseph Beuys for a leading Dutch magazine, it was immediately decided that you should be in the article too. The magazine reacted enthusiastically and promised ten colour pages.

A.W.: Oh wonderful...

L.W.: So nice, yes.

A.W.: Wonderful.

L.W.: So I thought we might do almost the same questions that Joseph Beuys has answered...

A.W.: That book was in English. Why was it in English?

L.W.: Because it can then go all over the world.

A.W.: Oh really...

L.W.: It will be going to Japan and...

A.W.: Oh great...

BOB COLACELLO: Where was it published?

L.W.: In Arnhem, Holland. A friend is the publisher.

B.C.: For which magazine are you writing?

L.W.: The magazine I was just mentioning is called *Avenue*...

A.W.: We get that magazine don't we? I thought that was an American magazine...

B.C.: No, that's the Park Avenue magazine.

A.W.: No, but we get one called *Avenue*...

L.W.: It's a large one...

A.W.: A large cover with...

L.W.: I gave my copy to Egon...

A.W.: No, no... I know that magazine, yes...

L.W.: It has a beautiful colour print...

A.W.: Yes, yes. It's like *Interview* it comes out...

L.W.: Monthly...

A.W.: Yes...

L.W.: I'll start with: How did you come to do the Beuys portraits?

A.W.: Well ehm. Look, when I first came to Germany, I guess when we were on tour for the movie *Flesh*, we stopped at the museum...Was it near Dusseldorf? *Andy Warhol asks Bob Colacello.*

B.C.: Darmstadt.

A.W.: Darmstadt...*Again asking Bob Colacello:* Was that the place?

B.C.: Well, that's near Frankfurt I think.

A.W.: And I saw his work there, years ago, in the museum. It was a Stroher collection, or something...And I always thought it was wonderful.

L.W.: When was that? Which year do you know?

B.C.: Seventy-one.

A.W.: Oh, was it seventy-one..?

L.W.: Oh yes...

A.W.: You know, and always I thought he was, you know, a wonderful artist...And I did not see him till...till all the people in New York used to talk about him...A gallery in New York by the name of Ron Feldman really did a big...

L.W.: Yes, I know, where he showed 'Neues vom Kojoten'...

A.W.: Yes...And then we met at the Hans Mayer Gallery...

L.W.: In Dusseldorf, yes...

A.W.: Then we came to lunch one day and I took a polaroid of him...And then somebody thought it would be a great idea if I did a painting of him...And...Who thought of the idea?

B.C.: Lucio?

A.W.: Lucio Amelio...

L.W.: From Naples, yes.

A.W.: Well, Joseph has about five people who really just adore him so much...and they're all really wonderful...And that's how it all happened. I was just going to do a portrait. You know, one portrait...and then people thought it would be great to do...

L.W.: A whole collection.

A.W.: A whole collection, yes.

L.W.: And Lucio was the person who...

A.W.: Yes, who thought of it. Lucio is just...well, I want to put him in a movie...I think he would be...well, he is...

L.W.: He was in a movie...

A.W.: Well, I know, but I ...we want to make him the star of a movie...

L.W.: He's fantastic...

A.W.: He's a wonderful actor...

L.W.: He has such a beautiful atmosphere around him, so warm...

A.W.: Yes...So that's how I got to do the portrait. But then...I had been working in diamond dust and...and I just didn't want to do another portrait, so I thought by using diamond dust this would sort of...I don't know...it would glow, and that's the reason why I did it.

L.W.: Is it very expensive, the diamond dust...

A.W.: No, no, it's just...it's left over dust...

B.C.: It's industrial dust. They actually use it to polish diamonds with.

L.W.: You don't happen to get it from Amsterdam?

A.W.: No, no. Well, it might come from Amsterdam.

L.W.: It is the big diamond city.

A.W.: Is it really? I thought Belgium was bigger...

L.W.: Antwerp. That's true, yes. But Amsterdam makes more publicity.

A.W.: Amsterdam does? Oh, there's a good reason to go to Amsterdam...

B.C.: *Asking Andy Warhol:* Have you ever been to Amsterdam?

A.W.: Well, on my trip around the world in 1955 I went to Amsterdam...

L.W.: That long ago...

A.W.: I know...God...

L.W.: They were saying that you're coming to Amsterdam.

A.W.: Well...

L.W.: Or is that not true?

A.W.: Well, I guess it's true, if it ever happens...

L.W.: No, it was the people at Avenue magazine. They said you were soon coming to Amsterdam.

A.W.: Oh really, when would that be? I might have a show...well, I mean, if somebody asks...I don't like to travel unless I do it for work, so...

L.W.: No, I thought there might be definite plans.

A.W.: There might be...

L.W.: Joseph Beuys says: 'The relationship between Andy and me is really a love story.'

A.W.: Oh, well... he kisses boys. That was the first time I ever kissed a boy...

B.C.: That's funny, whenever I tell people we are going to Europe because Andy has a show of Beuys paintings, they are thinking of 'boys', young men.

L.W.: Everybody thinks of 'boys' of course...

B.C.: He's not well known in America, except in the art world.

A.W.: But now he is very...within his art work he's very famous...Right now he is! It happened after the Guggenheim show...

L.W.: You were at the Guggenheim show, yes...

A.W.: Sure...

L.W.: What did you think of it?

A.W.: Oh, I thought it was wonderful...

L.W.: What did you think was especially wonderful about it?

A.W.: Ehm...Well, I liked it because it looked like the National Museum of History. It had a ...it changed the Guggenheim into a new look...

L.W.: Yes...

A.W.: And it was easy to see, because it was walking...I mean, they should get some ideas of that...Museums like that should get some ideas to walk around, you know, when you want to see artifacts, or, you know, things like that...it would be just kind of great, walking around in circles and seeing things... Somebody should be able...

B.C.: The Guggenheim is always like that.

A.W.: Oh I know, but it's for paintings and stuff...but this...this, you know...big...

B.C.: Objects.

A.W.: No, no. They weren't objects. They were...big...They were big tables with cases...you know, like the kinds of things that they show... ehm...

B.C.: At a store.

A.W.: At a store, yes... They were great. It was a good idea for a new kind of department store... But I always wonder why people don't commit

Louwrien Wijers photographed by Zontal at her home at 1 Herengracht, Amsterdam.

FILE Magazine, March, 1981 19

FIG. 97
"Andy Warhol talks to Louwrien Wijers"
In General Idea (active 1969–1994), *FILE Megazine*, vol. 5, no. 1, March 1981.
Photo of Louwrien Wijers by Jorge Zontel (1979 or 1980)

Photo: AA Bronson, 2021

> more inward. What is the real nature of the human "I" and the human mind? The human consciousness? Trying to control a country is rather difficult. Equally, to control the mind is difficult. But everybody is trying to control the external things. Many are making great effort. So, it is worthwhile to make effort to control our inner things. Like, you see, the arms control. These things are very good, but without being able to control anger, how to control these external arms? So, you see, real arms control is to control anger. It is essential to think more inward. Artists can express on this line. That's what I feel . . . You see, the clear weaknesses of human beings are anger and desire. On the other side are kindness and tolerance. These things, they grow without effort. Now, artists have their own way to express important messages, important ideas to the masses: to make a better human being, a better human generation, a better human future. The real peaceful harmony comes through making effort in various ways. The German artist's point is right, I think—even as an artist, not as a politician—when he remains a sincere, honest artist. Remain that and try to influence that good part into politics. That is very good.[2]

It was Andy Warhol who suggested that I should interview the Dalai Lama. Warhol came up with this idea probably because he had published the first interview with the Dalai Lama in the U.S. in his magazine *Interview* (Christmas 1979). I sent a letter to the Dalai Lama in exile in India and right away a letter came back saying, "Yes, come."

My interview with Warhol had actually come about because Joseph Beuys had suggested that I should talk with Warhol about the subjects that Beuys had brought up during my marathon interviews with him in 1978 and 1979.[3] Beuys and I covered a wide range of topics including: the Green Party; new structures for law, culture, and economics; his motto "Creativity is our real Capital"; the idea of a universal basic income, which he described as a way to make money flow like a bloodstream through the body of society; and his concept of Direct Democracy, which sought to get rid of government and political party systems, because for him democracy meant equal laws for everyone. These were among the activities that encompassed Beuys's idea of social sculpture, which viewed the world as a living sculpture;

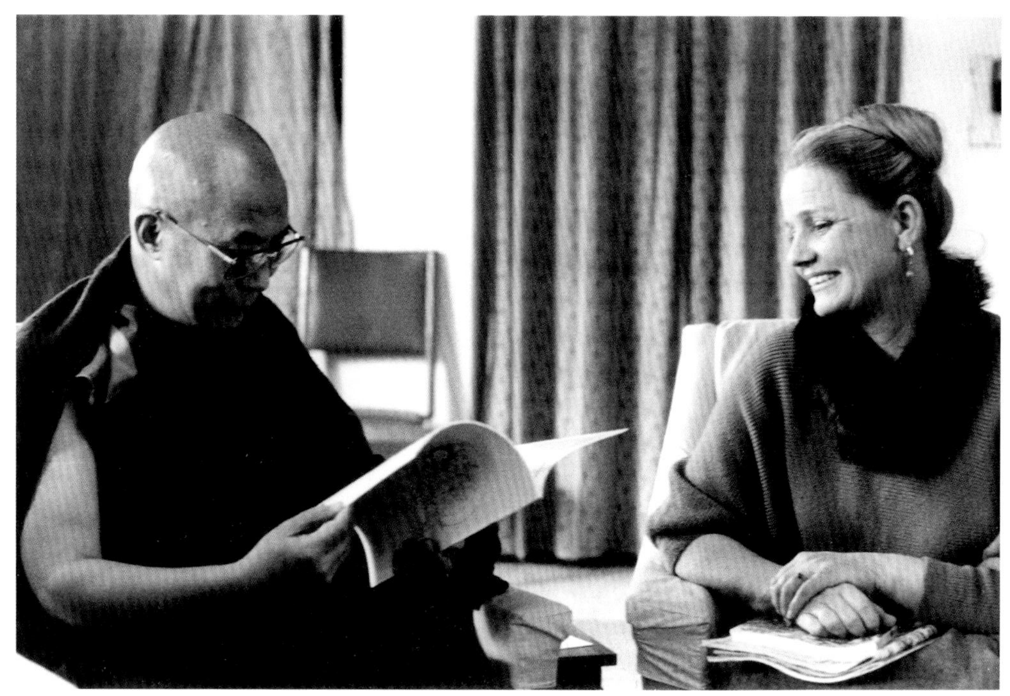

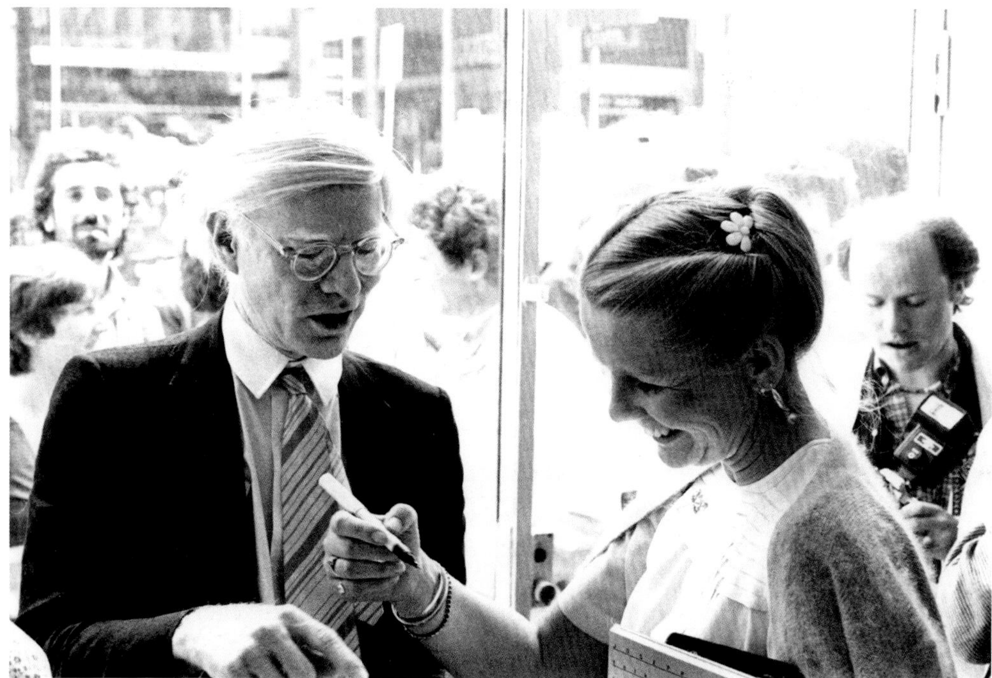

FIG. 98 (TOP)
Louwrien Wijers with His Holiness the 14th Dalai Lama
April 1982, Dharamsala, India
Courtesy of Louwrien Wijers
Photo: Jean-Paul Kool

During her third meeting with the Dalai Lama in April 1982 in India, Wijers brought with her the catalogue of Joseph Beuys's 1979 exhibition at the Guggenheim Museum, New York. The Dalai Lama carefully turned the pages and halfway through he closed the book and said, "The works by this artist are all about impermanence." In this photograph, Wijers shows the Dalai Lama a copy of *Maitreya Magazine* where she had written an article on Beuys.

FIG. 99 (BOTTOM)
Louwrien Wijers and Andy Warhol
June 1982, Geneva, Switzerland
Courtesy of Louwrien Wijers
Photo: Egon von Furstenberg

and his belief that "Everybody is an Artist," which is the most important insight that Beuys shared with the world. The final idea that Beuys shared in those interviews was this: "See in death the possibility of regeneration then we understand that the self is a free producer."

I interviewed Warhol in Geneva, Switzerland, on June 8, 1980. It was to be the longest interview that he had ever given. After my interview, I went to Beuys's studio at the Drakeplatz in Dusseldorf, Germany, to report on the meeting. I told Beuys that in answer to my question: "Who are the important people in the world right now?" Warhol replied: "All the people." When I asked: "Can you name any?" Andy said: "No, I cannot name them. My favourite people are anybody who really keeps going."

Beuys responded enthusiastically:

> "Yes, I admit. I would say the same thing. I express this in my idea that 'everybody is an artist.' So this fits exactly in my view. It has to do with the geniality existing in everybody and to find a way that everybody's creativity could find a participation and would then come to its most important development of his abilities. That is the basic thing to accomplish, to develop the ability of people and show that everybody is the most important element one can find in the world and that we should not come to some system where there are very important persons and the other not so great persons in the world."[4]

Beuys's idea that "everybody is an artist" resembles the basic Buddhist viewpoint: "Everybody has the Buddha-nature." Isn't that amazing?

When Robert Filliou talked with Beuys in 1969 for his book *Teaching and Learning as Performing Arts*, Beuys explained his view on reincarnation, saying:

> I perform something which the ratio can't understand, but which must be understood with another form of consciousness. Actually, this is a demand for an enlarged consciousness, the expanded concept of art. For instance, birth is not just a biological fact, [it is] possibly a process of incarnation. That is, man is born as a developing thing, a personality having gone through things not only from this earth, but also from other

spheres, bringing with him a great amount of experience. Birth and death are two important elements of my performances. All these actions were important to enlarge the old concept of art, making it as large as to include every human activity. The enlarged concept of art includes every human action, which can elucidate life before birth and the life which is present after death.

People are free, they are really independent beings. But very few people realize they have this freedom and actually personify this freedom. Man reaches beyond himself, he is not really an earth being. Only in part he is on this earth to achieve something. When I die I throw this carcass away and I myself move on with my thought. Thought therefore enters the world in a child, develops, and the body will later be discarded. Thought deals with this body through language. My speech is transmitted by sound waves. Thought to me is sculpture, where man can create things himself. Thought doesn't just extend into speech, but also becomes writing. Thus, writing is sculpture. Naturally I can take clay, fat or earth and form it. This is what sculpture is conventionally defined as. Intuition is the point of creation. Intuition realizes that man is free.[5]

When Robert Filliou spoke with John Cage in 1967 for this same book, the mind-direct method of education came up.

JOHN CAGE: The entire social structure must change, particularly educational structures. It will happen in all sorts of ways. One will become skeptical about what the function of education is. Ultimately what one will have to do is to give each individual from childhood a variety of experiences in which his mind is put to use, not as a memorizer of a transmitted body of information, but rather as a person who is in dialogue, A) with himself, and B) with others as though they were him too. New knowledge only comes into existence in our heads.

ROBERT FILLIOU: What I had in mind was the idea of permanent creation. There would be no difference between students and teachers.

JOHN CAGE: I think you have to begin with the notion that education is taking place without it being any effort. In the 12th century there was a great man, he lived in Tibet and his name was Milarepa. He went to a teacher who taught him absolutely nothing for years, just let him live in the house. By this process of not teaching, he ultimately educated him and Milarepa became one of the greatest teachers of Tibetan spiritual life. This story occurs over and over again in the annals of Zen Buddhism. It is this spirit of not-teaching which has been completely lost in our educational system. Our educational system in the United States is under the control of politics and economics. In truth we are forced into the accepted social structure. The educational system as it is at present distorts and enslaves the mind. The basic thing is to do nothing. The second thing would be to do what enters our heads. It should not be fixed in advance what that would be. Look at what is happening in music. Young composers distribute their music themselves. It brings about a community of individuals who have no one ruling. They are in an anarchic situation. Here the notion of basic economic security and of giving the necessities of life to all people on the planet is becoming a more and more prevalent point of view. We want a situation in which people do what they want, not what they are obliged to do.[6]

In 1977, Robert Filliou went to Canada, where he made a significant contribution to envisioning the potential of Canadian artist-run culture. Slightly later he connected art and Buddhism to a social vision. By chance I sat next to Robert at an AICA (Association Internationale des Critiques d'Art) meeting in October 1981 in Amsterdam. He had just returned to Europe from Canada. I had first met Filliou in 1964 as one of the group of Fluxus artists that met regularly in Paris. In Amsterdam I heard that Robert and his wife, Marianne, had become devoted students of Tibetan Buddhism. I informed them that their good friend Joseph Beuys wanted to make a permanent cooperation with the Dalai Lama and had asked me to help make that happen. "It's not surprising that we all find each other again," Robert replied.

Right after my April 15, 1981, interview with the Dalai Lama, I sent Beuys a "Free Tibet" postcard that said: "Dear Joseph, you have a brother here in the Himalayas, the Dalai Lama thinks exactly the same about the problems of today as you do." Beuys's

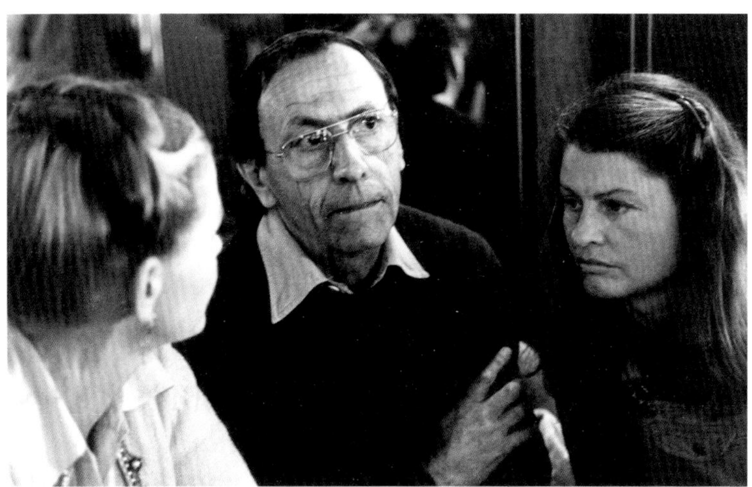

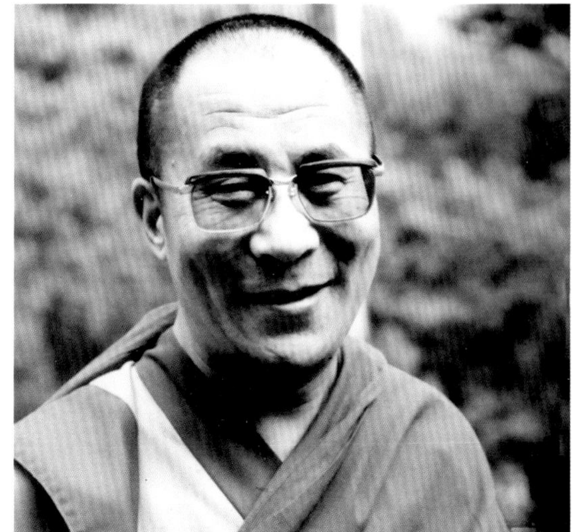

spontaneous reply when I later phoned him was: "I want to make a permanent cooperation with the Dalai Lama. This way we will make Eurasia happen and you have to do it."

Beuys was aware that Europe and Asia had always been connected. In his hometown Kleve the story was that Genghis Khan, Emperor of the Mongol Empire, had come as far as Kleve in the 13th century to accomplish his largest contiguous empire in history. Beuys had read many books when he was young about Genghis Khan, and his deep wish was to bring Europe and Asia back together. Many artworks Beuys made had Eurasia in their title. To restore the Eurasian culture was his goal.

On November 4, 1981, Beuys sent a proposal to the Dalai Lama to request a meeting, saying: "It is necessary to come to a permanent cooperation, a permanent embracement of East and West, that has to appear like a light from a lighthouse that everybody can see." Beuys explained he was working on his social sculpture and said that his Free International University would help with the execution of plans. Beuys informed the Dalai Lama that his other initiatives were his "Organization for Direct Democracy," his "Green Movement," and his Green Party. A positive answer came again, right away.

Filliou felt that to prepare Beuys for a fruitful private audience with the Dalai Lama, he should first meet Lama Sogyal Rinpoche, one of Filliou's teachers. I arranged for Beuys and Lama Sogyal to meet in Paris on January 29, 1982:

FIG. 100 (LEFT)
Robert Filliou with his wife, Marianne Staffels (right), and Louwrien Wijers (left)
October 27, 1982, Bonn, Germany
Photo: Cathrien van Ommen

Robert Filliou and his wife, Marianne, came all the way from the Dordogne, France, to Bonn on the occasion of Beuys's meeting with the Dalai Lama. Even though there had been no formal announcement of the event, the rumour had spread and a group of about sixty people gathered in the hotel where the Dalai Lama was staying. Those gathered had a chance to meet His Holiness briefly during a reception in the late afternoon.

FIG. 101 (RIGHT)
Jorge Zontal (Italy/Canada, 1944–1994)
Portrait of His Holiness the Fourteenth Dalai Lama, Dharamsala, India, April 1982
Photograph
Courtesy of Louwrien Wijers
© AA Bronson/Artist's Estate

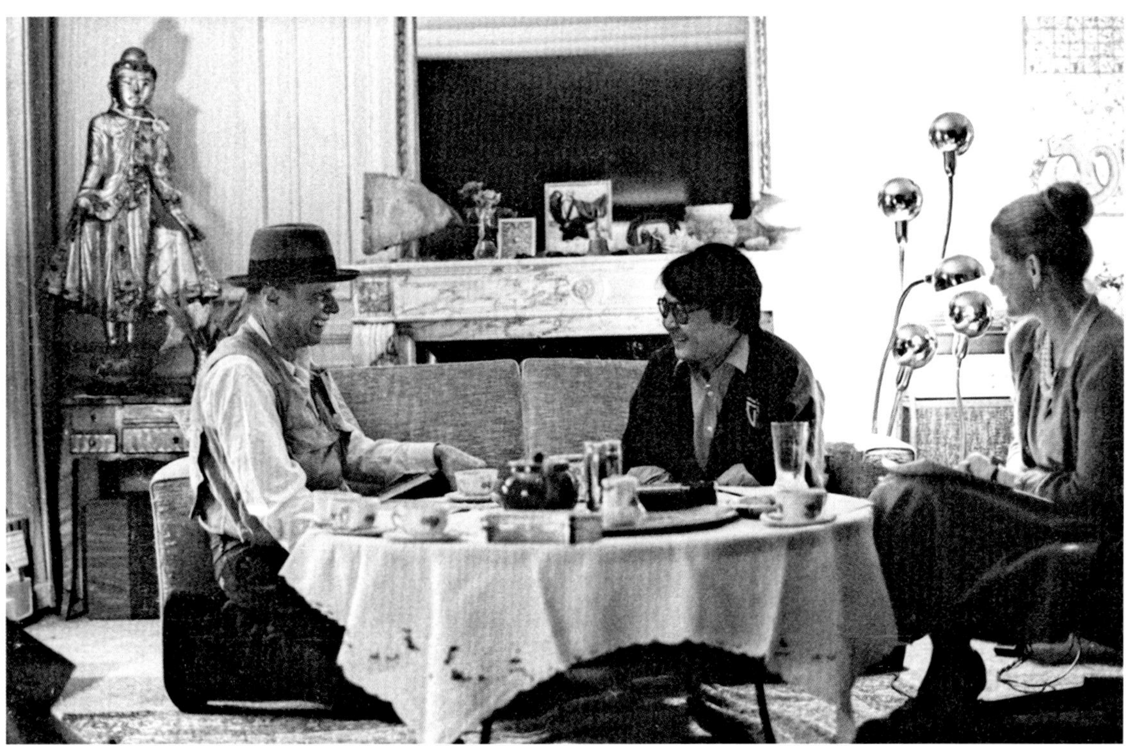

FIG. 102
Joseph Beuys with Lama Sogyal Rinpoche
January 29, 1982, Paris, France
© Anneliese Wolf

Louwrien Wijers recalls that Joseph Beuys's meeting with Lama Sogyal Rinpoche was very entertaining and demonstrated that Beuys knew a lot more about Buddhism than expected. The result was that Sogyal Rinpoche sent Wijers back to see the Dalai Lama to introduce him to the work of Beuys.

JOSEPH BEUYS: Firstly, we have to offer spiritual help. Secondly my Free International University should help to come to a real other concept of dealing with cultural ideas, economic ideas and law ideas, so we can come to a new idea of the human being.

I have an interest in the Buddhist philosophy and I am a friend of the tantric intention, and of incarnation and reincarnation. I have always felt that the tantric Buddhist form would have the most possibilities. I think it is almost a necessity that the Buddhas and Bodhisattvas work through life.

LAMA SOGYAL: Tantra is a spiritual art. There is some way of connecting that approach with art as it is happening now.

JOSEPH BEUYS: It has to come to a wider understanding of art, related to every person's doing.

LAMA SOGYAL: The tantric teachings is where really art could be carried on to. The artist has a tremendous original mind.

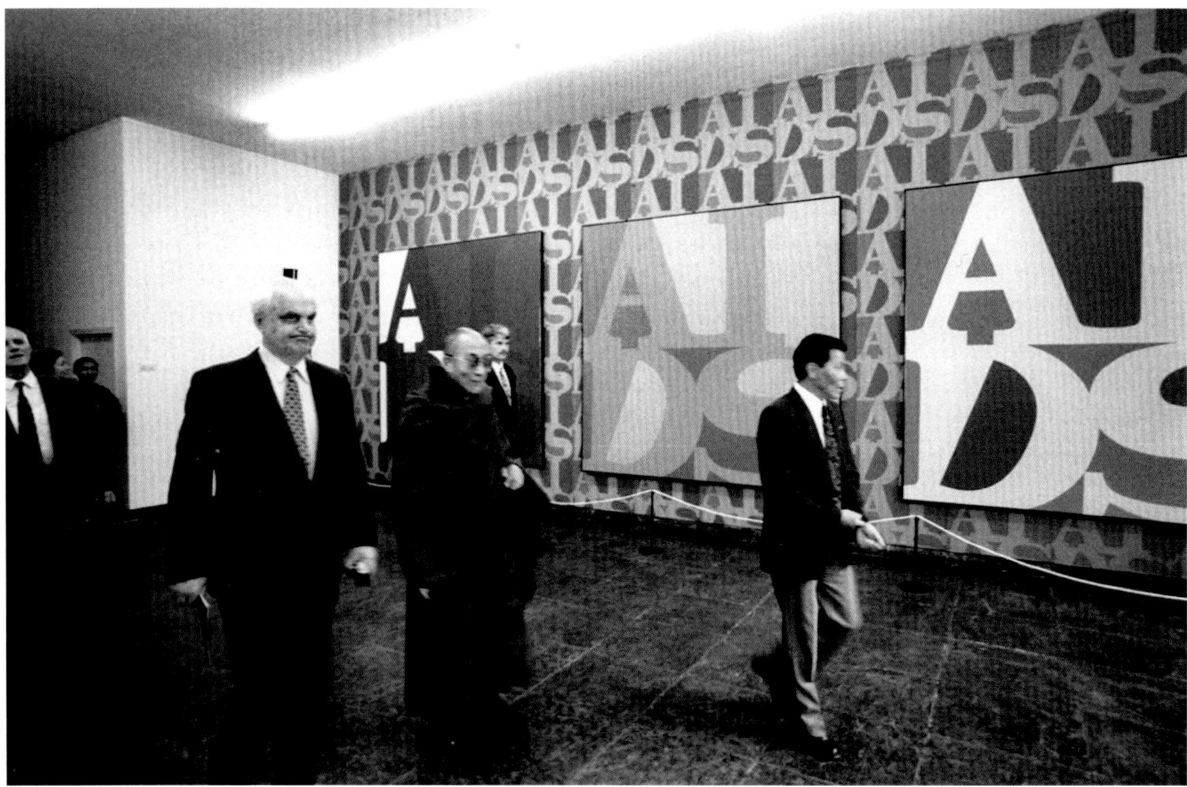

FIG. 103
His Holiness the Dalai Lama accompanied by Russian economist Stanislav Menshikov walking past the *AIDS* wall by General Idea at the Museum Fodor, Amsterdam, 1990
© Cary Markerink

JOSEPH BEUYS: Bring humankind and the world to another stage.

LAMA SOGYAL: In the highest teachings of Buddha, in tantra, in Dzogchen, it says that the transmission is first mind-direct, no signs, no words.

JOSEPH BEUYS: Unity itself.

LAMA SOGYAL: True, unity itself. Then by signs, then by word of mouth. The oral transmission is actually a mind-to-mind contact. And art; my personal understanding is that art draws a balance between pure mind and the expression.

JOSEPH BEUYS: That is really true. It comes to inner hearing.

LAMA SOGYAL: I think the point would be for Louwrien to again talk with His Holiness to explain about your work.[7]

I was given another audience with the Dalai Lama on April 12, 1982. General Idea from Toronto, three artists working together, who had published my long interview with Andy Warhol in their periodic publication *FILE Megazine*, were enthusiastic about my next meeting with the Dalai Lama. They wanted to come, foremost because Jorge Zontal wanted to photograph the Dalai Lama. AA Bronson, Zontal and I travelled together from New Delhi to Dharamsala. On the day before the audience we were given plenty of time to photograph the Dalai Lama, who had just come out of a three-week retreat. By far the most unique portrait of the Dalai Lama, I feel, was made by Zontal that day.

Because my teacher Lama Thubten Yeshe was in Dharamsala at the time, we went to visit him to speak about art.

I ASKED: Could Lama say anything about how contemporary art and Tibetan Buddhism could work together?"

LAMA YESHE: You see, Tibetans have already a history of art. Buddhism is gathering to express it intellectually; to express it visually we have art as thangka. It is very important to have artists to express the thinking picture into the physical form. Then people react. But when I talk Buddha dharma, like bla, bla, bla, bla. You know what I mean?...

JORGE ZONTAL: [*laughs*]

LAMA YESHE: And psychologically, how the mind is going, they get some kind of picture, you know. Human beings get a gross picture, but still don't understand. Therefore, we need, beyond concept and philosophy, we need artists to input—to give impact. You understand?

AA BRONSON: Hmm...

LAMA YESHE: Artists, of course, are the way. Artists can express. Oh, I think, artists you can tremendously explain the internal world, you know, deep philosophy, any level, any concept, lower and higher, or middle; on any level, you can explain, I feel. So, therefore, art is very important. What kind of lifestyle, what kind of thinking, what process to bring in this world. I think they are responsible. But unfortunately, you know, many artists in the West nowadays went completely samsara [cycle of birth, misery, and death caused by karma]. You understand? Completely grasping and stuff. Artists have to respond, because they are in demand. The public wants that kind of grasping object image. There is money, so there you put the energy. Isn't it?

JORGE ZONTAL: Yes. [*laughs*]

LAMA YESHE: Unfortunately.

JORGE ZONTAL: Yes.

LAMA YESHE: But it can be done the other way too. You know, something really pure, profound, deep and of universal level—a benefit for all living beings. I believe in that concept. Also, in Tibetan art, we think that the art of the appearance is speaking some reality. No words, you know. That is more powerful, that brings more reality, a more truthful result than just words, bla bla, but you don't make condition. Artists make condition. We are working together, you know. We bring some higher consciousness for the human being, isn't it? That is what we try...[8]

The Gelug Lama, Kyabje Zong Rinpoche, tutor of the Dalai Lama and Lama Yeshe's teacher, gave an important series of lessons in Upper Dharamsala. Bronson and Zontal came to listen but were late. The moment they appeared in the doorway quite near to his throne, Zong Rinpoche stopped teaching, greeted them with great respect, and asked the front row to make space for the two to sit right in front of him. Zontal later followed lessons given by Lama Yeshe and other lamas all over Europe. When I sat at his deathbed in 1995 I saw how he was able to keep both his hands in a mudra when his last breath had left. I admired him for this fabulous skill.

In 1976, I took the Trans-Siberian railroad to experience how large Eurasia is. It took fourteen days from Holland to Tokyo, where the line ends. I went into a Zen temple to do an intense retreat. In 1977, I found Tibetan Buddhism; lamas came to Amsterdam to initiate and teach us. I felt that Buddhism was nothing new but is ingrained in us. Buddhism has been with us

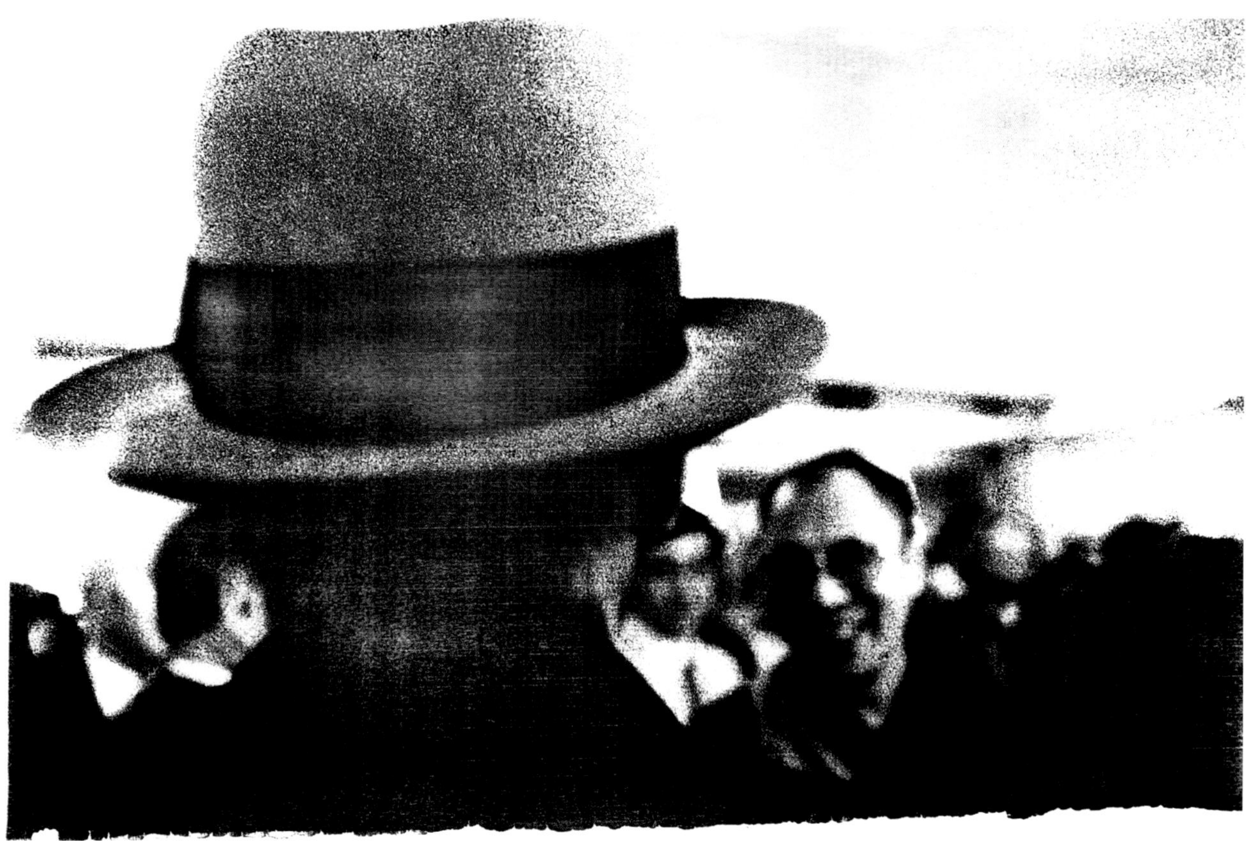

FIG. 104
Joseph Beuys and His Holiness the 14th Dalai Lama
October 27, 1982, Bonn, Germany
Courtesy of Louwrien Wijers
Photo: Ute Klophaus

This photograph was taken at the reception after the meeting between artist Joseph Beuys and His Holiness the Dalai Lama. When His Holiness entered the room, he immediately recognized Beuys and came up to him with a big smile to shake hands. Wijers explains that the photographs taken at the meeting could not be published. Therefore, aside from this somewhat enigmatic image, there is no publishable photo-documentation of the meeting.

and in us for ages. Maybe I must emphasize the concept of *budh*, "to awaken," the power to accomplish our enlightened mind, rather than Buddhism. It is *budh* that is ingrained in us, and may have come to us with different names in times before Gautama Buddha.

Beuys said in Japan in 1984: "To make human creativity definitive, humans should again be central in the world and step forward as creators, as divine beings." Beuys alludes to the connection between his idea that "everybody is an artist" and the concept that "everybody has a Buddha-nature." This connection is the basis of his idea of social sculpture.

The Dalai Lama affirmed: "The ultimate deepest consciousness is called the Buddha-nature. When you concentrate on that, the deluded mind becomes inactive."

That "everybody is an artist" resembles "everybody has a Buddha-nature" is finally not so amazing, because creativity can only be experienced when the deluded mind is inactive and our direct perception is active. Only in the very subtle consciousness of the non-dual mind can enlightenment be experienced and realized.

At my symposium *Art meets Science and Spirituality in a changing Economy* (1990), the priest and scholar Raimon Panikkar stated: "One of the crises in the present world is that we have relegated art to just a secondary role, whereas art is more essential than science. Man cannot survive without art. Competitive society is a natural outcome of the loss of the artistic dimension."[9]

The scientist Francisco Varela pronounced at that same event: "I have come to the conclusion that what the visual arts does is to draw out the invisible into the visible. Perception precisely is that drawing out into the visible something that wasn't there as visible previously. The creativity that a visual artist manifests is not unlike the creativity the evolution of life manifests to shape worlds. We can learn a lot from art. Give up the idea of objectivity. Western science evaporates."[10]

LOUWRIEN WIJERS (b. 1941) is a Dutch Fluxus artist who, through the 1980s and 1990s, was instrumental in making connections between contemporary avant-garde artists and important Buddhist teachers. Wijers considers writing and speaking as forms of "mental sculpture" where art and life coincide towards a social purpose. She undertook and published book-length interviews with key artists and Tibetan teachers (1978–1987), and in 1990 initiated the groundbreaking symposium *Art meets Science and Spirituality in a changing Economy*, hosted by the Stedelijk Museum, Amsterdam, and which was shown on television in fifty-two countries. These interviews, published texts, conferences, and associated documents define a form of social sculpture.

NOTES

1 Louwrien Wijers, "Robert Filliou talks about the Integration of Dharma into his work as an artist," in *His Holiness the Fourteenth Dalai Lama of Tibet talks to Louwrien Wijers*, (Holland: Kantoor voor Cultuur Extracten, n.d.), pp. 65–67.

2 Ibid., pp. 14–16

3 Louwrien Wijers, *Joseph Beuys talks to Louwrien Wijers* (Holland: Kantoor voor Cultuur Extracten, 1980).

4 Louwrien Wijers, "Joseph Beuys talks to Louwrien Wijers," in *Writing as Sculpture 1978–1987* (London: Academy Editions, 1996), pp. 93–95

5 Robert Filliou, *Lehren und Lernen als Auffuerungskuentste / Teaching and Learning as Performing Arts* (Cologne and New York: Verlag Gebr. Konig, 1970), pp. 168–173.

6 Ibid., pp. 114–118.

7 Louwrien Wijers, "Joseph Beuys and Lama Sogyal Rinpoche talk about a possible cooperation with the 14th Dalai Lama," in *His Holiness the Fourteenth Dalai Lama of Tibet talks to Louwrien Wijers*, pp. 78-91.

8 Louwrien Wijers, Lama Yeshe, General Idea, unpublished interview transcript (1982).

9 Louwrien Wijers, ed., *Art meets Science and Spirituality in a changing Economy* (London: Academy Editions, 1996), p. 130.

10 Francisco Varela and Raimon Panikkar, in unpublished transcript of July 2017 retreat viewing 64 hours' unedited film of the Art meets Science and Spirituality in a changing Economy symposium.

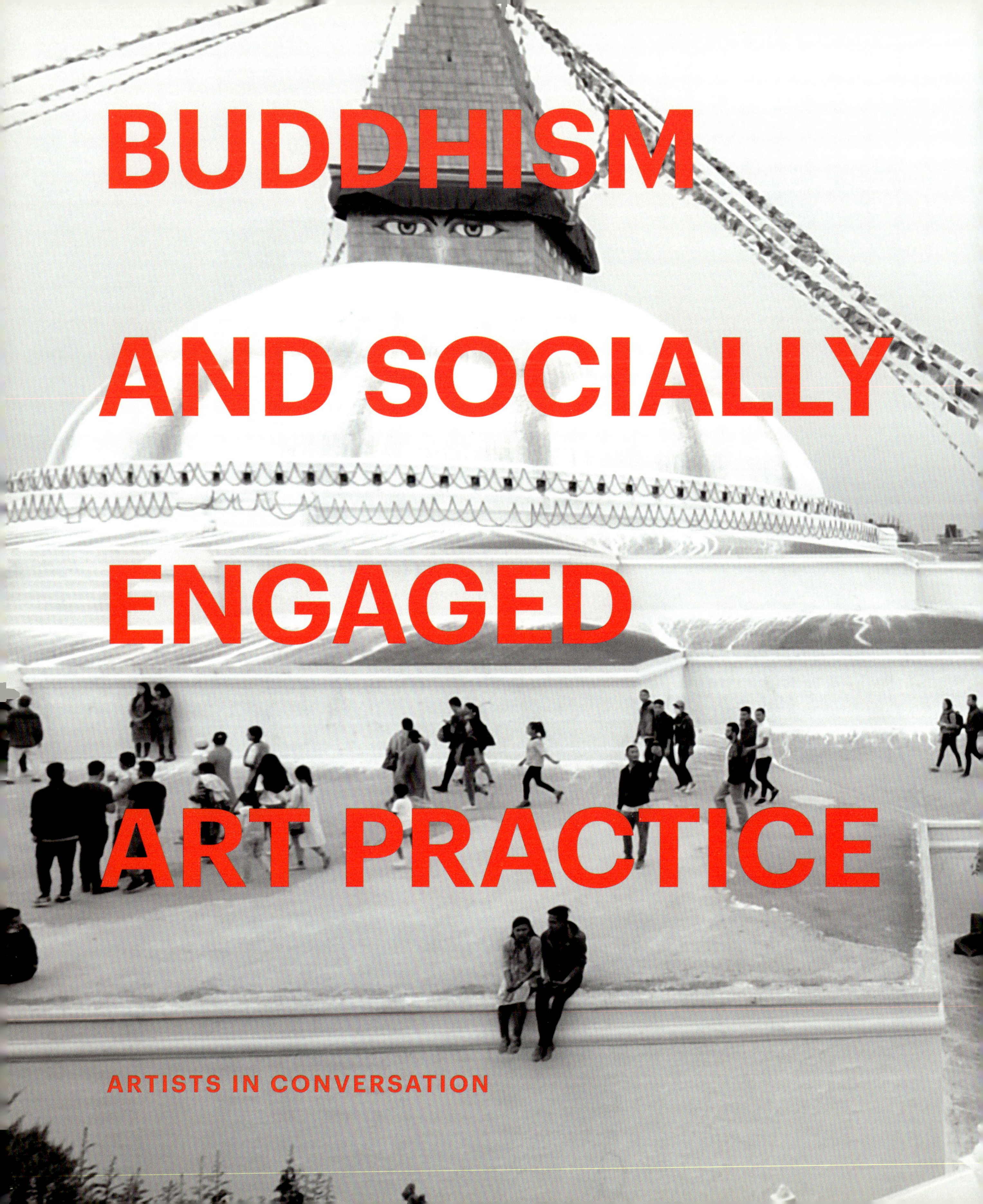

BUDDHISM AND SOCIALLY ENGAGED ART PRACTICE

ARTISTS IN CONVERSATION

THE FOLLOWING CONVERSATION took place on Sunday, October 27, 2019, at the University of Victoria as part of a three-day research convening designed to inform the exhibition *In the Present Moment*. The discussion reflected on the idea of Buddhism as a source for socially engaged art practice. In the late 1970s, the concept of Engaged Buddhism had a significant impact on artists concerned with social and civil rights issues. Engaged Buddhism, a term coined by the Vietnamese Zen monk Thich Nhat Hanh, proposed that the insights gained from meditation and Dharma teaching should have social and political application. Engaged Buddhists share the belief that mindful social action assists towards the universal relief of suffering. Since the 1970s, Engaged Buddhism has had an impact on approaches to socially engaged art practice and has informed ideas related to the role of the artist in society, including concepts of activism and notions of social change. This discussion explored how artists drawing on Buddhist concepts and methods situated new kinds of interpersonal and interspecies relations, examining the relationship between art and the broader social and environmental context.

PARTICIPANTS

Oliver Kellhammer, Lecturer in Sustainable Systems,
Parsons School of Design, NYC

Susan Stewart, Founding Dean, Faculty of Culture + Community,
Emily Carr University of Art + Design, Vancouver

Mali Wu, Professor, Graduate Institute of Transdisciplinary Art,
National Kaohsiung Normal University, Taiwan

Moderator: Marcus Boon, writer, journalist, and Professor of English,
York University, Toronto

MARCUS BOON: Hi, everybody. I never tell anyone this, but every time I speak, I say a Tara mantra beforehand, so I'm sharing my Buddhist secret with you. I also want to say, for myself, I dedicate my remarks to my friend John Giorno, who died about two weeks ago. John was a great American Buddhist poet, artist, and queer activist—going back to the Vietnam War and his activities with Abbie Hoffman. He had something called the AIDS Treatment Project in the '80s and '90s, where basically he committed to treating strangers who had AIDS, who needed money or love. So he collected money from different sources, and then without discrimination he would just give people whatever it was that they wanted, as much as he was able to give them, and that was the project. When I first started getting into Buddhism, I was excited to meet Buddhist artists and poets, so I started interviewing them. John was one of the first artists I interviewed, and he basically refused to admit that he was a Buddhist poet. He would just say, "I'm a Buddhist, and I'm a poet. I believe in compartmentalization." In other words, he didn't want the two things to mix, even though half of his poems were called things like "Guru Rinpoche." That completely stumped me—it was not what I was expecting at all. So I approached with trepidation, talking about Buddhism and art, and here we are. I'm going to ask each of the panellists to speak briefly about the connections between Buddhism, art, and social engagement.

OLIVER KELLHAMMER: I will start with an anecdote from very early childhood. So, imagine I'm about three years old, in a sandbox, in the back of a sixplex apartment in southern Ontario, near Toronto. My father worked night shifts in a Styrofoam factory. He was the superintendent of the apartment complex, and he made a sandbox for me and the other children who were living there. Our favourite thing to do with our little plastic shovels was to dig down into the sand, past all the cat droppings and everything, to where the earthworms lived. Our favourite thing to do would be to pick up the earthworms, cut them in half with our shovels, and watch them wiggle. We did this every day, and it was kind of like a weird demonic child torture practice. So one day my father came out of the building, and he looked at me, and he looked at the worms wiggling in my little plastic bucket, and he started sobbing. Now he was not really "sobbing," but I was too young and naive to understand that. He was saying, "Oh, I am

FIG. 105
Oliver Kellhammer
(Germany/Canada/USA, 1959–)
Healing the Cut/Bridging the Gap, 1997
Site-specific eco-art project
Courtesy of the artist

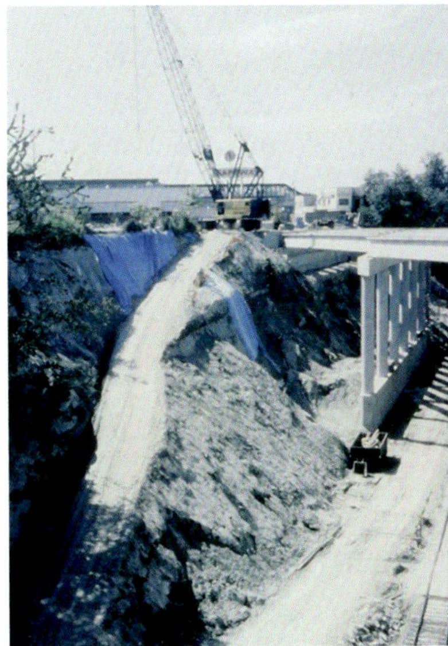

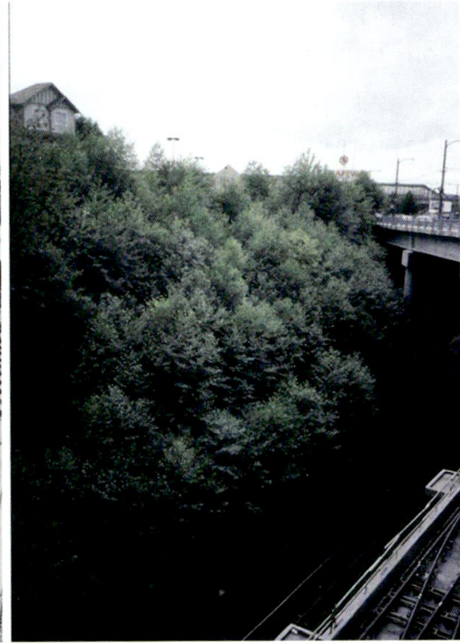

in pain, I hurt so much, you cut me in half and now I hurt!" Then I burst into real tears. That memory has stayed with me as an empathetic moment. It was when I first realized that there was suffering in the world, and that I could be responsible for the suffering of other beings, who I didn't understand had the ability to experience suffering. This was a really important moment for me, and ever since then I've been trying to do work that somehow addresses the subjectivity of the non-human, and also to try to reduce suffering in the world, as best I can.

The other topic that I was very moved by was, "Where do I end, and where does the worm begin? Where is the line between myself and other?" This has been troubling me as an artist since I got going. I eventually met my wife, who's a Zen Buddhist priest and novelist, Ruth Ozeki, who some of you have known. I was telling her all these things while I had been reading Bruno Latour or Donna Haraway, and going on about multi-species models and stuff, and she just says, "We do that. Buddhists have known this for two thousand years. Why is this new?" We were constantly having this conversation between art theory, my own mental torture about trying to do "good" in the world, and Zen Buddhism. So there have been remarkable congruences that I'm continuously discovering still twenty-five years after having gotten together with Ruth. So that's something of an ongoing thread in my practice.

Then there's this notion of ephemerality. So much of our practice as social practitioners is about starting something—working with communities, working with ecosystems, working with complicated situations—and then removing ourselves. I think that's a fundamental part of it. So, we're very non-monumental; we work outside of this notion of monuments, trying to decide, "What can I *not* do?" It's a very important question to ask yourself as an artist. We're so motivated by productivity, we've internalized Fordian notions of production, but to actually stand back and ask, "What can I *not* do? When is it time to let the intervention start to have its own life? When is it time to let the people and ecosystems that we have somehow affected or helped, start to take care of themselves and evolve beyond us as the artist?" The artist can then go away and be forgotten about. So, I think it's very important, certainly in my practice, to step back and say, "This is fine, I don't need to do anything anymore." And the older I get, the less I want to do. So really my ambition is to do more and more of less and less. So it's kind of laziness, but it's also a way of being able to do other things that you then too eventually remove yourself from. So that's been an ongoing theme.

These are little floating motes of ideas that hopefully we can build on—the idea of not making work that's *about* something but *is* something. So, my work is not about the environment, it *is* the environment, and after a while the environment doesn't need me anymore. So that's the difference between this kind of practice and other practices.

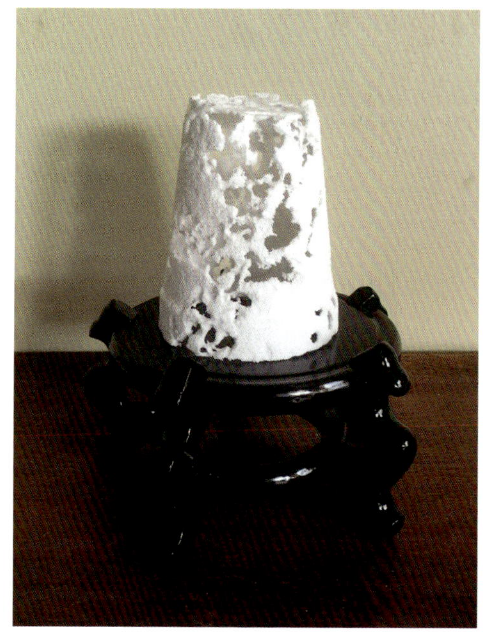

FIG. 106
Oliver Kellhammer
(Germany/Canada/USA, 1959–)
Plastivore, 2018
Styrofoam and wooden stand
20 × 10 cm
Courtesy of the artist

MALI WU: I really appreciate that Haema invited me to be here because when I got the invitation, I thought, "Oh, I am not a practising Buddhist—what could I contribute to a panel?" But in Taiwan, Buddhism is embedded within our whole culture, and within our daily lives. I've really learned a lot from the panels over the past couple of days, and they've reminded me of the paths I have gone down, so I thank you for that, very much.

The first thing I would like to share has to do with my learning process. I began my artistic studies in the 1980s in Vienna, and I stayed there for one and a half years before I went to Kunstakademie Dusseldorf Academy, where I stayed until 1986. While I was in Vienna, I was struggling a lot because I came from a totally different culture. I didn't study art in Taiwan previously, but I was very interested in theatre, so that's why

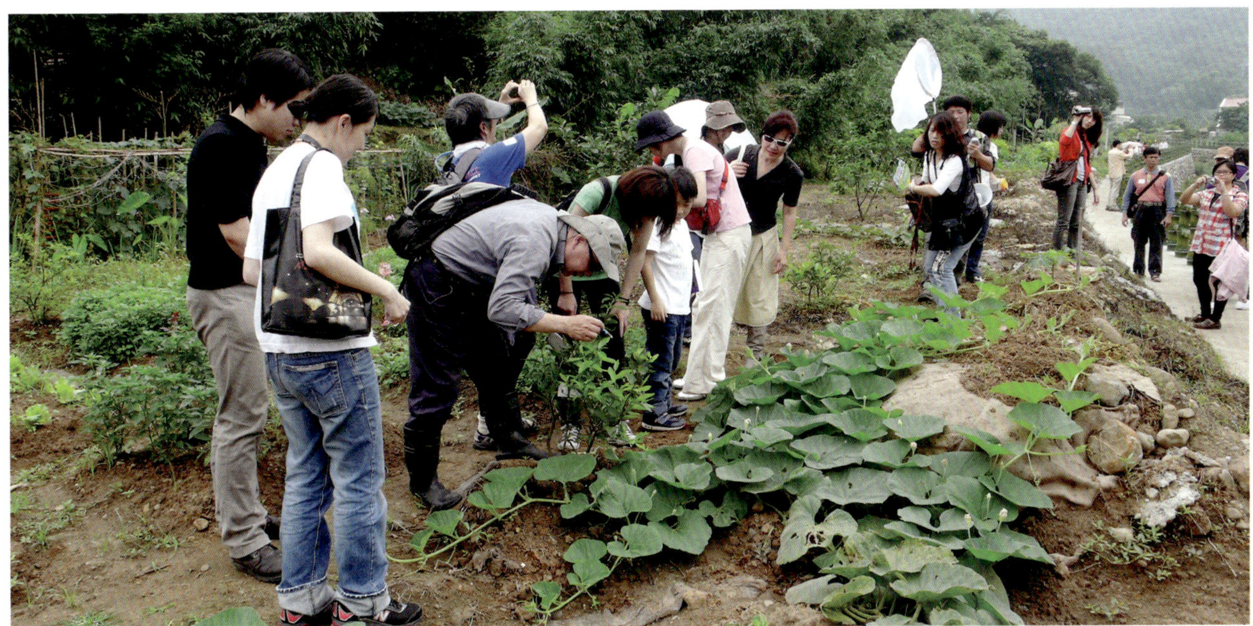

FIG. 107
Mali Wu (Taiwan, 1957–)
Plum Tree Creek Project,
2010–2012
Socially engaged art project,
New Taipei City, Taiwan
Courtesy of the artist
Photo: Bamboo Curtain Studio

I went to Vienna. While I was there, that was about the time when "action art" was gaining popularity, and there were many iconic male artists like Hermann Nitsch who had very strong egos to express. I found it very difficult, because I'm not this kind of person, but it really helped me to think of the cultural differences. I realized that I was trying to learn art in a Western world, but the art that I was confronting was actually from a totally different cultural background. I came from a world where, as I said, Buddhism or Daoism was really embedded in our daily lives. We were taught not to have ego, and not to be so egocentric. So I really had difficulties learning art in the Western world, because I realized that art is actually about individualism, about expressing your own ego. Then when I moved to Dusseldorf I learned of Fluxus and the group ZERO, and my professor was Gunther Uecker, whose work was really very meditative. At the time there were a lot of Fluxus events in the academy, so I began to encounter a kind of art that is really very different from the art I had experienced in Vienna. I began to read texts by these performance artists, and I realized that they were very much influenced by Buddhism or Daoism, and they really helped me to find my own path, to find a way that I could use art to express myself. So, I would say that this was a very interesting experience,

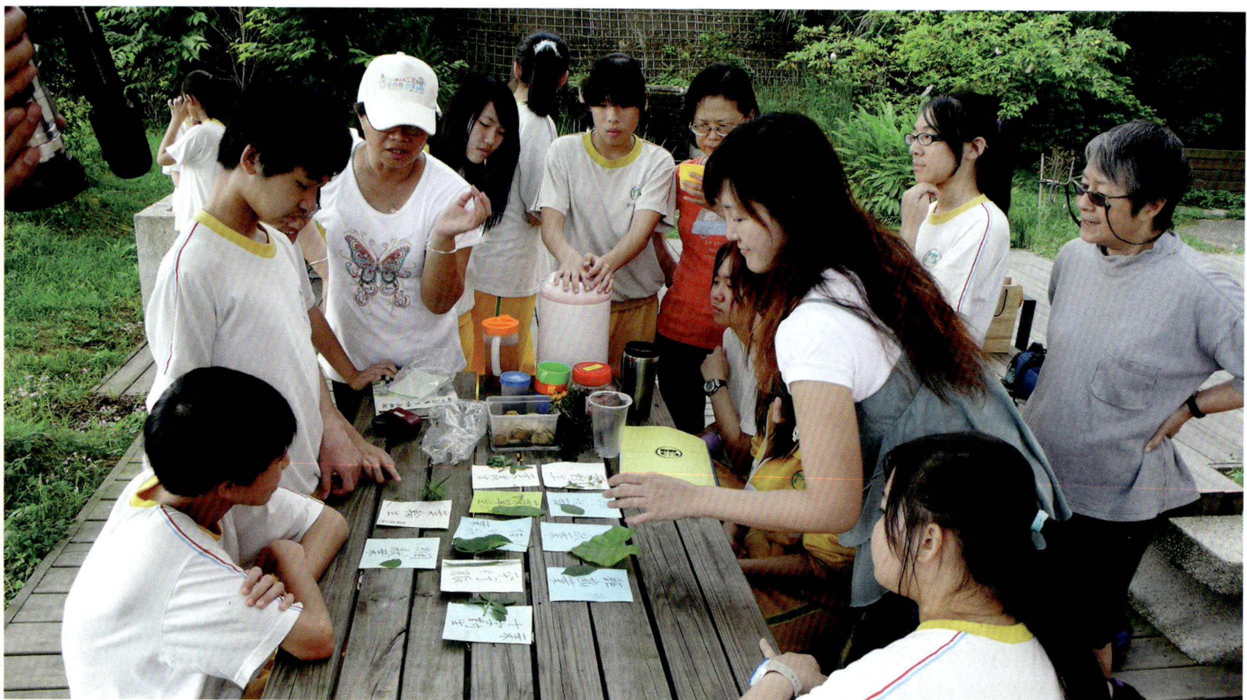

FIG. 108
Mali Wu (Taiwan, 1957–)
Plum Tree Creek Project, 2010–2012
Socially engaged art project, New Taipei City, Taiwan
Courtesy of the artist
Photo: Bamboo Curtain Studio

because over the past few days I've heard from so many of you who are living in the Western world but talking about Buddhism, while I come from the Asian world, where Buddhism or Daoism is really embedded in daily life—although it could also be a kind of ideology. So I felt that my learning about Zen, Buddhism, or Daoism actually came from Western art, through my study of the Fluxus artists. It really had an impact on my art practice, and my turn towards "social sculpture" particularly came from Joseph Beuys, who was also teaching in Kunstakademie.

The work I had done in Dusseldorf during this time was quite meditative and very playful. But in 1986 when I went back to Taiwan, that was the time when a lot of political protests were happening in Taiwan. I was confronted with tension in our society, and I was asking myself, "How can art deal with this?" So, that's how the term *social sculpture* came to my mind, as I was trying to understand the relationship between art and society.

In the year 2000, I was invited to conduct a workshop with a group of women who had non-art educations. At the very beginning they would say, "Oh, we don't know how to make art." So I asked them to begin by drawing a line, and try expressing

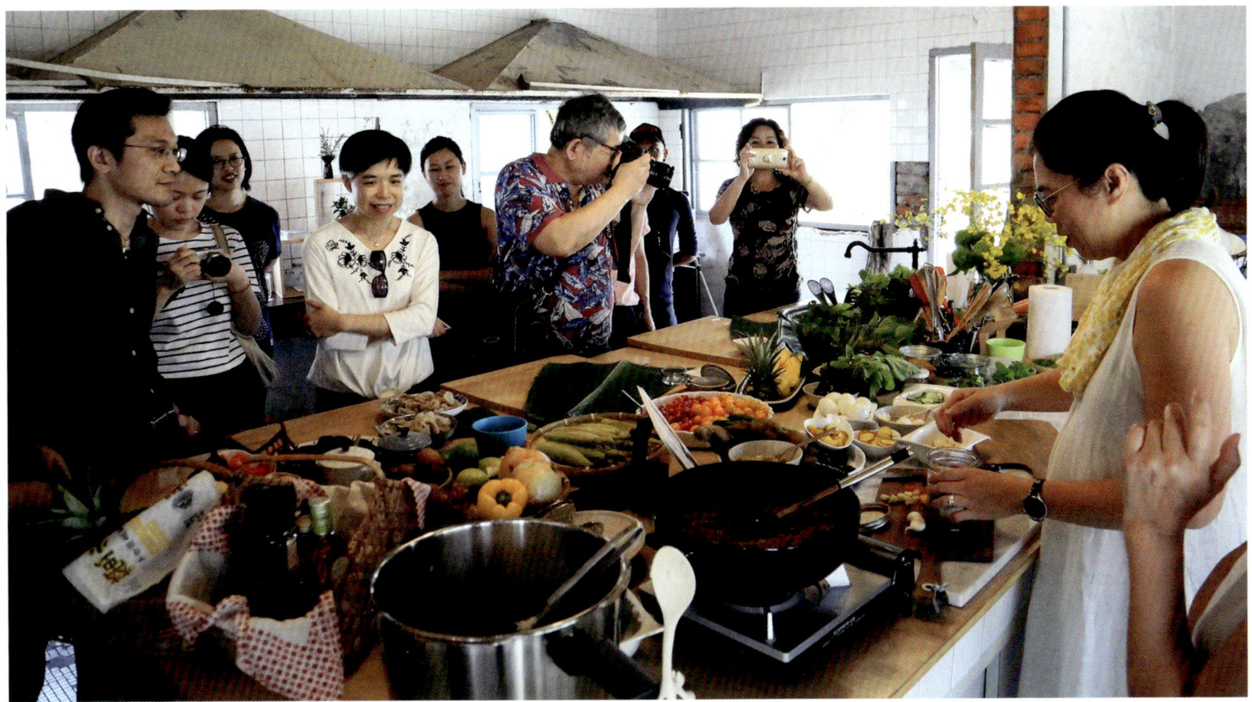

FIG. 109
Mali Wu (Taiwan, 1957–)
Cijin's Tongue, 2016–ongoing
Socially engaged art project in Kaohsiung, Taiwan
Photo: Ding-An Ji

themselves through simple lines. After the success of the exercise, everyone became an artist and could really express themselves very well. This experience was very inspiring for me, I felt that I had learned again what art means to us. These experiences help me reflect on the art education in Taiwan, because most of the art education was really focusing on producing artists, instead of helping people to understand or to appreciate art. So that's how I began to focus on how to engage the public through art. I was always asking myself, "Who is your audience? Whom are you addressing through art?" Through this internal dialogue I realized that art can be a platform for social interaction, and then eventually it developed into a kind of so-called "socially engaged art."

I really learned a lot from these kinds of relational art processes, because art is not just about the artists but about the aesthetic experiences: we share, understand, and appreciate with our different senses, our body and spirit. I also began to read books by Suzanne Lacy, Grant Kester, and, later, *Relational Aesthetics* by Nicolas Bourriaud, etc. I understand that I am working towards a different intention of making art; in some way it relates to education in arts—an art which is not about our own ego, but about communicating, experiencing, and sharing. It's an art of togetherness, about creating moments together.

SUSAN STEWART: I've been an artist for over forty-five years, so I'm in the same bracket as Oliver, Mali, and Marcus. In the beginning I was a very ambitious young artist, full of steam. When I emerged out of art school, I was ready to rock and roll, but I hit barriers immediately outside the gate: the barrier of sexism, the barrier of homophobia, and the barrier of class, and these were huge obstacles. So, the first twenty years of my career was spent battling systems. I found like-minded artist friends and together we pitched battles in these three areas—women's liberation, queer liberation, and class. It was an exhilarating time, but it ended up making me angrier in the end, and I was already pretty angry—to the point where things became very meaningless. I couldn't make sense of the world; I couldn't make sense of injustice. I know quite a few social practice artists, and I think one thing that we all have in common is a finely attenuated intolerance for injustice. It seems like that switch goes on as children, and never switches off in adulthood.

At the same time, I was also very curious about spirituality. I knew that I had this big lack of something important in life, but I couldn't quite put my finger on it. So anyway, twenty years in, I'm really angry—I'm kind of a spiritual seeker—I'm suffering a lot, I'm seeing a lot of suffering in the world, and I can't make sense of any of it. Then I discovered Buddhism and made a strong connection to Dharma. Soon after, I found a perfect teacher and the Vajrayana Tibetan lineage, and I just decided to go for it. I turned over everything and thought, "I am going to seriously look into this Buddha Dharma," because I had hit a wall, so why not? I went in 100 percent, and I spent the next fifteen years studying Buddhism intensively. Fortunately, I had a very good guide, so that helped with moving things along when I started practising. I started at the beginning, and when I heard the first teaching of the Buddha, I was totally hooked, because this teaching is on the Four Noble Truths, and the first truth is suffering, so, yeah, I related to it. The second noble truth is the cause of suffering, and I didn't understand that one for a long time. I spent several years trying to figure out these teachings. They are really good, but they're difficult. The third noble truth is that nirvana, peace,

FIG. 110 (TOP)
Susan Stewart
(USA/Canada, 1952–)
Boudhanath Stupa (Kathmandu, Nepal), 2019
Video
60:00 min.
Courtesy of the artist

FIG. 111 (BOTTOM)
Susan Stewart
(USA/Canada, 1952–)
Pilgrimage, Kaw Gon Cave, Hpa-an, Myanmar, 2016
Photo-projection
dimensions variable
Courtesy of the artist

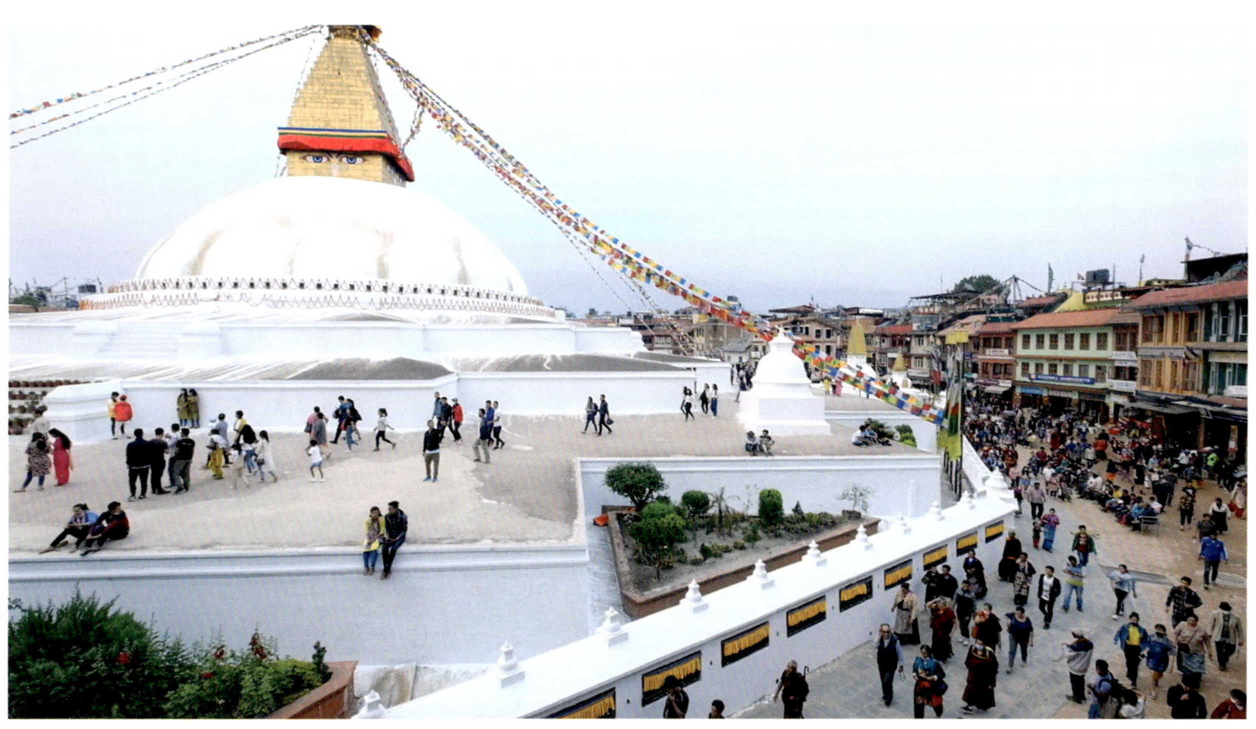

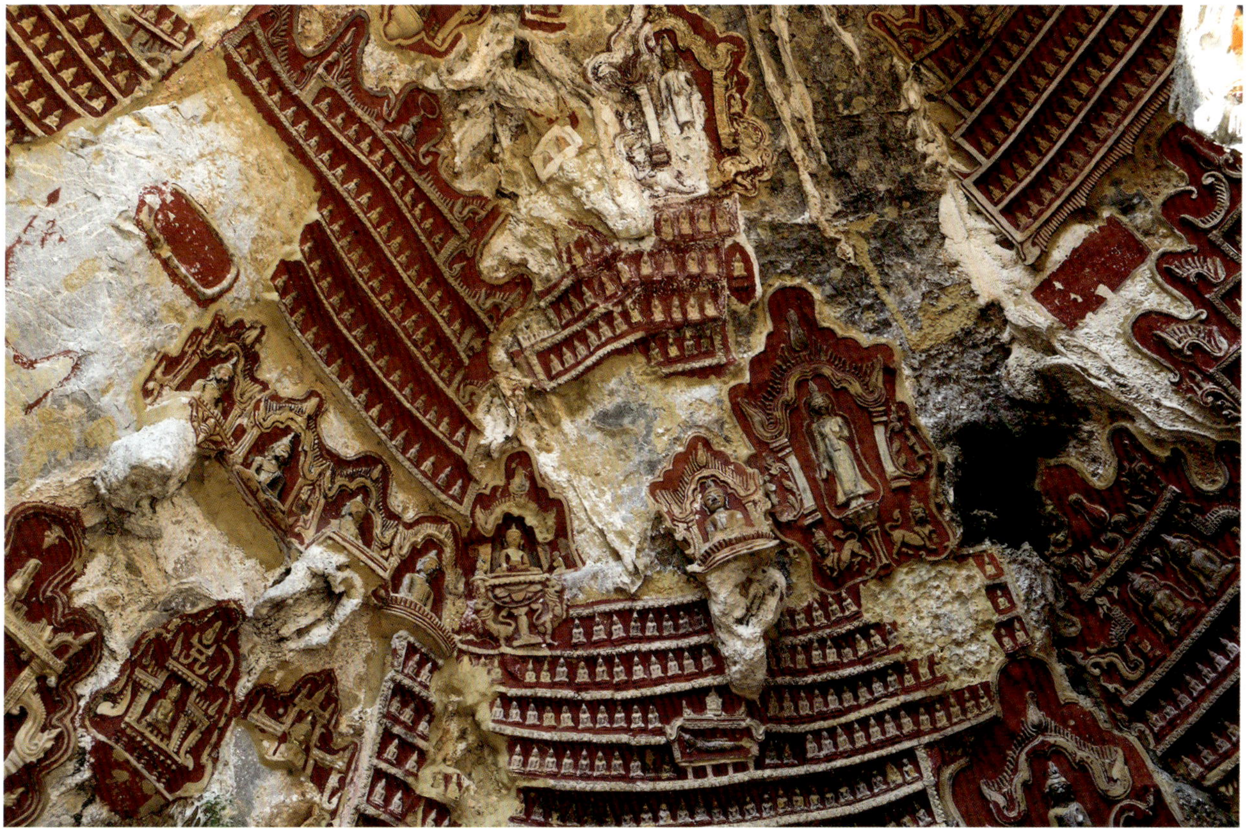

liberation, and freedom are possible—excellent news! Then the fourth noble truth is the path or the methodology to obtain that liberation—not such good news for someone who is on the lazy side, like me.

This became a twenty-year investigation, and I tried to divest art at the beginning. I said, "Art, you and I, we're kind of finished, I want a divorce." Art said, "No, not going to happen, I'm sticking with you." So I said, "Oh fine, but I'm not going to pay any attention to you for a long time." So, for about six years or so I tried to push art away, but it didn't leave completely, it was sticking. I moved along, and art was still there. So, what was the problem? When you start studying Dharma—in the beginning, the first wheel of Dharma—the foundational teachings teach how to not cling to yourself and your ego. Often, we cling with a tight fist, and one finger at a time we learn to pry it open, until the clinging lessens a little bit. You start with yourself in Buddhism. So, I did that for quite a long time, and I was practising and meditating on my own non-existence, non-self, and the non-existence of my ego. Yet how can I be happy when I'm empty, when I have no ego, when I have no self? For what reason would a non-self need to make a truly existent artwork? There was a contradiction here, because my understanding of art up until that point was that it was a "sign of self" at a particular point in my art career. In my case, I was an angry activist, so my signs were very political, but in my mind they were still signs of a self. So, I was having this contradictory striving for selflessness, egolessness, and emptiness, while dealing with the demands of art such as expression, presence, production, and action. During my foundational study of Buddhism, I couldn't deal with the fact that art was always demanding something of me. I had torn down my definition for art making; I didn't understand what art was at this point, or why anyone would do it. That was my John Cage period, for you Cageians. I was showing *4′33″* in all of my creative process classes. My mantra, which I would chant over and again, became, "I have nothing to say, and I'm saying it." That lasted for about five years, and I wasn't producing anything, so I felt like a total fraud as an art teacher.

After about a decade of study and practice, I moved onto Mahayana, which opened up the view of emptiness. Emptiness is the space of potential, of wisdom and awareness within the mind, where anything at all can appear, but where there is no

FIG. 112
Susan Stewart
(USA/Canada, 1952–)
Arctic Ice, 2017
Video installation (detail)
dimensions variable
Courtesy of the artist

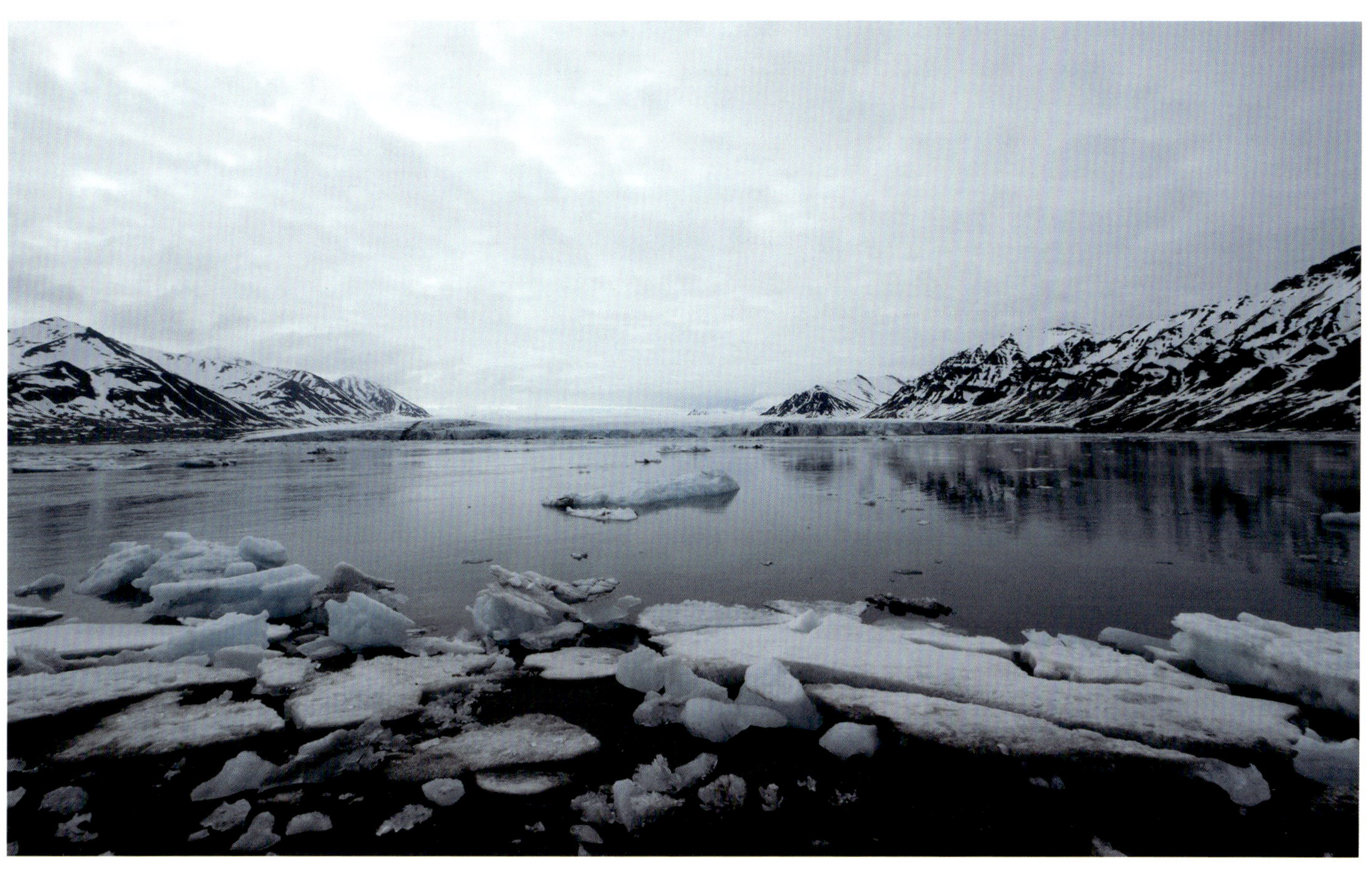

clinging to any appearances. We cling to appearances in ordinary life, generating desire, aversion, or indifference, which leads to negative actions and karmic consequences. When you start to experience the state of emptiness, you begin to get more in touch with your heart again. What obstructs the space of emptiness, awareness, and compassion are dualistic thoughts and concepts of self and other. When you are an angry activist, an open heart is one of the first things to go—at least this was so in my case. I couldn't feel anymore; I got very numb. So, the practice and the study of the Buddha Dharma will open up the heart. This means that we start increasing our empathy for all beings, and start imagining new ways of engaging with the world. In the Mahayana you start with the Heart Sutra, which we've been introduced to a couple of times throughout this research convening. The Heart Sutra is about emptiness; it's about "not this, not that, not this, not that," and replacing all of those "nots" with the view of emptiness and a compassionate heart. It leads to this bright awakening, and deep care for other beings.

When I became a little bit less confused I started thinking to myself, "Okay, art, let's give it another try. Let's see if we can do something here, but honestly I cannot make an object—I will not make anything that's a 'thing.'" So I began making art that didn't even look like art. I don't think my work was even readable to people—it was incoherent and illegible as art—but for me I was consciously entering back into art through social practice, a stream that was coming onto the scene as cultural discourse and which I felt aligned with. I started reading a lot of social practice material and, like Mali and Oliver, I identified with Fluxus, with happenings, and with performance art, as well as [with] the work of contemporary community-engaged artists. I took on projects that were illegible, but for me this was artistic practice. I won't go into too much detail, but one project was a seven-year administrative job at an art school, and the other was a study of the deep ecology of farming, or urban ecologies. So, those were my two projects, and for me they were social practice projects, but they wouldn't necessarily be read by the culture in that way.

MARCUS BOON: I'm interested in your thoughts on collaboration. In different ways, each of you are concerned with interdependence, and having some kind of art practice that emerges out of interdependence, and what it means to collaborate. How do you think about that? Or how do you think Buddhism changes the terms of collaboration, especially within socially engaged art?

OLIVER KELLHAMMER: That's a very interesting question because there are human collaborators and there are non-human collaborators. I continue to work with other people, working particularly with people from New York University in the Dear Climate Collective, looking at the psycho-social effects of climate change, discovering that the whole really is greater than the sum of its parts. This thing that is happening [to the earth] is so far beyond any of us as individuals, and that's what makes the collaboration so interesting and fun. Even my early work was collaborative, working with a painter named Janis Bowley, who was very influential in my early work. But then there's the non-human collaborators—like working with ecosystems. As artists we think about agency and we have ideas, but really everything has ideas. Lately I've been working a lot with insects, who have their own ideas. In 2018, I collaborated with hundreds of unnamed mealworms, *Tenebrio molitor*, who have developed a taste for Styrofoam, to create a piece called *Plastivore*. This piece is from a body of work which uses Styrofoam cups, and goes back to my father's sad life, because he got cancer from working in Styrofoam factories. Now this material has permeated my life; I'm still dealing with its effects long after he's gone. So, this material is essentially a collaborator, even though it's an obnoxious plastic material. I'm feeding it to insects who are creating these random absences of material—pieces of garbage that are full of holes that I now send to art galleries. As the artist, my name is on these pieces of garbage, but I didn't really make them—tens of thousands of mealworms are responsible. I guess I put it in the FedEx box, so I did something, but having an idea, that's a valid form of collaboration, too. Similarly, when you're collaborating with communities, you might have a sense of what you want to do, and some of your original idea may continue throughout the collaboration, but the serendipitous quality of all of the other agencies is really what makes the work much more interesting. As artists, we need to stand back from our work and say, "I didn't know that was going to happen, that's totally wild," and take ourselves out of the project. We need to start acting more as "good irritants," or homeopathic agents—as germs around which things can form. So how we situate our collaborations really depends on the metanarrative or the micronarrative. I guess the bottom line is that I don't like working by myself, and even though somebody has to start something sometimes, the less of me there is in the work, the better.

MALI WU: I work in many different ways, my approach depends on the subject. So, as I mentioned earlier, in the 1990s most of my work was very political—it was really a form of sociopolitical art, even though it wasn't collaborative. Then, in 1997, I began to develop a project about the stories of the women who worked in the textile factories. I began to ask myself, "What does this art mean to the women I collaborated with?" It's not just an ethical question, but also an aesthetic question: What does art mean?

Most of my work is centred on intervention, which means when I begin to do something, there's always a social, political, or environmental issue that I try to explore and try to bring possibility for changes in some way. So, I would initiate small-scale events at the beginning and invite people to join in. After a period of time, the work will become more abundant. And the meaning of the work emerges by itself. It's not a work done by myself, but by all the contributors. We are mycelium [a multicellular fungal colony that can create complex structures] in this sense.

SUSAN STEWART: I love collaboration, and I would say 75 percent of my practice has been collaborative. I seek it out when I can. I like working with other minds, especially when dealing with complex or difficult issues and questions. I find that working with collaborators you get unexpected results that are much fuller and much more interesting for the viewer. The other thing I've tried to do in my career is empower subjectivity. I'm a photographer, and I've done projects where I've worked with people where they have been the subject (either in a documentary film or in a photo series) and it's difficult, but I really try to make the power as equal as possible and honour the subject's side of things. From my perspective, that's actually more important. I still don't have anything to say, so when I'm working with people I'm much more interested in *their* side of things. Collaboration has become very necessary for me, I would say most of the time. The other 25 percent of my practice has become about practising presence, and that's why I love the title of this conference so much—In the Present Moment: I'm trying to be an artist who is present.

MARCUS BOON: I'll ask one last question ... I wasn't going to ask this, but the word *resistance* came into my mind. Unfortunately, I'm not an enlightened being, and if I ask myself why I am not an enlightened being, at some level within myself there is a resistance to being enlightened. And when I look politically at the world we inhabit and I ask myself why we are not liberated politically, and why we don't inhabit a kind of egalitarian world, at some level "resistance" manifests there. So, I wonder what the role of resistance is in your practice as artists, and how you work with the fact that often stuff doesn't change, we don't change, or the way reality is in its illusionary form persists.

OLIVER KELLHAMMER: This is a word that I think about a lot, and it comes up in my own resistance to pretty much everything that involves hard work, but there's a larger theme [for me]. The work that I like the most, and try to do, has a sort of emancipatory program. So, the idea that things are not what they might seem, that there's suffering in the world, that there's a voice issue—or as Marcus pointed out, issues of subjectivity—how can we as artists help intersubjectivity to evolve, to allow space for voices that aren't being heard? They could be non-human voices. One of the problems in the present historical moment—and this is me going back to the beginning of our careers during early to late modernism—is the object of the capitalist market. Increasingly, the figure–ground relationship between "What is the market?" and "What is not the market?" is harder and harder to discern. So our work—and certainly what I've tried to focus on most of my career—is to create the adjacent possible ground. The idea that there's an outside to the market system, like community gardens and crazy permaculture projects where the market doesn't apply. It's like Glinda the Good Witch coming down and going, "You have no power here!" Not that I am Glinda the Good Witch—well, actually, I do a pretty good Glinda—but [my point is] that there has to be an alternative to the sort of hegemony of the market. I'm responding to not just the oppressive nature of the market, but also to its monoculture, the fact that everything is a transaction, and measured according to its exchange value. So, in terms of intersubjectivity, to create subjectivity outside of the market aesthetic, I think, is a very vital part of my practice, and an important question for a lot of social practice people. The resistance to the market monoculture, the resistance to the power relationships that have defined life since we were born, is a key motivator, so that's where the resistance comes in.

MALI WU: I agree that art is very much about resistance because art helps things unheard to be heard. I see most of my projects as "art interventions"—to provide different perspectives. Although the world doesn't change quickly, or the change is only an illusion, I also agree with what Oliver was saying: nowadays, to rethink the role of art is important. Because too often it's seen as commodities as part of the "creative industry." I think that art should be about bringing the beauty back to life. It's not about a formalist idea, but about bringing positive energies into life.

SUSAN STEWART: I don't have a lot to add—I agree with what everyone has just said. I'm pondering this notion of resistance from a Dharma practice perspective, where ultimately it is about letting go of resistance. And what we're talking about here, from this perspective, is working with my own concepts of "resistance," and my own concepts of "other," and my own biases which force a duality of me versus them, or this versus that, and trying to actually bridge that space. The only place where I have any control at all is in my own mind. I can't control others, but I can control my relationship to others, at least from my side. I have no idea what enlightenment is either, but I've heard it said that the great Mahasiddhas experience something called "equality," wherein they regard all beings as equal, without any bias whatsoever, and I have that aspiration as well. I've been a political activist, so I understand resisting systems. This resistance still resonates with me, and it can get me going very easily. But from a personal, Dharmic, meditative perspective—and with the aspiration to become enlightened at some point in some lifetime—I think that a useful practice with resistance is to look at the resistance in our own minds and to penetrate this resistance by looking directly, and then letting go, opening up space for reconciliation and peace.

Thanks to Marina DiMaio for transcribing the discussion.

SELECTED ARTISTS' WRITINGS ON BUDDHISM AND RELATED TEXTS

Anderson, Laurie. "Marina Abramovic by Laurie Anderson." *BOMB Magazine*, July 1, 2003, #84. Available at bombmagazine.org/articles/marina-abramovi%C4%87.

Baas, Jacquelynn, and Mary Jane Jacob, eds. *Buddha Mind in Contemporary Art*. Berkeley: University of California Press, 2004.

Brauen, Martin, and Mary Jane Jacob. *Grain of Emptiness: Buddhism-Inspired Contemporary Art*. New York: Rubin Museum of Art, 2010. Exhibition catalogue.

Cage, John. *Silence: Lectures and Writing*. Middletown, CT: Wesleyan University Press, 1961.

"Deity, Demon, and Teacher: Thoughts on an Intervention with Michael Zheng." *BAMPFA News*, 2014. Available at www.michaelzheng.org/portfolio/deityDemonTeacher.html.

DiMaio, Marina. "Art as a Spiritual Practice: Q&A with Dylan Thomas." *AGGV Magazine*, June–August 2021. Victoria, BC: Art Gallery of Greater Victoria. Available at emagazine.aggv.ca/art-as-a-spiritual-practice-qa-with-dylan-thomas.

Giorno, John. *Cancer in My Left Ball: Poems, 1970–72*. New York: Something Else Press, 1973.

Greene, Vivien, Harry Harootunian, Richard King, and Alexandra Munroe, eds. *The Third Mind: American Artists Contemplate Asia, 1860–1989*. New York: Guggenheim Museum, 2009. Exhibition catalogue.

Kaprow, Allan. *Essays on the Blurring of Art and Life*. Edited by Jeff Kelly. Berkeley: University of California Press, 1993.

Lacy, Suzanne. "Having It Good: Reflections on Engaged Art and Engaged Buddhism." In *Leaving Art: Writings on Performance, Politics, and Publics 1974–2007*. Durham, NC: Duke University Press, 2010.

Larson, Kay. *Where the Heart Beats*. New York: Penguin Books, 2013.

Oliveros, Pauline. "MMM." In *Software for People: Collective Writings 1963–80*. Sharon, VT: Smith Publications, 1984, pp. 214–260.

Pearlman, Ellen. *Nothing and Everything: The Influence of Buddhism on the American Avant-Garde: 1942–1962*. Berkeley, CA: Evolver Editions, 2012.

Pujol, Ernesto. *Sited Body, Public Visions: Silence, Stillness and Walking as Performance Practice*. New York: McNally Jackson, n.d.

Ross, Nancy Wilson. "Zen and Dada." 1938. Notes for a lecture given at the Cornish School, Seattle, Washington. Nancy Wilson Ross Papers, held at Harry Ransom Center, University of Texas at Austin.

Tobey, Mark. "Japanese Traditions in American Art." Paper presented at the 6th National Conference of the U.S. Commission for UNESCO, San Francisco, 1957. Subsequently published in *College Art Journal*, vol. 18, no. 1 (1958), pp. 20–24. Reprinted in Wulf Herzogenrath and Andreas Kreul, *Sounds of the Inner Eye*. Tacoma: Museum of Glass: International Center for Contemporary Art in association with Seattle: University of Washington Press, 2002.

Tsutakawa, George, and Martha Kingsbury. "Oral History Interview with George Tsutakawa, 1983 September 8–19." Smithsonian Institute, Archives of American Art. Available at www.aaa.si.edu/collections/interviews/oral-history-interview-george-tsutakawa-11913#transcript.

Von Wiegand, Charmion. "The Adamantine Way." *Art News*, vol. 68 (April 1969), pp. 38–41, 72B–75E.

Westgeest, Helen. *Zen in the Fifties: Interaction in Art between East and West*. London: Reaktion Books, 1998.

Wijers, Louwrien, ed. *Art meets Science and Spirituality in a changing Economy: From Competition to Compassion*. London: Academy Editions, 1996.

Yanagi, Soetsu. *The Dharma Gate of Beauty*. Translated by Bernard Leach with the assistance of Mihoko Okamura. Tokyo: Japan Folk Crafts Museum, 2016.

INDEX

Captions indicated by page numbers in italics

Measurements of artworks are given as height × width × depth.

22 23 24 25 26 5 4 3 2 1

Cataloguing data is available from Library and Archives Canada
ISBN 978-1-77327-164-4 (hbk.)

Design by Naomi MacDougall
Editing by Steve Cameron
Copy editing by Stephanie Fysh
Proofreading by Renate Preuss
Indexing by Stephen Ullstrom
Front cover image: Charwei Tsai (Taiwan, 1980–)
Driftwood (Heart Sutra), 2019, Performance document: India ink on driftwood
90 min., Performed on October 27, 2019, as part of *In the Present Moment: A Research Convening*, Visual Arts Building, University of Victoria
Courtesy of the artist / Photo: Laura Gildner

Back cover image: Michael Zheng (China/USA, 1965–)
Mindwaves, 2019, Meditation wall drawing: markers on drywall, 243.84 × 365.76 cm, Document of performance presented on October 26 and 27, 2019, in conjunction with *In the Present Moment: A Research Convening*, Visual Arts Building, University of Victoria
Courtesy of the artist / Photo: Laura Gildner

Printed and bound in Canada by Friesens
Distributed internationally by Publishers Group West

Figure 1 Publishing Inc.
Vancouver BC Canada
www.figure1publishing.com

Art Gallery of Greater Victoria
Victoria BC Canada
aggv.ca

This book draws on research undertaken towards the exhibition *In the Present Moment: Buddhism, Contemporary Art, and Social Practice* originally scheduled for winter 2021 at the Art Gallery of Greater Victoria. Owing to the global pandemic, the exhibition is being planned for 2023.

We acknowledge the generous support of The Robert H. N. Ho Family Foundation

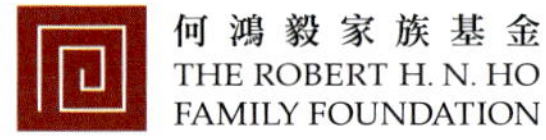